Writing And Reflections Volume 2

Writing And Reflections, Volume 2

Mary Catelli

Published by Wizard's Wood Press, 2026.

WRITING AND REFLECTIONS VOLUME 2

First edition. May 7, 2026.

ISBN: 978-1-942564-83-6

Written by Mary Catelli.

Foreword

The second volume of the collected works of Writing and Reflections.

I have edited them lightly from how they appeared them on, organized them as best I can to make their cross-references clear, and left in both my shameless plugs for my fiction and some redundancies between essays.

Some essays may continue to develop ideas that I originally talked of in the essays for the first volume, and so may improve on being read after that one. Still, I tried to make them all stand-alone.

I hope you enjoy them.

Ideas

We begin, as stories do, with ideas.

Ideas And Origin

The mysterious side of inspiration

One annoying side of writing is that once you have done enough—and enough is far less than is needed to master fiction writing—you may read some literary criticism.

Literary critics who are not themselves fiction writers show quite clearly that they have not, and would never be capable of, writing a competent work of fiction.

This shows when they take it upon themselves to talk about the writing process and the writer's inspirations. They are annoying in their arrogance. (Wayne C. Booth is an exception. There may be others. But the rule is very frequent.)

They take it upon themselves to decide what was the *exact* source of everything, and how the process worked.

It is of use only to boggle at how people can fool themselves. I could not recount to you the genesis of any work of mine with the confidence that they recount how a total stranger—possibly living centuries ago—wrote his work.

The first issue is that they assume that all works were published in the order written, and shortly before they were written. This gets truly amazing when a book is traditionally published, and the influences they impute to it occurred after the manuscript would have been submitted in the usual process.

Yes, some topical books are rushed through to hit while the iron is hot. Those require all sorts of special priorities to manage. The writer must write immensely quickly, people must be pulled from other jobs to edit and copy edit, and a new slot must be opened. It is wiser to assume that all books are a year old at the date of publication.

At least.

Assuming the writer rushed through the writing.

Which *can* happen, but it is wiser to assume not.

Tolkien took over a decade to produce *The Lord of the Rings.* Those who trace it to World War II overlook that he began writing before that war. (Certainly before any inkling of the atomic bomb.)

Even when it's chronologically possible that someone could have noticed something, that doesn't mean that he did. Every day writers decry claims that this, that, or the other thing came to their notice—claims based on vague resemblances, sometimes very vague indeed. (Sometimes seeing their own bugbear in the story with all the attention to evidence that led all manner of stories being read as solar myths in the nineteenth century.)

Partly of the issue is that the critics' notion of how ideas develop are out of whack. Yes, it is true that Phillip Sailor could wear his hair in a ponytail because he is a sailor, but you can't assume that. It's also true that he could be a sailor because the writer imagined him wearing that ponytail—perhaps even because he saw a work of art with such a depiction.

Perhaps everything else in the work of art has been removed or altered past recognition, but the writer can't shake the notion that this character wears his hair like that.

Which is another aspect of identifying inspiration. It is possible, in fact, to develop the story so thoroughly that even the writer can only rely on memory for inspiration. If an illustration depicts a king justly sentencing a criminal, the writer can run with the notion of its being a tyrant punishing an innocent, and conclude that the throne room does not make a good setting—and the original illustration vanishes entirely.

As for the elements that develop around it and push the throne room off stage, the problem is that the imagination can act like a supersaturated solution. It dissolves into itself history, stories, artwork, folklore, and many other things, and then one day the inspiration hits, acting like a nucleus.

Instantly, dozens, or hundreds, of notions crystallize on the nucleus.

Every step in the writing process may cause another such crystallization, and there's no telling where the original ideas came from, from a news article read the minute before or a story misremembered from earliest childhood.

Once that has happened to you, you will laugh at the idea of a literary critic, having nothing more than the story to go by, can even guess at the origins of the story.

Linking The Beginning To The Ending

Mushy middles

You have a powerful beginning. The villain burns a village and slaughters all he finds. The hero, having been away at the right time, is thrust into adventure and boldly seizes it despite the perils and his ignorance.

You have a triumphant ending. The hero throws down the villain and inaugurates the age of gold, or perhaps just wins his way to settle down again, this time with the love interest, in a new home to replace the one that villain burned, and raise a new family.

And something has to go into between.

Like seeing the near bank and the far bank, and not knowing whether the ford has mud, or quicksand, or water so deep it requires swimming even on horseback, or a strong current.

And because all metaphors are inexact, you know that you can bring the banks closer together, but that may ruin the story.

And you also know you have to throw something in the middle (which is why you need the distance). Something just about as large as the beginning and the end, something that will sharply change the journey.

Perhaps, instead of having no notion, you have a glittering if isolated moment in the middle. As well as, or instead of, a beginning or an ending. Even two or more.

On the whole, the more the merrier. Considering every idea that might fit in is wise. It is generally easier to join ideas together than to invent all the rest of the tale, even if you can make it a short story.

When building up, the important thing is linking them together. The ideas in the middle may not even indicate whether they come before or after each other.

But you do have to keep an eye out for whether you are forcing them together. Not all ideas are compatible, and it is the structure of the whole that matters. If it occurs to you that one idea would work best in a wholly human world, you will have to pitilessly cut the encounter with an ogre. Or the one with the wholly human world. Exile them to another work.

The real ugly business is when you have no good ideas.

You know the hero has to strive.

You know the villain has to flex his power, or at least some forces have to oppose the hero.

Sometimes it works out when I go to outline and stagger from "what happens next" to "what happens after that" until it reaches the end because some of the ideas are of greater import to the plot, thus making a structure rather than one thing after another.

Sometimes I have to grab a plot skeleton and see if I can throw ideas at it to find high points. Or merely connection points.

Sometimes I shove it all on the backburner and wait to see if something else pops up.

One story—*The Book Of Bone*—started with an ending that didn't satisfy me because it was told as the end of an episode, not a story, and also with the title. A Book of Bone points logically to some form of necromancy. Thus, I filed off the serial numbers to put in a new villain for the ending. Then I plopped him in the opening. Since I wanted the story, not just the episode, to end, the villain cursed something that would, once relieved of the curse, let the heroine be happy.

And then I pondered.

I pondered a lot actually.

The villain disappeared at the end of the curse, so searching for him and finding nothing was a conflict. Also, there was the book. Introducing it in a way that looked like progress and failed to resolve anything at that point sharpened the conflict. It also proved useful in the plot going thus forward. . . .

That story had a lot more work in the outline stage than in the first draft, juggling everything in between.

Backstory Ideas

Where ideas work

Some story ideas aren't really story ideas.

They're backstory ideas.

I was once trying to steal an idea where a hero lived in "secret" after an unjust conviction. It was the backstory of the tale, which was about a girl who learned that everyone was in on the secret, and that she should keep it, too.

Best sort of idea to steal. Since it's in the backstory, it's undeveloped and also unlikely to remind anyone of the original.

Except that then I poked at it. And poked at it. The unjust conviction had actually tied up his options quite tightly.

It may still become a story of mine, but the radical change needed makes it quite difficult to pry loose. It is in dire need of work on the legal system, a plot twist that makes a pardon reasonable, or a way for him to go into hiding before the conviction without changing the injustice of it much. So it's still in outline stage.

To consider a different example, let us take the story of Suppiluliuma, an ancient Hittite king, who received an offer from the widow of a Pharaoh, to marry his son and make him Pharaoh, and who did send his son, only for the son to be murdered. Suppiluliuma invaded Egypt to avenge him, and brought back many prisoners—and a plague, to which many, including Suppiluliuma himself, succumbed.

As a story, it has many problems, but as a backstory, it could have its uses.

Let us suppose that you are ripping off how Korea historically choose royal brides: the kingdom issues orders that there are to be no marriages until the bride is chosen, all the nobles must submit reports on their marriageable daughters, and one is selected.

Since this is a high fantasy story, the backstory is that the kingdom uses magic to protect its borders. One element of this is marrying within the kingdom. For its kings or princes to marry a foreign princess would open the border to invasion. Especially if he then fell in love, thus symbolically let himself be overcome by a foreigner.

The story of Suppiluliuma, artfully repainted to be plausible in the new venue, represents a warning to all kings of the disasters that can ensue if you try to intermarry with foreign royalty. Choosing whether the kingdom where the royal marriage in question is being arranged is the kingdom where the queen sent for the son, the kingdom where the king sent his son, or a third kingdom profiting by their example might affect various things. (Or might not, it may be history, or even history so old that people claim it's a legend.)

Or perhaps a warning to choose your bride with care. We have the actual text of the letter that the Egyptian widow of the Pharaoh sent, but we are not, in fact, absolutely certain who she is, because she uses only her title, not her name.

Obviously this could be expanded, and probably given some character. Explain, perhaps, that the king had married her because of her powerful family, only her father had died, and this was her desperate ploy to seize power without respect for the kingdom. The king must choose a bride who cares more for the kingdom, and possibly one with a less than powerful family.

Or, maybe it doesn't. The entire story could revolve about the foreign king's folly, or the widow's folly without reference to the details of her character, and be summed up in a sentence to warn your hero about the folly he contemplates.

Putting the ideas together would still require large quantities of reworking, since the cultures are too different. The motives of the character who elects to tell the story also influences the end result.

It would not, however, require anything to force the backstory to form an elegant story structure, or give characters motives, or anything else that distracts from its purpose.

Muddling From The Middle

Laborious invention as a writing technique

Sometimes, when the inspiration is in the middle, this is a problem. When I can't catch a plot bunny, or better yet, half a dozen, and stuff them into the beginning, but have to work back.

There is a dull slog of things, settings, characters, and events as I laboriously invent my way to reach the inspiration.

Sometimes I overestimate the amount of set-up needed to a situation until I fall back and consider. This created a rule for me: if I know something lies in the middle of the story, and I'm stuck, the next question is whether it can go in now.

The only downside of that is that, of course, often I have to invent more things to go after it. (Not quite so frequently as inventing events that lead up to it, but often enough.)

In some respects, this is incidental to the scene's being in the middle. It's just my bad luck that when I get inspiration in the middle, it's hard for me.

So, I settle into testing things. Throwing in new ideas, of course. But also trying to logically work out what my inspiration implies. What sort of magic. What sort of social structure. What sort of prior events would lead to this.

Sometimes—to whom would the event in the inspiration be deeply meaningful, and how can I show it beforehand? (That is, getting into character arcs.)

It is always wise to consider how much of it is necessary, whether you can cut to *in media res* and fill in the beginning as backstory.

But sometimes it is. If your hero is fleeing for his life from friends who betrayed him, their interactions before the treachery may be essential. The emotional wound is not real without seeing the relationship that was violated. Back-filling it means that the readers already know out it will turn out, and may eye it with jaundice. It also means that the back-fill will involve dramatic irony rather than identifying with the character. Perhaps the story works better without the irony.

Likewise, if a character is kidnapped, and the story is about the rescue, the character will be a MacGuffin unless there's enough time before for characterization.

Or if two characters meet in school, it is wise to give them some scenes that show their developing friendship before putting it to the test. Perhaps you could just cut to the test, since friends are a known thing, but if you need to open before they become friends, cutting to the friendship may not work, particularly if it needs to their bond needs strength.

All sorts of things need to be developed before the inspiring scene so that there will be objective reasons for the character's emotions.

You may need bridging conflict to get to the scene that inspired it all, and that means you need to invent bridging conflict if it does not spontaneously arise.

One odd thing about it is that you have to avoid getting too attached to your ideas, just as you have to avoid getting too attached to inspiration. While with inspiration the problem is getting too fond of the idea, the problem with these is that you don't want to go back and dredge up new ideas with all the effort involved in that.

Go back and dredge up new ideas if necessary. The dangers of trying to work out how things work is that the ideas that are most obvious to you are likely enough to be the most obvious. Cliched. Unsurprising to the audience and so undramatic.

On the other hand, the idea you so laboriously devised to support something may perk up and charge across the field of your story, pulling everything after it, until the original idea has vanished.

And on the third hand, in the finished work, you may not be able to tell, while reading, which is the inspired stuff, and which was the stuff you laboriously invented, constructed, and fit together to make it work. If you do not remember which you do, you may be as baffled as anyone else. (It's a bit frustrating.)

Such is the nature of writing.

Adventures In Art Inspiration

On this beginning

You start with what you start with.

If you start with a work of art, and develop it into a scene, and from there into a work, that's one way to do it.

There's a trick I've found, which is that if you start with an image, one thing to avoid is looking up the context. For instance, if you start with a print that tells you it is of the Great Ryogoku Fire, and shows you a bridge with two looming fires on either end—and your imagination roars off with the panicking people knowing that the conjuration of two fire elementals means the war is on again—don't look up the fire.

It may tell you nothing more than that two fires started at the same time, coincidentally, but it may tell you more.

Imagination is a finicky thing. If you perturb it with the knowledge that something is other than what you are building it up to be, it may be a problem.

This is more of a danger when working with illustrations, and art about stories, because those have already been fit in dramatic patterns, and usually been chosen to illustrate. (Usually. The Brandywine School warned against spoilers, but also observed that you could depict a scene not technically in the story that nevertheless summoned up the *spirit* of the tale.)

But if you see a woman on her knees with a man forcing her onto them with a spell, you might run with the notion that she's the innocent victim. Or that she's a nefarious villain being brought to justice. Or that they are opposite sides in a war, and both doing their duty. Or perhaps that she's just being trained in magical combat—the man's face is contorted in the image, but perhaps that's just effort—or perhaps he's trying to force her to admit she's not up to it.

If you run with the notion that she's in training, and perhaps he's trying to make her unusually tough because she can cope with unusual training, only she can't, and so washes out of the school—well, there you have a story.

If you learn, later, that she's just a villainess resisting arrest, it may not affect your imagination. Then again, it might. Such is the finickiness of imagination.

Referring back to the picture may be unwise, particularly if you do it frequently. As with any idea that you steal, you want to change it to fit your story. If it's not a public domain image, you want to change it as much as is feasible, for the same reason as when you steal from another story. Referring back may introduce a magnetic attraction to the original idea. Independence is best maintained with distance.

Especially if the image has things that fix it in time and place. Put a character in a tartan kilt, and there is no way to fix it without either dressing the character in something else, or putting the tale in, if not the actual Highlands, a Highland analogue. And if you are up on your history, a reasonably modern Highlands, because it is the modern kilt, not the historical great kilt, which was large enough to use part of it as a cloak.

On the other hand—and this may be a "your mileage may vary" sort of thing—if I go back to the image (or to any other source of inspiration) when I have run out of interest in the tale, it often can freshen my interest.

What makes this truly wacky is that it can refresh my interest even if I stripped out every element of the original, if only my memory allows me to know that this was the original inspiration. And it does so without dragging me back to the original elements, if I have it well-founded as my own story.

That is the sort of wackiness that imagination gets up to, which is why it is so tricky to handle.

History

An excellent source for ideas, and issues for world-building. Including how to make the world different.

Myths of Religion

A caution about sources

After advising reading primary source for research, and secondary source only secondarily—

Today, I advise against it. When world-building your religion, you may want to turn chiefly to secondary sources and give the primary sources limited inspection.

This is because for a good number of religions, the primary sources we actually have are the myths, and they are misleading.

Even if you read myths unhomogenized and from the source. I've read fantasies that clearly got their religion from neatened, homogenized, put-into-order myth books (probably written for modern-day children). Cicero's *On the Nature of the Gods* gives a pagan's eye view of their disorder, with mild comments about how many Jupiters there have to be, to match all the myths of his birth.

The homogenized ones, for instance, tend to start with the creation myth. Assuming you are prudently shoving the metaphysics off-stage, so you are using this with an eye toward the culture's myth, not the actual creation of the world—it's still unwise. Creation myths often have very little importance in the actual practice of religion. Witness the Greek myths take several generations to get to the actual deities that they worshiped.

(You will run across claims, to this day, that this reflected the conquest of peoples whose gods were earlier in the myths. I have not seen any non-circular evidence in support of this claim.)

But the unhomogenized ones—while they do tend to give the flavor of the wild discord of mutually exclusive myths, such as Athena being born from the head of Zeus after his splitting headache is relieved by Hephaestus hitting him in the head with a hammer, and Hera being angry that Zeus had a child on his own, and having one on her own after, namely Hephaestus—may not catch the actual views of the worshipers.

Compare any of the mythological tales you can run across about Ares, to this picture, drawn by the Homeric Hymns:

> Restrain also the keen fury of my heart which provokes me to tread the ways of blood-curdling strife. Rather, O blessed one, give you me boldness to abide within the harmless laws of peace, avoiding strife and hatred and the violent fiends of death.

Even the aetiological myth of the Areopagus, which explained the name from the myth that Ares was the first to be put on trial there. Poseidon prosecuted him for the murder of his son Halirrhothius, and Ares defended himself on the grounds that Halirrhothius had been trying to rape his daughter Alcippe. He was acquitted. And that's probably the most favorable myth.

Still, he wasn't that big in the worship. Sparta had more shrines to Pallas Athena (the Maid of Athens, quite likely) than to Ares.

Nothing like Mars, who was much bigger in Roman religion and the god of agriculture as well as war. There is, however, a small problem in looking at the differences in myths.

Many religions were not big on myths. The Romans imported Greek myths because they had virtually none of their own. The Egyptians had gods of locations; only when they unified into one country did the gods of the triumphant cities take on mythological, sphere-of-influence roles, and these tended to shift as the fortunes of cities rose and fell.

On top of this, even for cultures with myths, the problems get aggravated when the myths were only taken down by Christians as amusing stories. The Norse have the Elder Edda, written by pagans, and the Younger Edda, written by a Christian. The Irish stories are entirely taken down by Christians. This deepens the complications, because they wrote down what was of interest of them, and obviously could hardly help coloring them with their own viewpoint.

Furthermore, there has been a lot of mythologizing of myths. People inventing what the pagans ought to have believed, or projecting their own beliefs back in time. The Great Mother Goddess and the Triple Goddess appear to be not ancient but Victorian myths. There is no evidence that there was ever a religion of a single maternal goddess, or of a goddess whose aspects were Maiden, Mother, and Crone. (Check out Ronald Hutton's *The Pagan Religions of the Ancient British Isles.*)

Better than myths are primary sources about the actual religious practices. What rituals are actually performed. What festivals are celebrated. What acts are required, or forbidden. Reading a lot of these, even of cultures you have no desire to rip off base your story culture on, can alert you to the possibilities. Teach you such things that once-a-week rituals are, in fact, an uncommon eccentricity of certain cultures, for instance.

However, these are often rare, and have the added disadvantage of being elite. Roman and Greek writers have been known to philosophize about and even render the myths into allegories without affecting the ordinary religious practice in the slightest.

Then writers must turn to secondary sources. To read *Paganism In The Roman Empire* by Ramsey MacMullen and learn, for instance, that the Greek Tyche/Roman Fortuna was, by inscriptions found to her, one of the most popular goddess to worship. Do you remember any myths about her? Me neither.

Even for modern-day religions, the focus down on the individual worshipers in the act of worshiping is the most useful thing, since it will show what your characters should *do*. The good secondary sources talk about the difficulties and the evidence, and also give all sort of interesting details.

Such MacMullen's work telling how communities that received a useful answer from the oracle at Delphi would send choruses of nine boys—carefully watched over by adults—hundreds of miles to sing hymns in thanksgiving, as recorded in inscriptions.

Or to read *Portrait of a Priestess: Women and Ritual in Ancient Greece* by Joan Breton Connelly and learn how both men and women had tombs inscribed with a list of priestly offices, for all sorts of gods, over a lifetime, and how some priesthoods were simply sold.

These are the essential details, and you won't find them in myths.

Hobbies On The Side

What does your character do in spare moments?

Particularly on the road. Sitting around gives you advantages, if not great ones.

After all, hobbies can just be useful background noise. The sort of things that signal that this is a real world and not just the stage setting for your story, which can be crucial in giving weight to your world.

They can also be useful for characterization and for setting up plot devices.

On the other hand, they have to be realistic. True, having your character wager large sums on dice games, leaving him broke, can be a useful plot device, but we have to be convinced that this character is a reckless gambler, and his actions before and after must be compatible with it.

While we're at it, dice are accurate in many more eras than cards. If your character wagers large sums on card games, he's in an era of cheap paper, which has ripple effects. Mind you, vellum is excellent for making books that last for centuries on end, but since the first question for making a book is how many sheep you have to breed, even their durability does not make them common. Cheap paper, even if it falls apart in decades, means cheap books.

Thus opening a way for your character to have a hobby of reading. If, of course, it's in character. And it's more dangerous than most. If your character is an omnivore, or has the right kinds of interest, you can info-dump, but then, you have much more difficulty making for honest ignorance when that's preferable for the plot. Lugging around books makes this a more suitable hobby without travel.

Drawing also requires paper. It was a standard accomplishment for a fine young lady once upon a time. A lord, or gentleman, might also draw, and indeed, it would be more practical for him. An officer can't take pictures before cameras, and everyone knows how accurate a verbal description was. Much better if he can sketch whom he saw, and see if anyone can identify him, and draw up a picture of the fortifications.

Music is an easier one. A period-appropriate instrument can be lugged about, or the character can sing. Indeed, just about everyone can sing, or tell stories. In the absence of recorded or broadcast entertainment, everyone could do some entertainment, so in any gathering, people could switch off. Prince Esterhazy had his own orchestra, and Hayden for a composer, but he played a musical instrument at small parties.

Though given the notorious accuracy of ballads and other songs in fantasy, it may give you more issues with info-dumping.

It also allows people to indulge in dancing wherever the ground is clear enough.

Games involved some objects, usually, but not so many or so large they could not be lugged about. Balls, or cups to catch them, or blindfolds for Blind-Man's-Bluff. On the other hand, some games drifted into dancing, depending on the measures and what the dancers did. And all sorts of games would be played straight through adulthood, even at a royal court.

Sewing can be lugged about, but probably is not, properly speaking, a hobby. Most women sewed for practical use. Even the well-off ones sewed for the finery they needed for formal occasions, though there would be a certain sliding scale between those who do it only out of necessity and those who love it. Poorer women would be more likely to lug about a distaff and spindle.

Men, too, would be able to sew. Particularly rough, tough men. Soldiers on campaign. Foresters. Merchants who fared through wilderness. Anywhere, in fact, where no woman are likely to be found to mend things.

Scrimshaws are more likely to be their hobby in that situation. Carvings on bones were a common hobby among whalers.

Then, hunting is actually a hobby that befits from sitting about. All the moving about in search of the prey? It doesn't get you farther on the road. It gets you, if you do it right, and the circumstances add up, some catches. And then things have to be done to make them useful. It's possible that you might get a lucky moment on the road, but then you'd have to field-butcher it and hope you can do the rest in the next village.

It's a useful way to get a character far from the castle, to be sure.

Gardening is even more sedentary. As a hobby, it's very old. We have records of a Spartan sneering at King Cyrus, because he gardened for a hobby, and a Spartan, of course, considered any such thing below him. St. Augustine's gardening spurred him to philosophical reflections, given the burden that farming was, to many souls about him.

At least it will give the character a good eye for noticing flowers on the way, and for other people's gardens. Which is another way of tying the background color in.

What's Cooking?

How it changes

Cooking has changed a lot over the centuries.

Starting with how you learned it. Until nearly the twentieth century, all the cookbooks we have start with the assumption that you already learned how to cook—at some cook's elbow no doubt, even if she were also your mother or mother-in-law or aunt or grandmother—and could use some tips on how to vary your menu. (With tips on how to handle the seasonable availability of food.)

True, most people did learn. Aelfric's *Colloquy* has the Master tell the Cook, "We do not care about your craft, nor is it necessary for us, for we can ourselves cook the things that need to be cooked, and roast what has to be roasted." But not all.

At the tail-end of the nineteenth century, many American women were studying how to make the home better and easier to keep. One of them, Fannie Farmer, was a rich man's daughter precipitated into the kitchen after the family suffered financial reverses. When she wrote a cookbook, she wrote the book she wanted to have had, a book written for people who had never boiled a pot of water.

Thus began the recipe as we all know it nowadays.

She's also the person who decreed that a cup (of flour or sugar or anything else) was measured level. Ingredient measurements were rather haphazard in old recipes. After all, you could judge by the dish's appearance whether you had added enough, or you were no cook.

When writing of such an earlier era, or a world based on an earlier era, it may be wise to check out such earlier cook books. Fortunately, many re-enactors publish them with both the original recipe and the brought-up-Fannie-Farmer-standards version.

Some old recipes bring up other changes. "First catch your rabbit"—all the food arrived much less processed.

A lot more people would be involved in a large kitchen, but a lone cook might have to start with slaughtering the chicken, plucking it, butchering it to be ready before roasting it. A noble household of any size probably has its own slaughterhouse, and a butcher, too.

Vegetables might be quite fresh, pulled from the garden moments before, but then you have to wash, peel, chop, and cook before they get to the point of canned vegetables today. After you carefully remove any pests.

(Not to mention that the cat, of course, would have free run of the kitchen and pantry. Or cats. They fed themselves, of course, and were very necessary for that.)

The milk processing at least could be done in advance so that the cheese and butter could be brought out for the meal, or the cooking. Indeed, if you lived in a hot enough clime, it had to be done in advance.

Grain needed to be ground before you had flour. There were significant conflicts over the mill throughout the Middle Ages, millers not being noted for their honesty and lords setting high fees for their serfs, but it was an improvement over hand grinding—which peasants would still resort to when revolting against the lord's appointed miller.

And then there's the gentle art of cooking on a fire of some kind or another—and besides the danger to yourself, there is the matter that differences in fires translate to differences in cooking.

China's land is much more likely to be farmable than Europe's. Consequently they suffered more from lack of firewood and so have finely chopped foods; the labor is worth the decreased fuel. The roasts of Europe relied on its ready supply of wood so that they could spare the labor.

English perpetual ovens—an oven where the heat is applied during the baking process—were the most likely reason why pastry shops didn't take off as they did in France, where people were much longer engaged in the old process: heating up the oven with a big fire and then baking the dishes in big batches, in stages according to the heat required as the oven cooled off.

At that, one real disadvantage of modern electric and gas stoves is that you can not shape the heat. A cook used to arranging the coals in any shape needed would find fixed burners frustrating.

One real advantage is that the pots and pans do not get covered with soot, making cleaning them a real challenge—just when you didn't have modern dish-washing soaps. There's a reason why the scullery maid is such a wretched job.

And every night, you would put the cats outside. Not because the mice would not play, but because you banked the fire so you would not need to relight it in the morning. (This one, in fact, has wider applicability. Someone trying to move with even some degree of haste will not stop to light a fire on the way.)

The gentle art of cookery has had many changes over the years. Something to note before you make a character a scullery maid.

Replacing Itself

Where do your characters come from?

Does your world-building allow your society to replace itself?

Now, I grant you that many stories are not settings conductive to pregnancy and child-rearing. Wresting one's way through a snowstorm in a mountain pass, fighting a fire-breathing dragon, or descending to the otherworldly labyrinth are not places where prudent people introduce children.

In many fantasy words, the proper thing for the hero and heroine to do would be to conclude their adventures, have their wedding, and settle down so they can get a house and all that in order before the baby's born. In a good number, any child appearing in the story setting would be a reasonable grounds for panic.

Not to mention that if you have a family with two parents and ten children, you are already pushing the bounds of how many characters the story can reasonably hold.

If you look at nineteenth century fiction, you often have families of three, four, five children, without any suggestion that children had died. (To be sure, to an extent the writers would expect that most readers would take it as there having been a dead child or two in the family. Charles Dickens, since he was actually depicting the family life between the marriage of Charles and Lucie and the French Revolution, calmly gave them a son as well as a daughter and killed the son off in the only paragraph where he appeared.)

Still, many stories show enough of the world around the edges to make it very questionable. Especially cozy stories where the characters are in a settled place, exactly where people would have and raise children.

What do we find? Characters who are only children, or have only one sibling, when obviously many people are dying without children. Couples who have only one or two children. Worlds in which we are told that miscarriages and stillbirths have vastly increased, but in which no customs are in place to encourage or compel reproduction to make up for it.

There are cultures where a barren woman has been known to raise the bride price for her husband to have a second wife so he won't divorce her. A culture in which the reaction is a shrug is much more unusual. Divorce, or a second wife/concubine, is routine for handling the situation. Many disputes with the Church stemmed in the medieval era when a king, or a nobleman, wanted to repudiate a wife who had no children, or only girls.

If you take advantage of fantasy magic to decrease infant mortality, and to prevent infertility, you can make many changes. What you can not change is that if your setting does not reproduce itself, it will dwindle and die unless importing enough replacements—which means there has to be a location that not only reproduces itself, but which has surplus enough to overflow. And does overflow.

Countrysides have long been the source of inhabitants for the lethal cities. Country folk really do have more children—stork nests correlate with fertility for that very reason—and they do leave for the bright lights of the big city.

As a consequence, if your city is not reproducing itself, there need to be newcomers, and people who have not been settled long, and it needs to be a commonplace that very few city people did not come from somewhere else.

In Britain, in the nineteenth century, the Queen's List annually handed out noble titles among other honors. Yet the numbers of new nobles only replaced families dying out. Some people merely compared society to a lamp, burning from the top but being fed from the bottom, but others investigated and concluded the culprit was the nobles' habit of marrying heiresses for their money. The thing was, the fewer siblings she had, the more stunning the portion she could bring to her marriage. Then she would go on to have as many children as her mother had. If she were an only child—the best situation for the wealth—and the child were a daughter, or even if it were a son, and he died with no brother to serve as the spare, that was the end of the line. Old houses might be able to trace back to a cousin, but the cumulative effect was the extinction of noble lines.

Note that this set-up is entirely dependent on people desiring those titles. If your situation is dependent on new blood, your current population has to allow them in, and they have to want to come. And this will influence the size of the group.

I have seen online fringe groups discussing and belittling the idea that most children take after their parents on the grounds that they were mostly different from their parents, and not realizing that was why they were fringe.

Likewise, if most people who live in the Adventure Outpost never have children, their number will be severely limited by the rarity of people who are willing to drop their lives and everyone they know to trek to the outpost and its danger.

Demographers consider it an important transition when most people in a place are born there for good reason.

Character of Class

Birth, station, rising, falling

What standing does your character have in society?

This is an unwise question to consider in a vacuum because it is too vast. What status will serve the story turns on so many other factors.

Is it enforced by law?

Does it restrict what occupations he may go into? And that may be because his birth is too high or too low.

Can he marry as he chooses? If he marries as he chooses, are his children his heirs? Will people sneer at his mesalliance, and what effects will that have?

Can he travel? Bear a weapon? Wear certain clothes? Eat certain foods? And notice that he may be too high-born for things as well as too low-born. Or, of course, both, for different things.

What is the correlation with wealth? Many societies have tried to declare that the merchants are the lowest of the low, far below farmers, but their unquestionable wealth keeps perturbing that.

If he resorted to witchcraft, what sorts of animals can he change into? (In Aztec lore, only nobles could change into jaguars. Commoners had to settle for more lowly beasts.)

Trying to start a story with social class opens a whole can of worms.

I did start with one, once, because of an open call for an anthology, where the condition was lower class in a port, but that one was a real pain. In fact, I gave up the notion of trying before another idea collided with it. True, *The Turtle In The Sea of Sand* did ensue, but it was the other idea that really drove it.

Part of it was that the society came with it. Social class is tied so closely to its society that it doesn't really make sense to talk about class in the abstract. A young woman who is gentry in an equivalent to Georgian England—an impoverished and orphaned third cousin of a nobleman at the end of the Middle Ages—an impoverished scholar of good family at the university in the middle of the High Middle Ages—all are shaped by the society around them so much that their relative status is loose.

And those are three relatively close societies.

Still, if it's not a good starting point, it may bear some consideration. Since a story turns on conflict that is difficult but feasible for a character, social class is implicated in all sorts of stories.

Could your character feasibly bring a legal action against the villain? Would he be bound to lose because the judge won't take the testimony of a lower-status character? Or because his oath is not so binding as a nobles? Or because he can't afford a lawyer?

Can he appeal to the king? That depends on the size and formality of the court as well as his own status.

Can he rise in status? Would a title get him scorned among the nobility as a new creation? And if so, how scorned? A few sneers? Not be presented at court because not all of his great-grandparents could be thus presented? Able to join the army in the artillery because technical skill is more important there, but never ever in the infantry? Would he have to conform to aristocratic practice, but if he did, would be acceptable? Or at least his children would be?

Is that why your hero lives in the marches, with monsters beyond? Because there, no one cares who his great-grandparents were, or whether he can name them, just how good he is while fighting monsters?

It still may be a sharp point, where the wizard recounts how his grandfather was a prince of the realm, but his marriage was morganatic, and still his children had to flee for their lives on his death, and the survivors settled here.

Just as the former street urchin may still find it a sharp point that he had no honest way to make a living except to flee to the marches and use the tricks of skullduggery against monsters instead of men.

And even there, in the marches, social classes will evolve, from the skill in adventurers, from profiting from supplying them, from instructing the newcomers. Newcomers are unknown; a family of adventurers for the last seven generations has a heritage to live up to, but also to speak for them.

Consider how and why the society your characters move in organizes its structure, and classes will spring from that, and they will affect much.

School And Studies

Subjects and scholars

And off your character goes. The second age of life, as Shakespeare puts it:

> Then the whining schoolboy, with his satchel
> And shining morning face, creeping like snail
> Unwillingly to school.

Historically, of course, private tutors, or governesses, were relatively much more common than they are now. Partly because many more children (relatively) went uneducated.

Still, you may find, if you look at a society, that it has a lot more education, and a lot more of it happening at schools, than you think—or may have been told. In medieval times, Paris ordered all schools to subscribe to principles by which women could only teach girls. Nevertheless, a third of the teachers who assented to the principles were women. Obviously a lot of girls went to school.

Indeed, there are medieval works for girls that hold up saints as particularly admirable for academic studies, telling them they should emulate St. Agnes, who went to school, and the standard iconography of the Virgin Mary as a girl, with her mother, showed her mother teaching her to read.

On the other hand, you do have to consider the extent of teaching at those schools. The ones Shakespeare described often taught reading and basic arithmetic. Not even writing.

I note here, because I have seen some confusion about it, that you do not need to read or write to send letters. If you can read without writing, you can read yours, of course, but then you do what an illiterate person would do to read and then return a letter. Get someone else to do it.

In nineteenth century France, market days would include a row of professional letter-writers. They would read you the letter you received if you needed that, and then write the letter you wanted to send. Which, among other things, gave value to the basic literacy.

One notes that in China or Korea of the day, the basic arithmetic was far less likely. Numbers were the tools of *merchants*. In Europe, on the other hand, the *quadrivium* held four of the seven liberal arts, and though taught after the *trivium*, was held to be *all* numbers: arithmetic was pure numbers, geometry was numbers over space, music was numbers over time, and astronomy was numbers over space and time.

This is the sort of thing that makes it very difficult to think of schooling in general terms. Learn about schools in the eras most like those your high fantasy setting, and apply spackle as needed to make them fit your society and serve your purposes.

Or, of course, realize what kind of schools you need, and build the society to match.

And do not neglect their info-dumping usefulness. Not all classes are equal for that.

Basic arithmetic has little utility, but word problems can do a little from the most basic (a merchant buys grain for this much, and sells it for that much, after a river voyage that costs this much, what was his profit?) to the positively creepy (a mental institution was built for that much money, how many loans of this much money could have been given to newly-weds if the money had been spent there, instead?).

History is far more useful, especially since the conventions of the genre allow it to be far more accurate than would be plausible in real life. Though of course if it goes on too long, it will be dull. Give and take helps, but only some. Bear in mind that different societies select differently what to teach in history. Not just what events, but how they treat them.

Geography can also help, though it's less likely to be taught.

Magic and science can have a lot of theory explicated in the classroom, with the same problems.

There are also subjects in which the subject matter does not matter. Composition, for instance. Or handwriting, when the child is set to mimic a perfectly written sentence in a copybook. Or foreign languages. Set the pupils to translate a passage. Or elocution.

I have recently read some nineteenth century works by Charles Walton Sanders. The early books in the series are about learning to read—though even those might be useful in info-dumping—but the later ones present selections to be read aloud.

There, you must take care to provide such selections as your society would deem wise. Even the selections in a copybook will be of wise proverbs. Elocution samples can range from biography to rhapsodies over nature, from stories to poetry, but they will be chosen to form character as well as practice elocution.

Which is one more way to build the world.

Only The Dead Have Seen The End Of War

War, and why

In a book I read recently, in the background, the prince was a great hero for having conquered many other countries.

No *causus belli* was mentioned. Indeed, the tone of the tale strongly suggested that no such thing was considered, let alone deemed necessary.

Which is to say, it was a normal international situation: international anarchy. No one is in charge. Everyone does as he pleases, and if you want to conquer your neighbor, that's your neighbor's look out.

In many ways, all the armies, generals, and forces of civilization did not fundamentally change warfare from the raids. They were all out to get other people's stuff. It was more likely to be land once it was warfare, but it was still simply grabbing.

After discussing in *Federalist Papers No. 3,* how the Constitution's unifying elements would help prevent other nations from having just cause to war on the United States, John Jay goes on to observe, in *No. 4,* that

> It is too true, however disgraceful it may be to human nature, that nations in general will make war whenever they have a prospect of getting any thing by it,

To be sure, there never was a time when the problems in this were not known. In a hunting and gathering culture where the mode of warfare was still raids, one woman told an anthropologist, "The men fight, and the men die, but the land remains. It exists in its own right. It does not ask anyone to fight over it."

And Jay's very discussion shows that people were aware that some causes were more just than others in his era.

In fairy tales, the tales will just say that the king had to go to war—eliding the issue—or else that another king was coming to attack him, thus giving him a just cause. (One wouldn't want to go into too much detail anyway, since this is either to separate him from his queen, leaving her in peril, or to allow the gardener's boy to save the day disguised as a knight.)

In a less pared-down tale, you can give a *causus belli* anyway. "Another country has invaded ours, bent on conquest" is, of course, a legitimate one in any world. In order to make it justify conquest, you would need to elaborate it some: Perhaps the foreign king will not admit defeat, and so you must overrun his country and take control.

Or perhaps this is the third time in a quarter century that his kingdom has attacked, and it is clear that nothing will stay him from violating the next peace treaty as soon as he sees his way clear to a more victorious war—and he's quite foolishly ready to see such a way in the teeth of the evidence.

A pirate kingdom, or a kingdom where bandits run wild and attack travelers from your kingdom, also offers an only slightly less clear reason.

Then there is the option of leaning more into the international anarchy. This does require bringing into the foreground, because the situation must be made clear in its complexity.

In that condition, all security is a Red Queen's Race. You can make your nation stronger: build up its wealth, increase its army, improve its armaments. But all your neighbors can do the same.

Assuming that the world-building gives the countries neither magical nor technological means to beef up defense in way that can't be countered by your neighbors' offensive abilities, there is no way to better your safety, really. Not for longer than it takes for your neighbors to realize that you have lessened their safety with your new capabilities. They will race to catch up, and try to surpass you, for their own safety.

Alliances, diplomacy, treaties, and even diplomatic marriages can do only so much to keep people at peace. And those measures can also lead to war. Your alliance with Ruritania does you little good if you don't join the war when Graustark attacks Ruritania. Thus, keeping the alliance drags you into the war.

For the ultimate result of such tangles, see World War I.

A novel in which the international situation is laid out clearly make it feasibly to portray conquest as the only reasonable form of self-defense. It would, if course, need delicate handling, with the other countries being actual threats to the kingdom. But it would give some reason for the conquests, which would lend some sympathy to the character's actions.

Courtship In History And Story

Whether they woo

How likely is it that your high fantasy hero and heroine are dating?

Very unlikely, actually. Even if you stick to a European-ish era between the Middle Ages and the nineteenth century.

And not just because the era would speak of courtship and wooing, though you would be wise to use those terms. (Or a local, informal term. "Stepping out together" or "sparking" perhaps. Further, they should probably be "sweethearts", or he should be her "beau", or some such.)

Every era and area has variations on how young people marry. Particularly over social classes. The poorer your characters are, the more likely it is that the hero can actually woo the heroine. Their marriages are of less import, and their personal opinions matter more to those about them (who are, after all, of the same status) because their labor matters more.

Not to mention there's an entire spectrum of arranged marriages between being marched to the altar to free choice.

When, at summer festivities, while the young people frolic in a game, a young man and woman meet and like each other, they follow it up by having the young man, and perhaps his father as well, call on her parents, and the parents thrash out the details of their marriage because they are both landed proprietors, and everything must be clear down to her dowry going to their mutual children.

Or when, in town, the merchant and his wife propose a fine upstanding man, of good status and prosperity, to their daughter, and the advice books solemnly enjoin the young woman, while she gravely considers the choice, that she must of course reject the man if she concludes that she could not come to love him.

Or an advice book tells a gentleman that he should place his daughters in the households of respected lawyers and other professionals so that they can attract respectable rising professionals as bridegrooms.

Or the upper-crust family is scrupulous about introductions, and so when the daughter sweeps into a ball, and her father introduces her to the young men, who then talk to her, she knows that it is safe to talk with them. Her father, or uncle, or other relatives will investigate further if they seem to be serious, before she commits her honor by accepting an offer, but she can let them woo her in the ballroom. As one becomes her beau, they flirt on the balcony to the garden at balls, and he comes calling at her parents' house in his fine clothes—well, fine for calling, not for balls.

Calling on the family was an acceptable mode of courting in any level of nineteenth century society where calling was practice. Hence in *Little Women,* Alcott has Jo notice:

> "Dear old fellow; he couldn't have got himself up with more care, if he'd been going a-wooing," said Jo to herself; and then a sudden thought, born of the words, made her blush so dreadfully, that she had to drop her ball, and go down after it, to hide her face.

Other practices might include going for walks together. While the upper-crust from New York City gathered at Newport during the summer and carefully chaperoned their unwed daughters, the Bostonian blue-bloods scoffed at that Europeanized prudery and went Down East to Bar Harbor, where their daughters went on walks in the local pine woods with young men, or let the young men take them out in rowboats—though they did have to stay within sight of the docks. Furthermore, the boat had to be a rowboat because if it were a sailing boat, the couple might be becalmed. Being out all night was an inconvenience for a gentleman, but a scandal for a lady and a gentleman.

Plus of course all the regular calls and dinner parties, and dances and balls. Social events were regular occasions for courting. Check your era carefully, with comparisons to historical situations, to consider whether the young people organized their own, or the sober married couples arranged them, and the young people flirted at them.

Even working events. A sewing bee would not, since it would be all women, but a corn-husking gave plenty of time to flirt. Unusual ears of corn might provoke traditions about kissing or other forms of flirting.

This can even combine with walking together. A young man offers to see a young woman safely home from the hoe-down, and they have a chance to be alone together. Unless, of course, that is culturally imperative that they not. Perhaps a group of young women and their young men?

Or perhaps while the family is going to church, the young man wanders by, and he and his sweetheart walk five or six paces ahead of the family. Enough to keep them in sight at all time, and to require them to speak in low voices to not be overheard.

There's a whole range of activities, and none of them are dating.

Ancient Tomes

Where the secret lore lurks

When your wizard ponders the works in his library, the ancient secrets of magic of long ago ages—how ancient is your wizard's tome, anyway?

Perhaps his era uses the term "ancient" rather more lightly, but the sense of the magic older than remembered history is effective in what it makes the reader feel, not in logical quibbles that something a century old has sometimes been called ancient.

Still, there are problems with a tome that ancient.

Skipping lightly over the magical things that could be done to fix the issues—here are some of the issues they might need to work around.

If you are in a medieval situation, there's a hard limit to how old the book is, if the work is a codex—which is to say, as a spine with the pages bound into it. (Though sometimes it's used inaccurately. The Aztec "codices" are not in this form.)

Codices came in with Christianity. Indeed, with Christians, who apparently liked that format more than anyone else did. As in, archaeologists dig up libraries, and more than ninety percent of the Christian works are in codex form, and more than ninety percent of the pagan works are in scroll form.

You occasionally see a fantasy wizard's workshop with scrolls, but they chiefly have codices.

That, of course, is a technological innovation, and doesn't require much technique. If you want to have books several millennia old, and still codices, you can simply posit that they devised it millennia ago.

The material that it is made of matters rather more. Books were rather cheaper in antiquity than they were in medieval times. This is because in antiquity, they were made of papyrus, and in medieval, of parchment.

Papyrus was made from a river sedge that grew in Egypt. Papyrus meant gathering the plant, if you were in Egypt—or importing it if you were elsewhere, which is why the switch.

Parchment, from sheepskin or cowskin, being basically very, very thin leather. Parchment required starting a book by calculating how many ewes need to be bred. (Though it's also important to not over-estimate how much they cost. We have medieval books that were commissioned by gentry—not even nobles—for the daughter's education, and even works that were clearly meant for a minstrel to refresh his memory as he prepared to recite a chivalric romance to a noble household.)

But, within a few decades, another difference becomes apparent.

Parchment is tough. I mean, really, really tough. Graduate students are allowed to handle centuries-old books made in parchment with no more precautions than gloves. Millenium-old parchment books are readable.

Papyrus rots within a century except in rare conditions, such as Egyptian desert. Any book that is not recopied within a century vanished. As a consequence, most surviving books from antiquity were books that people cared enough to transfer to parchment before the papyrus rotted away.

This produces an interesting effect on the secrecy of magical tomes. A tome that has to be continually copied to achieve "ancient" status has difficulty maintaining "secret" status. Though it would explain why your manuscript of ancient magical secrets is a codex—it's a copy.

Also, where there are copyists, there are copyist errors. Imagine a wizard painstakingly gathering every single copy of a tome that he can find, and comparing them all, to reason his way to the correct, original spell. One hopes that he knows enough of the theory to deduce which is more likely to be correct even if it's the less common variation. Or that the error won't burn up a continent in fire.

Putting it all in parchment form makes it last longer. On the other hand, secrecy is even harder when you have to get all the parchment and thus all those animal skins. Perhaps surreptitiously removing sheets from a place that produces books on a regular basis?

The cover, of course, would have been done by hand. Solidly into the era of printing, in fact, readers would buy a sheaf of paper from the book-seller, and bear it to the book-binder, who would bind it to their specifications. A man who had all his books bound in uniform brown could have the exact same books as one whose shelves showed only red covers. Which at least will disguise the contents from the casual eye.

Your wizard might find the disguise more troublesome in that it can conceal exactly what he wants to know. Such is the problem with secrets.

The Whig Interpretation Of History, And Other Problems

Teleological readings

Among the many perils of viewpoint that lurk in your path when you read history, one of the nastiest is the Whig Interpretation of History, and its variants, and other teleological views.

The original interpretation, popular in British history writing of the nineteenth century, was that all of history had been aiming for the wonderfully wonderful wonder that was nineteenth century Britain. And if it was not quite so smooth as a train ride gliding over well-laid tracks, it was unnecessary to point out minor details.

The most disastrous effect, for the reader, is that the things of the past are described for their presumed effect on the progress toward that aim. They were not described for their actual effect on the era, or how they appeared to the people of that era (possibly more important for the fiction writer), which is what a reader using them for that era needs. Down to and including excluding vital details as unimportant.

(Obviously, "development of what they regard as progress" books are more or less resistant to this, though they can press some very odd things into the service of their thesis, and sandpaper off quite a bit of things they deem anomalies. It is when it colors works about something else—or nominally about something else—that the peril really arises.)

Plus, of course, any coloring the viewpoint gives them in regarding the people of the era as stepping stones toward the ideal future. In particular, the heroes and villains are assigned not for the moral character of their deeds but whether they sped history along the right path. Frequently enough, any openly and clearly stated motives by the historical figures will be breezed over for the "real" motives according to the historian's agenda. Some quote the primary source and not even apparently noticing that it contradicts the agenda before writing as if the historical figures' intentions matched the agenda.

H. G. Wells, in *The Outline of History*, gets all starry-eyed about any attempt, or success, at union between countries because he's looking forward to the beneficent World State, regardless of how the union was imposed, and what its consequences were, and again looking with a jaundiced eye on any division regardless of how justified.

It would be easier if the issue were limited to the historians of that school, but, of course, anyone who regards history in light of a progress toward the wonderful present—or future—will have the same issues. World War I hit the original Whig interpretation quite hard, but the Marxist interpretation kept roaring along, and is not quite dead yet.

And you can see all sorts of people tut-tutting over things where their notion of the end is in play. I have literally read a lament that during World War II, and as opposed to the stories before it, women characters in a certain magazine's stories were less likely to pursue their own ends and more likely to lend their strength to the war effort, to the point where I grumbled, "Don't you know there was a war going on?"

You can, of course, get the same effect in people who lament a decline. A marked tendency to track everything to how things failed. You can see this with particular ease in discussions of the Dark Ages. Especially in discussions of the Dark Ages that regard the entire medieval era as being the "Dark Ages." The nineteenth century is still rife with them, even though modern historians regard the recovery from Rome's fall as being pretty much accomplished by the year1000.

This one is a little harder to find, but not much harder to diagnose.

The real interesting one is the writer who unconsciously picks up the influence of the theory and occasionally lets it leak in comments that imply that the winner *deserved* to win, and the loser to lose, on no more evidence than of victory or defeat. Or some such assumption. Nothing but practice will ward that off.

All of them, of course, constitute primary source when you are considering the *historian*'s era. The view of the "Dark Ages" was closely connected to an uncritical view of the Roman and Greek classics, and hence an undue adulation for eras that followed them uncritically.

Just one of those things about reading history.

Blue Blood Begins

How nobles become nobles

Among other matters of social class—between the commoners and the king stretch the blue bloods. From the dukes of royal blood through the lower ranks of titles, down to the gentry who may not even be descended from a titled lord.

This is a useful group for characters.

Conflict in a story stems from the character trying to do something feasible but difficult. Picking the exact position on the scale is specific to the story—and to its setting and era, and any adaptations you have made to its practices from history, including mix and match from various cultures and eras—but it's a good part of the social system for many plots, both for the hero to come from and for his opposition. (Though, obviously, his opposition tends to be higher in status.)

Then, the era will determine many things about those characters. And their plot devices.

For instance, what makes a character noble?

In practice, of course, a character is noble if born into the noble class—because everyone knows what that is. The actual legal definition? There's a lot of variation.

Exactly how defined is the hierarchy your character is dealing with? A Dark Ages sort of setting has some variation in title, but often the title depends on your ability to back it up by force. A man might claim a higher title only for a more powerful man to insist on a lower one.

Or, of course, grant the higher one as a concession. In medieval usage, "Your Majesty" was for emperors only; kings were "Your Grace." The first use of "Your Majesty" for kings was when a medieval king and emperor signed a treaty, and it treated them as equals.

Then, in any era where social structure was well-defined enough to have aristocrats, there was also the possibility of being born to it. Your father was a duke, you are a duke; your father was a king, you are a king; your father was a baron, you are a baron.

Plus, the character could also attach himself to a born lord or king of sufficient power, and receive a title and lands to support it for his services. The big difference in this era and more structured ones is that any powerful man could set up his underlings in positions.

At the other extreme from the chaos, the noble structure may be set in stone. A literal caste, such that moving in or out has been unheard from time immemorial. One is a kshatriya by being born of a kshatriya mother and father. The only way in is fraud. Or, perhaps, taking yourself off to a more flexible region.

But European systems may, in practice, be only a little more flexible. Everyone may know in advance how the great-grandchildren of two characters will stand in relationship to each other even if the king decides to grant honors to the lower-status one. There were Germanic courts in the nineteenth century where, to be presented at court, all your great-grandparents had to be fit to be presented at court.

The advantage of this system is that it occurred when society was relatively peaceful, expansive, and prosperous, and thus if your character is not born to the aristocracy, you can perfectly well situate him in the circles of wealthy merchants, academic scholars, or bold explorers according to his situation. A character can be noteworthy and famous without blue-blood.

In between the poles of being able to claim the title by violence and being excluded, the king, the font of honors, may grant characters a noble position. There is a certain lack of status in being a new creation, but not relative to being common.

Long-established nobles may attack those newly granted titles for services to the crown in the course of conflict with the king. Attacking the new nobles as a bad influence is a way to attack the king without actually attacking the king. So it does have its perils.

On the other hand, in this state, there are a good number of aristocrats, namely second, third, fourth, or lower sons who will not inherit the estate. The second one has some chance in the modern era; hence the expression, the heir and the spare. The younger sons had more of a chance in the medieval era, where mortality was much higher and more evenly spread over age groups.

Still, if your older brother is grown and has sons, you, as a younger son, may be out to seek your fortune. There's no particular reason why you would not associate with young men also seeking their fortune as possible candidates for honors. At that, you yourself might seek a peerage in your own right. If you do inherit your father's estate in the end, your own title would just be added to the line-up.

This would give your friends a connection into the world of aristocrats, always useful during adventures. Since the point of being, or aspiring to be, noble during the course of the story is the plot device use.

Fakelore And Holidays

The perils of origins

I mentioned the myths of religion.

Another thing to watch like a hawk is accounts of folklore. Particularly its origins. All accounts of the origins of things, even in primary sources, should be suspect unless evidence can be verified. And this is a prime example, visible in glowing colors and great clarity.

Because a lot of what you see spread about—in books, in newspapers, in blogs—nowadays is very much fakelore, a lot of it provably invented in the nineteenth century or later.

Take Halloween—All Hallows' Eve or, in more modern English, All Saints' Eve.

Back in the earliest days of the Church, there was a feast to celebrate all the saints.

In April.

When St. Patrick brought Christianity to Ireland, the Irish adopted this practice. They also gave up Samhain, which none of them would have regarded as related to the first, because it was nothing to do with the dead. It was just the end of the harvest season. It also was not generally "Celtic"—only the Irish had celebrated it.

Later, the Germans started to celebrate All Saints' Day in November. It spread from there. The Irish were, in fact, very late adopters, and the Orthodox have not adopted it to this day.

In the nineteenth century, people, many of them overtly bigoted against Christianity, who wanted to insist on "pagan survivals" circularly claimed that Samhain was about the dead because it was on Halloween, and that Halloween was still Samhain.

This is, obviously, chronologically impossible, but you will find people to this day babbling about how Halloween is "really" Samhain.

Christmas is worse. Partly because they tend to miss that in some parts it was celebrated on December 25th and in others January 6th. But even going with just the December date—

The claims that Christmas is "really" Saturnalia are rife. The problem is that Saturnalia started on the 17th. After a time, it grew longer, until it stopped—on December 23rd. Two days too early. You can't appropriate a date without, well, appropriating a date.

Likewise, there are claims that Christmas is really the feast of Sol Invictus—which was, actually, celebrated on the 25th. Unfortunately, the first reference to its being celebrated on that date comes from the fourth century, in a document that mentions that it was also when Christians celebrated Christmas.

Meanwhile, there are references to Christians celebrating Christmas on December 25th at the beginning of the third century.

Given how Christianity spread in those times, it is quite possible that Sol Invictus was created as a counter to Christmas, but not vice versa.

And then you get people claiming Christmas is Yule.

Celebrated in the north. Past the bounds of the Roman Empire. Where the missionaries had not even reached at the time of Christmas being celebrated on December 25th. Certainly long before they converted them, or these people from the North could have influenced the customs. (As they did—oh—All Saints' Day.)

Besides clearing up those dates and things, remember this when reading about the origins of things. Never accept a claim, even when made by a primary source, about the origins of things. People do not know where their customs come from.

Slow Motion

Applying history to story

Travel is hard.

I mean, it is really, really, really hard. Roads are terrible. If they exist. Bridges fall down, or get flooded out, or simply do not exist. Crossroads may bear no markings, and so your choice may be life or death, with no knowledge, and you may not learn you went the wrong route for days, weeks, even months later.

Your speed is limited to your own plodding feet, or perhaps a beast that can carry you, but if you go by beast, you may not go much more swiftly because the beast needs rest and food and is incapable of traveling relentlessly all day. (The swiftest travel requires relays of horses. Or runners, but that will work only for messages.)

Not to mention the adventures dealing with war, or royal officials, or bandits, or just suspicious residents.

Land travel is difficult enough that traveling by sea is better, even with all the problems of waiting for winds, storms, becalming, rations, water, and shipwreck.

The consequence of this is that whenever someone travels, his family and friends lose contact with him.

One particularly eerie aspect of the banshee was that when she keened for the death of someone in your family, you might not hear for many months of the death that happened the next day.

Even mundane tales are rife with such things as brothers and sisters failing to recognize each other because they had been so long parted. (No doubt helped by the way that the age gaps could be much larger, since historically, couples went on producing children as long as they could be conceived.)

And yet I stare at the page and wonder whether the story as plotted works.

The heroine does indeed live at her parents' estates, in the mountains, in the borderlands—at any rate, some out-of-the-way corner where few travelers go.

She does indeed go on a pilgrimage, and if it's not the extent of, say, one from Norway to Rome, I could certainly make it leave the kingdom.

Then she gets involved in politics. And politics that have gotten violent, over the succession. And once they have gotten violent, they can't back down.

Perhaps I shall make the border regions fall under the control of the other faction—her involvement having forced her onto one side.

And the prince leading the faction she's in is reluctant to send a messenger into dangerous lands for reasons that will not benefit him in his fight.

So I look at this pile of reasons and wonder whether I should pile it higher, or perhaps work harder on explicating it for the benefit of the readers to whom this is all strange and alien.

Because after she goes on this pilgrimage, she returns home with a husband and two children in tow. Year-old, twin children, but children. And they had never met her husband before. She had never met her husband before she entered the prince's service. It took her at least several months after falling in with the prince to get married.

Can you really convey that no news came back about their daughter until she showed up?

All right. Deep breath. And fall back.

What is needed is *foreshadowing*.

And what that needs is for her to not be the only fish in the ocean.

People are gone for long times. News is scarce. Perhaps the hills in which she lives are particularly derided for their lack of news.

Perhaps I can rip off the Peach Blossom Spring tale. Actually having a valley in which people are unaware that they aren't still in the reign of a long-dead king would be overkill. But someone could tell it.

On the other hand, if I do that, it's probably going to have to be significant in the struggles. Both factions need to have serious troubles about knowledge. (All the more in that, for another reason, the heroine has reliable knowledge that she can't justify.)

Not to mention all the world-building effects. Only on rivers or other bodies of water is any real degree of famine relief possible. Control of the borders of even your kingdom is precarious. Your emissaries have to have real authority because they can't check with you.

Writing is full of these things. You start with a scene you want, and you end up dictating the world-building all over.

World Building

Putting the world together from all that you've gleaned.

Reliability vs. Dragons

Whether your infrastructure withstands monsters

How reliable is your world?

It is of vital importance because nothing influences the society more.

Hunters and gatherers rely on food sources that can be fugitive. They hand out their finds to many people in their bands in hopes of future generosity when their own luck turns bad. Then, their efforts will have immediate rewards—or not.

Only in wildly fertile areas could they remain in fixed abodes. The vast majority had to move regularly because an area could not reliably produce enough for all even of the small bands. This had effects, such as making the development of pottery with all its advantages impossible. Pottery is bulky and hard to lug about.

Farmers face more certain rewards and ability to reap them in a fixed location, but only months in the future after relentless labor. Consequently, they reap, and then they keep what they reap for themselves.

Indeed, in cultures where both are practiced, people often keep all that they farmed while sharing after hunts or gathering.

Then, farming is often struck with disaster—weather, locusts, and many others—and hunting and gathering follow seasonal patterns, such that it has been suggested that the famous Neolithic cave paintings are calendars to track the behavior of animals.

In a fantasy novel, if magic forecasts weather and insects, or even controls them, the greater regularity works wonders. Crops are more bountiful. Gathering is more plentiful. The weather knowledge lets boats transport the food more widely. True, people in marginal farmland may have to change their crops or even give it up entirely, but people will eat.

On the other hand, if fae magic makes time pass faster or slower from one spot to another, there is no point in planting seeds because the wheat field may be an ancient oak forest the next time you see it, or even when you finish your meal. Characters living in such a place would grab whatever food they can see, on sight, if they could live there at all.

Things that require more reliability will be even more difficult.

I was thinking of factories and supply chains.

Transportation from far away—remember when the Suez Canal was blocked? There is bound to be some way to cause that much trouble for magical transportation, whatever it is. And thus reliability fails.

That sort of failures affects supply chains for factories. Many fantasy worlds would affect factories beyond the difficulty of developing the necessary technology.

I once read a book in which the knights traveled by motorcycle. And were needed. Enormous monsters—chimera, gryphons, dragons, what have you—would appear out of nowhere anywhere at all.

And this was the way it had been for generations, long past the ability of people to scavenge what was needed, even without noticing that the book did not have the scavengers where they would be needed to supply the knights, or the locations to be scavenged on stage despite much travel.

So how on earth did they keep the factories going?

What did a chimera tromping through your factory do to your production? What if it breathed fire on combustible material? How about explosives?

What about the gasoline you need for your motorcycle? What if a dragon merely flew by and breathed fire?

What did a gryphon sitting on the train tracks do to your part supply? Would it leave the tracks undamaged?

What would a unicorn do to your chemical vats? When it purifies them of their poison, what do you do to fix them?

Godzilla and his ilk are a similar problem. Real-world kaiju would lead to massive alterations in the world. Cities would be massively decentralized. Institutions would spread out their infrastructure to avoid concentrated damage. Factories would be set up in defensive locations, probably far from shore, and probably with as few factories as possible. You do not ship gears by routes that could be endangered—if you can. Though you still have to get raw materials in and products out. And you may have to have parts factories for the size of the plant.

All of that, of course, would aggravate transportation and communication issues because of the way people are more spread out, and so delivery must be. One hopes you have the technology or the magic (or some combination) to deal with it, but you might not. You might just have to live with the limits.

Would the limits allow for motorcycles with all the infrastructure requirements? To build them in the first place? To build their spare parts? To provide the fuel?

For good and for evil, magic is not just an epiphenomenon on your world, something that dances alongside all the stuff that makes this work. It affects all kinds of things, and their reliability.

The Sun, The Moon, And The Stars, And Other Observations

Things you don't realize you don't realize

Once upon a time, someone set out to create a world with a dualism at its base. He wanted to base it on a different dichotomy, an unusual dualism, so he decide to make it Sun vs. Moon. Everyone born by day was Sun; everyone born by night was Moon.

He went off and elaborated from there, how all this Sun and Moon thing played out, but I stayed there.

I thought of twilight.

I thought of solar eclipses, and lunar ones too.

Finally, I remembered that in the ordinary way of things, the Moon spends as much time in the day sky as in the night.

Indeed, you can quite frequently see it. Mind you, it's a half moon, or gibbous, or (if the seasons are right) full, and it can be tricky to pick out because it looks like a small cloud, unusually neat in form.

No, if you want a Night luminary, what you want is the Stars. Lots of contrast there. The Sun is brilliant and drowns out all else, to be single. The Stars are multiple and more chary of their light.

The Moon can either make it a three-way system, turning on its fugitive and changing nature, or perhaps be demoted to a servant between the Sun, the power of Day, and the Stars, the power of the Night. The Moon could go from the Stars to the Sun and back, bearing messages.

Perhaps some people were born as Moon people, either night or day, to work as a go-between.

But still, there's twilight. If people are born between the faintest stars starting to vanish from sight and the first peak of the sun over the horizon—even if it's the mathematical horizon, not the visible—or conversely, between the last bit of sun vanishes over the horizon and the faintest stars becoming visible, what happens then?

Actually the only real problem is civil twilight, when things can be seen clearly. By nautical twilight, while the horizon can still be made out, the stars are clearly visible. (Hence the name. This time is very important when navigating by stars.)

But it's there. And only for one of the twilight times in any given day will the Moon shine.

Will there be evening stars and morning stars? Can people be Evening Star people or Morning Star people?

Do your characters know that these wanderers differ from the fixed stars?

Does your world have evening and morning stars because it has wanderers that differ from the fixed stars? Or not?

Then, your world could be all sorts of things, including flat as a pancake. (With all the interesting effects of a sun that either remains perfectly high during the entire day, or one that comes much closer to land in the evening. With particular effect for that land. Or maybe it warms up until noon and cools up after.)

Indeed, you could have a world where the moon is full every night, rising as the sun sets. You still would have to work out twilight—unless perhaps you abolished that, as well. The same moment the last bit of sun ticked under the horizon, the first bit of the moon ticked up.

You might have to work out whether there are tides, and if so, what controls them. That would be a problem with a flat world, too, since tides stem from the way the earth and the moon rotate about their common center of mass, but also with the ever-full moon because it can not be rotating in accordance with Newtonian mechanics.

There's a whole range of things you can do. Easiest one is to make it the Sun people and the Stars people.

Religions in High Fantasy

How to build them

Questions of metaphysics and fictional religions raise questions of fictional religions.

Fictional religions where the gods do not appear. Where you *might* glean a riddle from an oracle and try to puzzle it out at most. In fine, ones that could (in theory) appear in historical fiction.

Most religions in fantasy are very badly written. One major reason is that most fantasy religions don't really exist. And the other one is that, insofar as they do exist, they don't fit together.

A conglomeration of Bad Guys Out To Do Bad Things is not a religion.

Three religions, one of which worships the sun, another the moon, and a third the evening star, are not religions. If only because they offer no reason for their exclusivity in worship. All the more when they have lifted elements from monotheistic worship, including persecution. (In fact, except for cosmetic elements, chiefly persecution.)

One commonest errors in polytheistic religions in fantasy is that you have characters who worship one god in a pantheon while acknowledging the existence of all the others. This can be possible if the gods are gods of locations—I live in Thebes and worship the god of Thebes—or ancestral in some way, but most fantasy gods have spheres of influence: god of kingship, god of oceans, goddess of fertility, goddess of marriage.

Euripides's *Hippolytus* depicts how the actual polytheists view a man who worshiped only one god, the goddess Artemis in this case: a dangerous lunatic who will bring down the wrath of the other gods. Hippolytus's exclusive worship of Artemis is his tragic flaw.

In a real polytheistic religion, you would worship any appropriate god. The king would of course worship the god of kingship, but because he would want heirs, the goddess of fertility as well, and because he would want his country's merchants to do well for tax purposes, the god of oceans, etc. etc.

Indeed, we have inscriptions where the worshiper recounts how he raised this altar to Zeus at the command of Apollo. Priests and priestess may be in charge of propitiating all the appropriate gods. Even priests dedicated to one god would act as worshipers of other gods as appropriate; the idea that a priest of the marriage god should not participate in a harvest festival would be regarded as very dangerous, it might offend the god of the harvest.

Consequently, given the visible limits of the luminaries, you have to have some reason for the three religions. Perhaps they each claim descent from the luminary god and so are engaging in ancestor worship. Perhaps each god relates to a way of life.

But they are more likely to regard it as a danger to themselves if the other people give up their worship of the luminary. It is dangerous for a god to go without propitiation.

If you look at actual religious practice, you will soon find that there are two types: religions that are fully integrated into their societies and have no rivals, and religions that grow in contrast to other religious beliefs. Hinduism, Shinto, and Greek/Roman paganism are instances of the former; Christianity and Buddhism of the later. The first class don't have names until an instance of the second class comes along, if then; Hinduism and Shinto were named in contrast to Buddhism, and since "pagan" means a person neither a Christian nor a Jew nor a Muslim, Greek/Roman paganism hasn't really been named YET.

The first class tends to be highly syncretistic. That is, it pulls in all sorts of gods and practices from other regions and even other religions. This can be done by identifying gods with other nation's vaguely similar gods: in the Roman times, the god Mercury was identified with the Greek god Hermes, with the Egyptian god Thoth, and—get this—with the German god Odin. This sometimes happened with the second class; in Japan, a oracle of the sun goddess Amaterasu (Shinto) identified Buddhist priests as the correct people to perform funeral rites. People who practice this type of religion in the absence of a contrasting religion of the second type aren't aware of their practices as religious.

They also tend to be lacking in philosophy. One notes that both Plato and Buddha calmly dismissed the gods worshiped about them as *irrelevant* to the matters of importance.

Also, they seldom have sacred texts—at all, or in the sense that most people think of them. The teachings are passed down parent to child, or through a sacred caste of priests, or by special officials.

Obviously, since the second class comes in to being by contrasting with the first class, it defines its doctrines more stringently and obviously excludes a great deal more, since exclusion is a necessary part of definition. They come much more naturally to philosophy, and they are much more likely to have sacred texts to define things.

Which class you pick will have a lot of effect on your society. There are, in fact, a lot of options in history and sufficient worldbuilding could generate more. But there needs to be an actual religion, and then its institutions have to fit.

Mastery of Mankind

Why aren't elves ruling the world?

In your average high-fantasy role-playing game, in any GameLit world, and in a great many high fantasies—the fantasy worlds abound with civilized races. Sometimes to a ludicrous degree, dwarves, elves, gnomes, halflings being merely the minimum that high fantasy worlds are seldom without. All of them live openly, without any masquerade, with commerce and diplomacy, with schools that teach all sorts of species, without any vulnerabilities to sunlight or iron.

And these worlds are dominated by mankind, not elves, or dwarves, or trolls, or halflings. Despite, as many complain, the dominant race's being the shortest lived of the intelligent civilized races.

Fundamentally, the great reason is because most gamers and most readers are human, so there's an element of ease.

Given the out-of-universe reason, this tends to be treated leniently. Really, many post hoc explanations would cover it. Assuming, of course, it comes up. It doesn't have to. Most characters would accept the world as the way the world is.

Still, it might affect things that the characters don't realize, so it may be wise to determine it.

One reason, which games even make canonical, explains that human characters are more diverse. Which does play into the aspect that a non-human race has to have a commonality to make them something other than humans with pointy ears or short stature or what have you. Then, if the players are running the characters, they are likely to turn into humans with cosmetic differences.

Still, other reasons are possible.

The world suffers magic droughts, and it turns out that mankind is the only race that can really live without magic, and takes over the world during them. The other races survive in oases in these times.

Mankind was there first, and filled it up before the others arrived. (Which may also have effects in that the others aren't really native to it.)

Mankind is actually the only race. Every "non-human" race was derived from them by magical alterations to them. Possibly caused by naturally magical lands. This would, at least, explain the ease of interbreeding among them. Also, it would mean they came after, here, too.

Conversely, if it serves the story, the trope can be lightly tossed aside. Mankind with their short lives might be as marginal as goblins and ogres, while long-lived elves reach the highest levels at civilization and power.

But even in typical game lore, there's a lot of reasons why mankind might rule the world.

Indeed, the way the typical game sets up religion, such that the gods are literally dependent for their very existence on worshipers, produces the obvious cause that the gods favor them. Not *like* them, but favor them. Mankind frequently serves several pantheons in one setting. Elven, dwarven, etc. pantheons are constant throughout the worlds, where worlds with only one human pantheon may have gods unique to that world.

A god with only a subset of humans needs to keep their favor. A new god has no choice but to woo human worshipers because no other race will give the worship a chance. And if the gods dislike showering mankind with favor, they have nowhere else to go. Plus, once the humans predominate, they are also the biggest source of worship.

Other worlds, more rational than that about metaphysics, can use the same long lives to keep the other races from taking over. The longest-lived races may also be the greatest procrastinators. Never put off to tomorrow what you can do today? Pshaw! No one but a human would consider tomorrow putting something off. You could wait a century and still do it.

They may even think it beneath their dignity to worry about the humans and their civilizations, which come and go like mayflies. (Perhaps after some centuries it dawns on them that civilizations may go, but they are replaced in some form or another. By that time, mankind has established a position strong enough that dislodging them is hard.)

Foolish non-human characters could also flaunt their long lives and produce interesting backfire.

One elf telling his fellow wizard apprentices that he will be alive centuries after they are dust could produce a lot of wizards who want to ensure that centuries from that day, people will still ask him if he knew that great archmage when they were apprentices.

If most would forget that ambition before doing anything, if most of those left would produce no real impact, if most of those left didn't get remembered for their impact—still, it would produce a cumulative effect because the impact was real even if not remembered.

Not to mention that if one wizard succeeded, everyone would remember not the unremembered fellow apprentices, but how everyone asks the elf whether he really was an apprentice with that one. Selection bias will encourage them.

Or—perhaps its nonhuman culture that's to blame. Human cultures tend to be indifferent to the particulars of power. Non-human?

After an ancient red dragon and its clutch of wyrmlings, and all its minions, are dead, the heroes sit about their conjured feast, and the human cleric speaks warmly of returning home.

The elven barbarian considers how her fellow elves will hear she killed a dragon, sniff, and say, "But can she write a villanelle yet?"

The dwarf sorcerer contemplates how they will talk of how he uses magic, and not even magic he learned.

The orc wizard envisions being held up of an example of how magic deludes weaklings, he thinks he's great because he killed a dragon, but only with magic.

The gnome paladin realizes that some gnome will ask her whether the dragon was named Joy, because she's certainly a killjoy, and they will all laugh like it's funny.

The halfling rogue knows they will tell her to get to work helping put up the new chicken coop after the wind blew a tree over the last one before bothering with her tale.

So they resolve to return to the large human city where there are many non-human enclaves, of their own kind more in tune with humans, and lots of humans who will at least recognize what they did.

Perhaps humans picked up the generalized respect from an era when they were as marginalized as orcs or ogres.

Consider that if they are that marginal, they can not quibble about what you do to fight, as long as you fight. They won't even quibble about your not being human. Non-human adventurers may find themselves more welcome among mankind than among their own.

At that, members of other races, wanting to fight monsters, have to come to human lands to do it. That's where the frontier is, and therefore the monsters. Therefore, you have to at least tolerate mankind to adventure.

This would also influence the willingness to switch gods whenever something looks better. This is logical and even necessary if you are living on the edge.

Not to mention that the scorn for a marginal race—or touchiness about their history of being marginal—could feed into the the scorn for the short-lived, and thus increase the anger and the desire to show them.

Once they grow powerful enough this way, they can slowly take over while the other races continue to care more about their own preoccupations.

No doubt many other fun histories could be devised for it, but this one would work.

Pondering Punk As A Post-Fix

Technology in your fantasy

Ah, the wonders of semantic drift.

How "-punk" means nothing at all in terms of the original meaning of "punk", despite the intermittent efforts of various souls to try to drag it back and insist that all the -punk genres should be dark, gritty, and cynical, and take the position of the essay's author about society.

I agree that as a term meaning anachronistic technology, "-punk" is about as bad a term as can be devised. However, unless someone else comes up with a better suffix, and everyone decides to adopt it, "-punk" is what we are stuck with. We can just read bright, colorful, cheerful, idealistic, hope-filled "punk" and try to not think about that side of things.

We can, instead, think about the use of technology in fantasy. This is, in fact, a more reasonable use of the various technologies. The steampunk computers in the original, alternate-history tales would not have worked for as long as they did. Even though they theoretically could work, they would need a larger supply of coal than was actually available.

As such, magical technology works elegantly. The energy supply needs only to be plausible to the reader, as a rhetorical trick, and can still be impossible. You do not need steampunk and billowing clouds of smoke; you can elegantly have clockpunk and finesse that the springs can not power it.

Indeed, if you hail all the way back to the days of chivalric romance, when magic and technology were not so divided, you find works with automata doing this and that. A hero's father wants to convince him his beloved is dead, and he should make a more useful match. He builds a splendid tomb, with two figures of a young man and a young woman, and the romance tells us that when the wind blew, the figures would embrace each other.

There are also tales that the magician Virgil—you didn't know that Virgil was a magician? now you do—created an automaton that patrolled a city. It also complained when threatened.

-Punk technology can, of course, do some of the same work that a highly advanced magic can do in preventing the unpleasant sides of reality from intruding, but not the same sides. Magic can do the healing and the preventing crop failure and famine, but technology is probably more closely bound to the same paths as ours is.

Not absolutely, but it's hard to make another path, especially one distinctly different.

When you read nineteenth-century stories, you can see that health has little improved—writers have no difficulty killing off characters and saying he just died as a plot device—but the effect of improved communications and transportation is heavy. Adventures have shifted venue, and adventurers often have to be explorers. Or, like Sherlock Holmes, find secret, hidden adventures in civilized lands.

It is not merely the callbacks to the chivalric romance that put most high fantasy in a sorta-medieval setting. Nor the influence of *The Lord of the Rings*. (Though, granted, that was not trivial. Lin Carter, digging up old works of fantasy to reprint, found they succeeded in exact proportion to their resemblance to *Lord of the Rings*. Chesterton's *The Man Who Was Thursday* crashed. Evangeline Walton's *Island of the Mighty*, which crashed on its original publication, launched her fantasy career in this new era.)

Nowadays, tackling the issues is much more common. That does not mean that the issues aren't there, or that they can't make your story absurd. Rampaging monsters would destroy factories. Dragons have to learn to live in harmony with mankind, or in secrecy.

Which is why the masquerade grew so much True, it is much older than "-punk" levels of technology. Still, its advent matters. Monsters must move away, or live in relative peace, or hide.

I had some fun with the "relative peace" in *Dragonfire And Time*. Central to the story is the dragon. Dragons have agreements. Kings and their governments will not object if the dragons deal summarily with thieves in their hoards and, furthermore, will hunt down any thief who manages to escape. In return, the dragons remain in their lairs and send indignant word when a thief escapes. Thus, the heroine is assigned the task, and travels by train to reach the place.

Summer's Over

Seasons and time and magic

Summer is over.

And yet people still chirp that the *official* date at which summer ends is the equinox.

To which I respond: then who is the official who decreed that? What office does he hold? Who appointed him and gave him the authority to decree that?

Is the summer solstice called Startsummer Day? No, it's called Midsummer.

(I've never even gotten an answer.)

Mind you, that was probably more accurate back in the days of the Julian calendar, when everything was slipping back in seasons, when St. Lucy's was the longest night of the year, and Easter was steadily drifting out of spring and toward summer.

Shakespeare was eminently reasonable when he wrote

> Shall I compare thee to a summer's day?
> Thou art more lovely and more temperate:
> Rough winds do shake the darling buds of May,
> And summer's lease hath all too short a date;

because May was clearly summer weather.

But still June is clearly summer before the solstice.

Odds are great that your characters consider that seasons are governed by the actual climate, not by the stars. If this means that the seasons vary in length, it means they vary in length.

Indeed, there is reason to believe that the Romans started out with a ten-month calendar. It started in the spring (March 25 was the date fixed, quite possibly later) and went for ten months, and after that came winter, not divided into months.

A perfectly plausible calendar would be to start based on some natural occurrence, and then run the rest of the year through. Provided you don't have issues that don't turn on the natural seasons.

Most people didn't. A continual struggle to construct a calendar that fits the actual seasons has occurred in many cultures. In China, issuing a calendar was a grave issue, an imperial prerogative, and that the Jesuits could make a more accurate one was a point in their favor.

Even bureaucrats can manage such shifting calendars. Egypt managed for centuries working on the period of the Inundation of the Nile occurred.

Then, in a fantasy world, there would be more people who would find a fixed year useful.

Imagine a culture in which spring starts with the little snow-star blossoming in the woods. Suppose that everyone formally turns a year older on that day.

Then imagine a wicked sorcerer blighting it, so that the flower does not grow. Formally, grown men and women are still boys and girls, and not allowed to marry, or go to war, or engage in trade, or own land.

The best thing that could happen to them would be for a prophecy to take advantage of the liminal status of being actually adult but formally a child to exploit a weakness in the sorcerer's protection.

Or take your canonical Dark Lord. If he overshadows the land as Sauron did in *The Lord of the Rings*, and then conquers—well, if there are magical means by which they can continue agriculture, or otherwise raise food—they are really going to need some kind of formal calendar.

At least it will be a useful tool to fight against the endless blur of days together. All the more if the Dark Lord's food raising trick causes harvests to be an unpredictable measure of time.

Then, if you have the traditional Snow Queen, you have a real problem with food. It might be plausible to work around the light problem, but cold strikes me as a deal breaker.

On the other hand, the sun, the moon, and the stars would be visible, thus giving you a celestial time to contrast with the utter lack of terrestrial time moving forward.

Fantasy calendars would be complicated. (And the question of magic that can change relative times would—be too large for the tail end of an essay.)

A Brief Account of Days of Labor

Setting your calendar

Does your setting have days in honor of labor? Can you fit one in?

Well, kinda, sorta—look, first world-build your religion.

Medieval guilds, for instance, would have festivities on the days of the patron saint of their profession. Attend a service, pray for blessings on them and their work, and hold a feast.

For the vast majority of people who worked the land, there were the agricultural feasts. St. Distaff—there was no saint named Distaff. It was a reference to the way that, with the twelve days of Christmas being over, everyone took up work again on January 7. Women's spinning being one of the most pervasive and time-consuming, and season independent (women would even take spindle and distaff along to spin while on journeys), the distaff served as synecdoche for all labor.

Then there would be Plough Sunday, the next Sunday, where a plow would be brought to church and blessed.

Agricultural labor would also bring harvest festivals, such as Lammas (Loaf Mass) to have a service in thanksgiving. (Harvest festivals have the charm of being easy to feast at.)

And then some religions are polytheistic. In which, we note, there are often gods of occupations. Weaving. Blacksmithing. Agriculture. Especially agriculture.

We note that the Spartans, who were noted for being particularly scrupulous about religion, had no temples to, or festivals for, Demeter or Dionysus. Those two were agricultural gods. That was helot work. That was, in fact, so thoroughly helot work that we had the story of a Spartan's unfavorable reaction when he heard that Cyrus gardened as a hobby. Utterly absurd for *a king* to do that sort of thing.

So we can deduce that other places, having those temples and those festivals, probably did have a modicum of respect for the job involved in the rite.

Indeed, one Greek city would ritually put out all fires, send for new fire from Delphi, and perform rites. Then, they would distribute the fire with particular attention to those whose work was with fire.

So you can have a day in honor of a particular kind of labor, but you have to build the world carefully.

A god of labor in general? Not likely. Polytheistic gods tend to proliferate, and also a god's other spheres tend to control which occupations honored him. Mariners for the sea god, bureaucrats for the kingship god, scribes for the writing god. . . .

If you want a *civic* holiday in honor of labor—or of particular occupation—choose a model that postdates the French Revolution, and pick with care. Prior to that time, the idea of a civic holiday with no religious element would be regarded as absurd. (Witness that the term derives from "holy day.")

And even since the French Revolution, you have to pick your models with care, depending on how much religion you want. Totally secular ones need the right model.

Or else the application of a lot of spackle to make the world-building work.

Funny Fantasy Money

Fantasy coinage

Ah, the gold piece, the silver piece, the copper piece. Such an effect that RPGs have on fantasy economics. The bland workhorse of the economy is those three—sometimes a few more, but not a thousand and more different coins with the heads of different kings or other insignia on them and, worse, varying values.

Not that I can blame them. The novels follow the games because the plot device effect is the same for both.

The stories that would benefit from the characters having to line up and change all their money for the debased coins of a region that legally requires you to use them its borders while they are worthless outside it—and pay for the privilege—are very few. All the more in that likely it would happen several times.

Even trying to reckon the value of coins found in several different realms' coinage would be tedious. (Perhaps they could figure out dates by the monarchs? Or realize there are symbols in use that they don't know for a nice Chekhov's Gun?)

And a random grab bag of coins is entirely plausible. In early modern France, peasants who dug up Roman coins in their fields would simply use them as coins.

This reflects a common problem. Money is, of course, incredibly useful when it has any value. As long as it was made of precious metals, the lack of supply was a problem. There simply was not enough money for it to pass from hand to hand to facilitate trade.

And not just the large coins. One Roman emperor decided to spread his fame by minting a lot of small coins with praise for a victory of his, and an economic boom ensued because of the greater ease in making change.

On the other hand, those minting coins were profiting by it, but they wanted to profit more. The constant temptation to debase your coins, including less and less of the precious metal, devalued them. Both Athens and Egypt mandated that their own, debased coins be used in the lands they controlled, and no one would accept them outside their regions. Hence, the need for money changers when going in or out of them.

(Not that they were alone in their lack of scruples. Milling coins—putting ridges on the edge—was introduced to prevent people from clipping the edges of coin for the precious metals before spending the coins. This was introduced by Sir Isaac Newton. Before, it was a chronic problem.)

Inflation still ensued whenever the money supply increased. In devalued currency, of course, but also when there was a strike of silver, or a gold rush.

That is one thing that the games get right. Gary Gygax described the price list as being based on a gold-rush sort of economy, owing to the influx of treasure brought back by adventurers. If this then spread out and stimulated the economy—which it appears to, since in many ways RPG worlds are far better than medieval—inflation may not ensue, since the goods increase.

But why the constant coins?

The only real way to nail it down is magic. In the standard RPG universe, a god of justice whose clerics can create small enchantments that test coins. (Perhaps weights and other measurements?) They would have to be permanent and widespread to have good effect, being effectively magical objects. In a world more distant from games, wizards known for probity.

Hmm—perhaps a magical object that validates something to evaluate things to standards. Perhaps only coins, perhaps weights and measures.

Coins could be made a particularly urgent matter. Perhaps dragons have been known to burn down cities in revenge for the mint there producing inferior coins. Plus anyone who originally gave the dragon the coins, thus giving anyone who might conceivably need to bribe a dragon incentive to ensure that all his coins are good.

No doubt there are other reasons why it could be made moot where the coins came from. (And hey, you can still use the particular details to the coins to tell when they were minted, and where, and still be standardized coinage, just for fun.)

The Course Of History

History changes.

Kings rise and fall. Kingdoms rise and fall. Cities rise and fall.

Cold weather and drought turn lands to desert, or to grassland. Warm weather and rain turn desert to grasslands, and grasslands to forest.

Rivers silt up, and worse, harbors. Floods scour out new routes for rivers.

Those who notice those sorts of changes may still maintain that, in the long run, nothing changes. There's an ancient Greek tale about a land where every thousand years, a land is utterly changed from a lake whose fishing villages thinks it has always been there, to a grassland whose nomads think it has always been there, to a city whose inhabitants thinks it has always been there—to a lake whose fishing villages thinks it has always been there.

This view gets harder to maintain when technology or knowledge changes. Steam, or electricity—or iron, or bronze, or, no doubt, newfangled techniques in chipping flint—or writing, or what have you.

Not for people in general, mind you. Notoriously, people take for granted technology introduced before they were born, or even when they were relatively young. Many even take for granted the marvels of modern medicine and machinery, and the wealth and prosperity of the modern day, where the threat of famine does not hanging continually over everyone.

This, obviously, is much greater in people of two or three centuries ago, or earlier. Partly because technology changed so much more slowly, partly because the threat of famine hanging over your head is an excellent distraction, partly because the vast majority of people were uneducated because it did not help prevent the next famine.

Oral history, it has been found, is not really accurate when it's over a century and a half, even when you have trained professionals trying to transmit it. Without the trained professionals, it's closer to a century.

Consequently, nothing is odd about the peasants saying that they have always lived in the shadow of the Storm Lord who extorts their crops and surrounds his mountaintop stronghold with unending thunderstorms, regardless of whether it's been a century or millennia.

It is even possible that your hero can reach the summit and slay the Storm Lord without the question of whether it's been a century or millennia arising.

But if it does—

Suppose the Storm Lord also has petrifaction magic. The heroes who tried to overthrow him, the rivals who tries to usurp his place, the victims he captured—all were turned to stone. When the hero slays the Storm Lord, they all come down the mountain, and they complain of the changes over the course of centuries—and you notice how little there have been.

Take Pern. A 400 "turn" time leap—and their turns can't be too far from years, given how old the characters are at given ages in turns—and the Old-Timers grumble.

But what, really, has changed? The Guilds have grown a little more powerful, but there have not even been any new ones founded—possibly because they have made no noteworthy technological innovations.

All the Keeps are still in place, and there are no new ones, and no people spreading past the Keep's bounds. This in a heavily agricultural society, favoring fertility, and low infant mortality. One lord went and conquered five keeps, but this was an anomaly, and they split instantly on his death.

There have not been any four centuries on Earth in any civilized region where there have not been vastly more changes. (And I wouldn't bet on the uncivilized regions, either.) It makes the world seem more shallow.

True, a fantasy novel can implement means to keep kingdoms more stable, such as spells that rely on the royal family's blood to keep things prosperous. Elves who like to keep things the same. Or ancient wizards. Kings and emperors who reasonably (or unreasonably) fear that changes would endanger their thrones by empowering their enemies inside and outside their realms. But, if characters are consciously reflecting on the passage of time, such causes can be mentioned, and should be mentioned, or at least introduced. Perhaps the repressions are significant enough to be mentioned, and thus avoid shallowness.

It can be done in science fiction, too. George Phillies's *Mistress of the Waves* shows that the society is constrained to keep that way.

Or, of course, you can introduce enough history to suggest what is needed. More or less depending on the story. In my own *Queen Shulamith's Ball*, the City was built to give kings a place to negotiate together. (It's called the City so as not to use the name from any given kingdom. That would be undiplomatic.) Now it is also a place where royalty go to take refuge from revolutions—though it's still vital enough diplomatically that some constitutional monarchies have kings solely to gain access to the City.

All of which could be worked around the edges—somewhat aided by my use of omniscient viewpoint—and while moving the story forward. It helped to give depth.

Strange Things Happening To Strange People In Strange Places

On balancing your strange

When making your character, setting, and plot interesting, it helps to throw in strange things. Because they are novel, and distinctive.

But, you need to realize you have a limit there. Too many strange things makes it just a jumble.

Worse is when they are at random. If your hero can work magic that no one else can with rubies, and then with emeralds, and then with sapphires, it at least points to a reason. If he can work magic with rubies, talk to daffodils, and fly, the reader's eyes are apt to narrow.

Especially when you realize that the limit doesn't expand much when you have different characters getting different strangenesses. Some, yes, there is more plausibility about an odd thing happening to each of half a dozen characters than half a dozen odd things happening to one person. On the other hand, you also have to factor in that you are giving the reader more strange things to juggle.

If you don't provide some good reason for them to all meet and work together, that is, in fact, another strange thing that uses up some of your reader's attention.

So—watch how strange your characters are. Think of it in terms of a budget. Things may be cheaper by the dozen, but they aren't free.

Furthermore, the strange things need, on the whole, to be relevant to the story.

Indeed, some of them *must* be relevant to the story, or it will run afoul of the great principle of fantastic writing, whether science fictional, fantasy, or superhero: a story that can be told mundanely should be told mundanely. If you can remove the non-mundane elements without fundamentally changing the story, there's no point to them.

(All right, some can be essential for mood or theme, so that the same events and characters will have different impact. But be wary of that.)

But even once the story clearly must be fantasy or SF or superhero, peripheral strange things need careful handling. Otherwise they will distract.

More or less. Much depends on how artfully you handle it. And it does need some balance. If absolutely everything strange serves the story, these things do tend to flaunt their plot device status. So some things may serve the story solely by being a distraction from it, and others are of trivial import.

If some songbirds fly about and shine while in shadow, it can indicate that you have passed into a different kingdom. Or that you are near to the enchanted forest you seek.

If the thunderbird was sighted, it may be impossible to get a cart, because they all belong to farmers who are frantically trying to get the harvest in before the threatened thunderstorms.

If a garden has flowers that open precisely at the hour, forming a far more accurate flower clock, it may indicate only that they have magic that skillful. This, of course, needs care.

Artful use is needed to downplay and elide things that are to be local color.

If your character glances over headlines on the paper, reporting on gryphon migrations in Suddene, a dragon warlord in Serica killing merchants, and the sudden reappearance of the prince of Norroway with his new wife, the reader will take those as important. Even if he grumbles about the irrelevance, the reader may take the very grumbles as a way of highlighting their importance, and ironically giving the character a chance to be forewarned, thus building up dramatic irony.

It may help to give it more purpose in the scene that it occurs. The character glances over the page to ensure that no news of the Black Hound leaked out, even at the bottom of the page, knowing that most people won't read further in. Or perhaps he glances over it in fury, knowing that none of this will be relevant to more than one in a thousand readers, but no one is warned of the dangerous Black Hound.

I hit on this in *The Princess Seeks Her Fortune*, when I wondered if the story made it seem like Alissandra was the center of the fairy tales of the world, at least in one lengthy passage. So I threw in a bit where swans were carrying a carpet across the sky, so far off that she didn't even see the princess it carried, because *The Six Swans* went on parallel to her, and she wouldn't even be a bit character in it.

It was a throw-away bit of world-building, but much to my surprise, it got singled out for comment in one review, about how rife the world was with fairy tales, that she could see this and not even think to mention it to the characters she worked and lived with.

So juggling strangeness like this, with all its difficulties, can definitely aid your work.

Maps, Distances, And Travel

Some considerations

Look at some maps of ancient empire. Babylonian, Egyptian, Persian.

One notes a degree of contiguity between the regions involved.

Odd shapes, to be sure, sometimes with a tendency to follow coastlines, and probably other geographical features.

Still, the empire is a shape.

Now, compare to the British empire. Splotches here and there, far apart, with no visible connection.

Other empires of that era show the same trait. The regions are connected by the ocean, which is open to all mankind, and not feasible to lay claim to. Consequently, no degree of contiguity is to be expected.

Now, look at some science fictional interstellar maps. What do they look like?

Blobs like ancient empires. And not even so odd in shape. Just someone slapping some paint on the map.

Now, from the viewpoint of a map, what outer space consists of is hard vacuum. Atoms, let alone planets or stars, are rounding error.

It would take an enormous innovation in science, far past mere faster-than-light travel, to enable anyone to exclude anyone else from that space. It is open to all mankind.

Much more likely would be a map where stars are in color, and it looks like pointillism, only much more mixed.

Now, some forms of FTL would mitigate this. Worm holes, for instance. If you travel between star systems by finding one of the rare worm holes, if most systems have one, or two, or three, the empires will spread along the web of worm-holes. Network stars with scores, or a dozen, or half a dozen stars, could leverage their position to attain power over trade.

BUT—

Most works assume that wormholes will tunnel to the next star system, thus producing blobbing. Fine if you really want it.

Literally nothing prevents a worm hole's going anywhere in the universe. You could have a universe in which a worm hole necessarily goes to another galaxy (or equivalent but smaller stellar group). You could have a universe in which your interstellar empire needs telescopes to see other members but can pick out a dozen other empires by eye.

A map would look like pointillism, only much more mixed. To be sure, you would probably "map" it to a chart with vertices of stars, and wormholes as lines between them. All distances set by difficulty of travel, not physical location.

A fantasy world turns on its level of technology, or magi-tech. Less powerful eras look like ancient times. More powerful, steampunk ones, like the nineteenth century.

More powerful still?

Dirigibles, winged horses, and other forms of taking to the sky are unlikely to make it work like space travel. (Fantasy space travel would, of course, work like SF space travel.)

On the other hand, some forms of magic work more like wormholes. Traveling into other dimensions such as Faerie (or hyperspace) and then hopping out again. Or portals.

This would produce a curious effect because the reason for such plot devices in science fiction is that you can not travel the distance without them.

True, a fantasy world might be impossible to traverse without them. Different lands actually being in different worlds, so you need a portal. Seas filled with monsters, including flying ones. Towering mountains.

A quite different effect would be produced by the ability to walk through a portal, or conversely decide you just want to walk, and reach the same region in days, weeks, months—years.

Much depends on how expensive the form of instant (or speedy) transportation is, and how much it can bring. If you can march armies through a portal, that will have a large effect on your ability to maintain an empire, as opposed to being able to send letters on a regular basis. (And conversely, to end empires. You probably don't want the portal within the city walls for that reason.) Letters will require that you march the armies, and thus change the empire again. (Then, do not underestimate communication faster than travel. The telegraph was world-shaking.)

Also, if portals are hard to erect, or require specific locations, other forms of travel have a chance against them even if once built, they are cheap in themselves. Particularly if the locations with them abuse the power with high tolls. Cheaper access to spices drove much of the Age of Exploration.

Trade being the other thing that heavily turns on transportation. Cheap portals make it easy to move bulk goods.

Ironically enough, portals may produce a burst of other forms of transportation. Horses increased greatly in Great Britain as the railroad advanced, because what you could not economically send by horse, you could send by train, with the horse economically hauling it the final mile. You may see new roads and bridges built precisely for the portal use.

On the other hand, hinterlands whose sole attraction lies in lying on the trade route have less attraction. Particularly if they charged high tolls, because they will only continue if they are cheaper than the alternative portal.

At that, exploration becomes much more of a quirk than a policy. Perhaps you will find something worth trading for in a new region, but that's the only reason, really. You might find a Northwest

Passage, but it will be of little interest unless you found a firebird, or a new spice, along the way.

You need to fit your empires and trade routes to your mode of transportation. Or the transportation to the empires, either way works.

Fairy Tales

The source material for so many stories, and stories within stories. And the gentle art of using them

How Much Magic Does A Fairy Tale Need?

The lore and the lack

How much magic do you want in your fairy tale? How much do you need?

Consider this tale:

Once upon a time, a nobleman had a daughter but no son. He ignored her, and when she was grown, he went to arrange her marriage to anyone who would take her off his hands. She demanded three marvelous dresses to consent, and then a coat of catskin. Whereupon she wrapped the dresses up in a bundle, donned the coat, and ran off. She found a job as a scullery maid in another castle, and when they had a ball, she wore the marvelous dresses to three, and so won the son of the house. Later, after the cook she had served at jeered at her son as a beggar's child, she tells her husband about her father, her husband tracks him down, and he is all alone in the world and wishes he could see his daughter again, so they are reconciled.

Now, this tale, *Catskin*, is obviously a variant of *Cinderella*—though it's ATU type 510B, not 510A, because her father is a problem—and it holds *no* magic at all.

It is also a clear folktale, told in the British islands, and collected there in various forms. Marian Roalfe Cox, doing pioneering morphology work in the nineteenth century, used it as one of the three base types of Cinderella (plus two others, the miscellaneous tales and the boy tales).

Part of why *Catskin* is still treated as a fairy tale is that it fits so neatly into the 510B type, and many other tales of type 510B do have magic. *The Egg-Born Princess* does, indeed, feature a princess who was born from an egg. *The Bear* gives the princess the power to turn into a bear, and a wheelbarrow that will carry her wherever she wants to go. *The King Who Wished to Marry His Daughter* has the princess demand, and get, a chest that can travel over land and sea. At the end of *Tattercoats,* the heroine is magically transformed out of her rags, thus convincing the court that their prince had indeed chosen a lovely bride.

One notes that in *Tattercoats*, the magical transformation comes out of the blue. She does not get dresses up front from her fairy godmother or her mother's grave. The prince has already met Tattercoats, in her tatters, and fallen in love with usual swiftness of fairy-tale prince. You might think that the playing of the gooseherd's pipes—the very way that her clothes are transformed at the end—might magically aid the romance, but the story holds no hint of it, and given the other *Cinderella* tales, it is not necessary. Such minor magics do not change that the brunt of the tale is non-magical.

This is not the only one to show that rendering some elements mundane does not require all of them to be thus changed. *Richilde*, a literary form of *Snow White* (and the oldest German form of it), has Richilde as the wicked stepmother, and she still has the magical mirror, but Blanca survived because the doctor Richilde had ordered to create poisons had created sleeping potions instead.

So, in fact, removing magical elements and substituting other plot devices is a grand old tradition, a solid strand in the fairy tale tradition. Gioachino Rossini agreed to do a opera, *La Cenerentola*, based on *Cinderella*, with no magical elements, which eased staging it, and there's no reason why any other writer can't.

Some are easier than others, of course. Snow White, of course, might fall into a coma, but Sleeping Beauty—well, you'd better turn to science fictional notions about cryogenics or other forms of stasis if you want to keep the time the same.

Likewise, if the secret prince can not conjure up a force of knights to bring with him to battle, it is probably better to have a tourney instead. It's far more plausible that he will do well by himself while jousting than that he can single-handedly win the war.

Assuming, of course, you don't opt for larger changes. That's another old tradition. There's no particular reason for anyone to be able to recognize the tale by the time you're done with it.

Either way is part of the great tradition.

The Fairy In The Tale

Fairy tales vs. fairies

If it's called a fairy tale, where are the fairies?

If you say at the christening, or helping the heroine go to the ball—you do realize that those are literary versions? They have spread far and wide by the usual means, but they are not the only options, or even the common folk version.

The Brothers Grimm even took out the fairies between the first and the second edition, and put in wise women instead, for their *Sleeping Beauty*, and many other variants never had the fairies. In *Asheputtel*, their Cinderella never was aided by a fairy godmother but by a tree that grew on her mother's grave, which is more typical.

Some tales of the Fair Folk are told among the fairy tales, such as *The Shoemaker And the Elves*—but a story where the shoemaker and his wife accidentally chase off their helpers by giving them clothes obviously does not fit the normal tropes of the tale.

There are indeed more typical fairy tales with more folkloric fairies—occasionally. There is Rumpelstiltskin with his desire for a child—though it's a bit odd that he doesn't just take the baby, if he's a fae. In the British Isles, the spinning is carried out by a rather more brownie-like being, who calmly shows the bridegroom how spinning distorts the spinner, so that he will not demand his beautiful bride spin forever.

Or you could have the fairies in *Kate Crackernuts*. The prince dances every night in the fairy hill, as the princesses in *The Twelve Dancing Princesses* in their underground ballroom, but where they just wear out their shoes, he collapses in exhaustion, thus matching a folk explanation of tuberculosis, nightly fairy dances wearing out the victim for want of sleep.

The Green Lady may take on the heroine, and later her stepsister, to work, just as Mother Holle does in German tales, but both girls spy through a keyhole to see her secrets, and are blinded for it in the best Fair Folk manner. With a return to the fairy tale, the heroine is cured because she helped others about the household, where the stepsister stays blind.

What did the girl eat? Do you wonder how she managed to not eat fairy food while working for this Green Lady? The tale doesn't mention it because it does not matter. There is no talk about cold iron, or changelings, or the peril of fairy food, or all the other to-do about the Fair Folk.

This is because fairy tales eat up any characters put into them, and turn them into fairy tale characters.

Even religious figures. The Brothers Grimm have a story about St. Joseph in the forest, and St. Joseph acts in it like any beneficent fairy tale donor in the Kind and Unkind Girls: testing the girls, and dispersing fitting rewards and punishments. The only odd thing about it is that there are three girls, and two are extremely kind, and reasonably kind, to get generous rewards and moderate rewards, the third girl being the usual failure.

The Devil is far more common—but he's not a devil. True, he may make a deal with a character, but in the manner of a fairytale trickster. And often he's just a stupid ogre with a daughter, to be outwitted with her help.

On a simpler matter, dragons are rare in fairy tales. Much more common is the ogre who will hold a princess prisoner until the hero comes to rescue her—except for Eastern European fairy tales. This is because Eastern European fairy tales have dragons that will hold the princess prisoner until the hero rescues her.

So likewise with fairies. The figure in the tale may be called a fairy, but whether the donor or the villain or the magical helper, or even the king (the person who sends the hero) or the princess (the person the hero marries), the fairy nature will be subordinate to the character.

This is probably why they are seldom either the king or the princess, and never the hero or the false hero, in my experience. Even when the girls take service with the Green Lady, they are helped (or not) by the other beings about the household, never by the Green Lady's son. Occasionally, a maiden who helps the hero is a fairy maiden, but she knows no more magic than the ogre's daughter.

Which means, of course, that "fairy tale" is a very bad name. I suppose most of you knew that already, but here's more evidence.

Fairy Tales, In Light And Dark

How grim is authentic?

Once upon a time, there were a pair of brothers, by the name of Grimm. They collected fairy tales.

In one fairy tale, a girl's parents forbid her to go see a witch in the forest. She disobeyed. She was terrified by apparitions of men, black and red and green, on the way and then by seeing the Devil in the witch's house. The witch caught her, questioned her, explained away the men, but finally exclaimed, with the account of the Devil, that the girl had seen the witch in her true form. So the witch turned the girl into a log of wood and tossed her on the fire. The End.

In another fairy tale, a girl gave away everything she owned, first her coins, then her clothes, down to her shift, and was alone and naked in the dark night forest. Stars fell on the ground before her, and she found herself wearing a fine linen garment, and that the stars had turned into silver coins by her feet, and she lived off them for the rest of her life. The End.

You hear a lot of nonsense about the original grimness, or lack thereof, in fairy tales.

The truth of the matter is that fairy tales are a subset of folktales. And folktales reflect the folk in all their aspects. Sometimes good, sometimes evil, sometimes scoundrels who get away with it, sometimes fools with dumb luck, sometimes rewarded for what they did, sometimes reforming after they are shown clemency, and sometimes returning to be still more villainous after such clemency.

Fairy tales are, to be sure, a subset of folktales, distinguished by certain plots. Still, even within a plot, the range is great.

Sometimes the false bride who usurped the bride's place after turning the bride into a bird is brutally executed—at her own suggestion, perhaps—and sometimes she's sent home and suffers nothing worse than being heckled by children about what she did.

Sometimes the third prince's older brothers are executed for their treacherous and murderous conduct toward him, or only escape execution by fleeing for their lives, and sometimes the third prince rescues three princesses, and marries the most beautiful, while the other two marry his brothers.

Sometimes, after the ball, and after the shoe has finally fit, Ashenpettel's sisters have their eyes pecked out for their envy, and sometimes Cinderella arranges fine marriages for them. And sometimes the marriage of the heroine ends the tale, and sometimes the stepmother comes to substitute her daughter for her stepdaughter, and murder the stepdaughter, after the stepdaughter has given birth. (Be very wary if your stepmother has only one stepdaughter. Two stepsisters are, believe it or not, safer.)

There is, in fact, no standard of light-heartedness or of grimness that any given fairy tale may fall above or below. There is just an enormous range of tales from the frivolous to the deadly serious, from the deeply cynical to the severely just to the overflowing with mercy and generosity.

When writing your own tale, you do so in reaction to any given tale. Or, for that matter, to a given artist. From Hans Christian Andersen, from the *précieuses,* from Disney.

Just be aware that whatever your reaction is, the odds that it will take you out of the natural range of fairy tales are very slim. So are the odds that the original story, that you are reacting to, had made it out of the natural range (and so you are not getting back to the original).

Fairy-Tale Romp

Compatibility and other issues

Here's a land where all the fairy tales are true! Can it work?

Well, maybe. If you make it a large enough saga, with scope to fit a vast world.

There's a reason why I blurbed *The Princess Seeks Her Fortune* as merely taking place in "a land where ten thousand fairy tales come true."

To fit all of them in—well, in a large enough canvas, you can have a tale where the heroine's virtuously giving away everything she owned brought her a linen gown from heaven and star money to support her for life, and a tale where an unscrupulous scoundrel told his mother he'd rather have a full loaf of bread with her curse than half with her blessing, and proceeded to, through tricks and knavery, win the princess's hand in marriage and the kingdom after the king died, and lived happily ever after.

Or a tale where older brothers murder the youngest, only for him to be revived by his talking fox companion, and to win to court, where he reclaimed the wonders he had brought back, and his brothers had stolen, and another where the murdered brother's body grows a reed that sings of his murder, but all that can happen in court is that the murderous brother is put to death, and the murdered given a decent burial.

Not that just deserts are the only thing handed out unevenly. In most fairy tales with animal brides or bridegrooms, burning the animal skin when the character has shed it to assume human form is a disaster. It means that the attempt to break the curse has broken, and the other spouse now has a long and wearisome quest to reclaim the beloved.

Sometimes it's rather shorter. Burning the animal skin merely kills the cursed character.

On the other hand, it's also rather shorter in the versions where that's just the right thing to do. Burning the animal skin breaks the curse and lets them all live happily ever after.

You would have to define the magic rather more than most fairy tales do, in order to depict the different cases. Perhaps the witch who is the hero's stepmother and wants him to marry her daughter sets up the quest—he does generally end up being forced to marry by the time the heroine tracks him down—and the others don't bother. Perhaps the freed-by-fire version is intended as a slap on the wrist, or the witch is negligent, or weak. Perhaps the killed-by-fire version is uncommonly harsh, or miscast, since it was meant to drag the character off to marry another.

But if you want *all* the fairy tales to be true, you have to have all three variations. Plus those where the bridegroom—or the bride—is disenchanted by other means, such as the hero's following the frog's directions to go to his father's house and tell everyone that his bride is arriving after, or the curse is extended by other means, as when the bride looks at him by candlelight when he is in human form and asleep.

And, meanwhile, you have all the other variants of all the other tales to deal with. There are tales where a woman's sisters, or mother-in-law, or both working together, steal her babies and expose them, and then tell her husband the king that she gave birth to puppies, or kittens, or stranger things. After she is punished for many years, and her children have adventures, the children come to the king's attention. They invite him to a feast and offer him cucumber skins stuffed with pearls or the like, and claim that's the way they grow. He denies this is possible, and they demand to know why, therefore, he believed that his wife gave birth to puppies.

The problem with that is, of course, in fairy tales women are perfectly capable of giving birth to puppies, or hedgehogs, or bears, or crabs, or stranger things. Even to a sprig of myrtle. So she could very well have done so.

The large canvas might give you scope to juggle that. Perhaps the resentful sisters might run away and study magic, and start causing women to give birth to creatures whenever they foolishly express a wish to have a child, even one that's a crab. So from becoming impossible, they make it possible. Or perhaps it's a regional quirk. Witches in this region are fond of cursing women for their folly in wishes, while in that region, they prefer cursing little children for laughing at them.

And this is only brushing on the incompatibilities of the tales.

On the whole, fairy-tale mash-ups pick their rules and filter the tales accordingly, and are wise to do so.

The Fae Godmother

Tropes and tales

I was thinking of *Cinderella*.

Now, fairy godmothers, as a class, do not show many signs of being—ehem—*Fair Folk*.

Even past the way fairy tales eat up characters and turn them into fairy tale characters, fairy godmothers are strikingly like nobles of the French courts at which the *précieuses* wrote fairy tales. They are powerful connections—it's just that some of the power is magical.

And you must keep up all the normal courtesies, especially since your godmother is apt to be more powerful than your parents. Your real-life, non-fairy godmother. Your parents would want the most powerful connection they could get you (and the rest of the family) that way. Fairy magic is an added bonus.

There's a fairy tale in which the fairy godmother flatly refused to help her goddaughter because she was not consulted about her marriage to an ogre, though she relents later.

And another in which the king and queen in exile lose their three princesses in the forest for fear of hunger, and the youngest princess's fairy godmother helps her—only to be insulted by the goddaughter not strictly obeying her, thus leaving her on her own for the second movement of the story, where she gets to play Cinderella.

But, to return to Cinderella herself, as Perrault wrote her—and Disney followed—the fairy godmother is indeed uncommonly beneficent for one of the Fair Folk.

On the other hand, she's nowhere up to the standards of the usual assistance, from the dead mother, or a talking animal.

In *Aschenputtel* and *The Wonderful Birch*, and many others, the heroine gets help from the beginning, with all the housework, by going to her mother's grave. Then, when her stepmother imposes an impossible task, she gets help with that. Finally, when the stepmother reneges, she gets help going to the balls.

Talking animals are often much better than the mother's grave, even. They will actively feed the heroine when her stepmother tries to starve her. Indeed, there's a grave danger that the stepmother twigs to the assistance when the stepdaughter no longer desperately eats the burnt scraps she's offered.

Neither in Perrault nor in Disney is the fairy godmother that useful.

Disney gives Cinderella talking animal helpers in the old style, though they do less than the usual run of help. Making the dress is at least the traditional help with the impossible task, though they do not do much to ease the housework, and they can not help with attending the ball.

So the fairy godmother shows up.

There are variants of Perrault in which she actually has to introduce herself to Cinderella. At any rate, she has done nothing all the time Cinderella suffered under her stepmother and stepsisters. Only when it is time for the ball does she bother.

Isn't that just like a fae?

A truly fae version could do more with it. Perhaps, as is also frequent in the Cinderella variants, the trouble is her sisters, not her stepsisters. Her mother—hmm, let's say her mother was widowed and could no longer get a good godmother for her daughter, and thus in the grand tradition, goes to look for anyone. Instead of getting a queen traveling in secret, or Godmother Death, she helps a fae and gets a fairy godmother, and there's nothing to be done.

She tries to parley her older daughters' godmothers into matches, and has the youngest serve as a maid of all work because that way, her sisters might manage marriages, and then they could take their youngest sister into the household. After all, who would marry the goddaughter of a fae?

Or perhaps the mother dies, and the older sisters do it. The logic is the same.

And then, after both her older sisters go to their godmothers to be escorted, in hope the ball will get them a good match, the fae shows up to send Cinderella.

Then, if this is really and truly one of the Fair Folk, there is the little question of how the prince, and everyone else, can be kept from dancing to exhaustion at the ball. Or dancing all night only to discover that, in reality, they had danced for a century and will crumble into dust on leaving the dance hall.

Perhaps Cinderella can pick up something from being the goddaughter. Even if the fae ends up as furious as Godfather Death. It will, of course, be a fairy-tale-based story, not a fairy tale, once that happens. Such is the consequence of introducing other elements.

Speculative Fairy Tales

Tales within a tale

What sort of fairy tales do your characters tell to their children?

If you are telling them in a science fiction setting, you should notice that fairy tales are noticeably resistant to technological changes. You can introduce foodstuffs easily: turkeys and pumpkins do not change the setting.

But trains? Steamships? Airplanes?

Well, the fairy tale is not impervious. I have read a tale—rather like *All's Well That Ends Well*—in which the hero travels by train and the heroine by plane, so she reaches the city before him.

On the other hand, the plot logic pulls in the mode of transportation and preserves itself, so that the hero has no legal problems locking up his wife and leaving, and inexplicably, though he's clearly some kind of powerful noble, she can evade his locks without trouble. Airplanes, yes, but neither modern law nor modern locks were allowed.

Go ahead and have the heroine carried to the ball by a gourd turned into a space ship. Have her wear neutron-star diamonds. Let her shoe be caught in an airlock. But don't fundamentally change the tale as long as it's told as a fairy tale. If it ends with the wicked stepmother turning her into a deer and putting the stepsister in her place, run with it rather than trying to invent a science-fictional trope to replace it.

If, on the other hand, your characters are telling them in a fantasy story, you should note you do not have to change the magic. If the fantasy world does not have talking animals, or shape-shifting, or wishes, their fairy tales nevertheless can. Indeed, you can open the tale with "Once upon a time when animals could still talk" and do nothing more than many fairy-tale narrators do in the real-world.

Though you could. If you told a fairy tale in a world very like Harry Potter, the stepmother could take away her stepdaughter's wand, but the house-elves recognize only the stepdaughter as their legitimate mistress, so they help her with the housework and to attend the ball three times.

Or even the daughter could run away because her father wanted to marry her, and bring along three gowns, and thus, once she has a job as a scullery maid, go three times to ball and win the young lord without a single use of magic. After all, that's what happens in *Catskin* as told among us Muggles.

What could get really interesting is when the magic does—sort of, kind of—match but the fairy tales prettify it until it is dangerously misleading. Just as a tale of a bear may mislead people into thinking a real-life bear is not dangerous, *Cinderella* may mislead a child into thinking that a fae offering to help is innocuous, or actually friendly. This is—unwise. *Kate Crackernuts*, where the prince has to be rescued from evil fairies dancing him to death, is more prudent.

Vampires would be worse. *Sleeping Beauty* and *Snow White* may have parents pause and reason that they do not want their children to think that anyone who rises out of a coffin, or from a state like death, is harmless. *The Princess in the Casket* at least has the princess rise from the coffin and be dangerous, but on the other hand, has it feasible to disenchant her and bring her back to life.

In a world where fantasy is overt, this may lead to quarrels between parents and the little old lady they have watching their children during the planting and harvest, who tells them old wives' tales.

In a world where the masquerade is in effect, parents who deal with the mundane world have a conundrum. On one hand, they may not want to isolate the child with only magical connections. On the other hand, small children may blurt out inconvenient statements at the oddest of times. Statements so severe that they could bring the enforcement to bear severely.

The wisest thing to do may be to introduce the child to many, many, many fairy tales, so that if he blurts out that it doesn't go like that, the parents can laugh heartily and tell him to not be so rude, and tell those who are listening that he reads a lot of fairy tales, and they must admit that he's quite right in that most *Cinderella* tales do not go like that.

Probably wisest to shelter the children with others who are in on the masquerade until they learn more judgment. Such are the complications of juggling magic and tales of magic.

Philosophy

Many matters. Metaphysics, ethics, epistemology.

Philosophy vs Alternate History

Choices, choices

Various forms of alternate history have been used for various purposes, some more philosophical than others. One of the more philosophical is to explore the meaning and significance of choices.

At first glance, the genre would seem ideal. At second glance—

There are various forms of this trope, but the commonest one is that people making choices are the splitting point for the worlds. A magistrate is ordered to exile his son for treasonable correspondence, and he both obeys and disobeys—in two different worlds. The consequences follow.

As long as you do not think too much about it, you do not realize that means that all the characters in the alternate history are either the lucky ducks who made the right decision, or the unfortunate ones who were stuck with the wrong decision.

In *Lord Kalvan of Otherwhen*, for instance, H. Beam Piper has the Paratime Patrol warn its patrol members to avoid the timelines near the one where Kalvan landed, where the prince's intransigence means his lands will be overrun and handed over to his enemies, but the slaughter there gets no more mention.

And still more, the proliferation of timelines stemming from Kalvan's decisions in the kingdom is completely ignored.

Does he, rather than rally forces against an attacker, stay out of the initial attack and get taken for an enemy seriously, instead of the friendly-fire accident that has little consequence? Does he grow angry over the friendly-fire incident? Does he decide to bend his mind to getting back to his own timeline? Does he defect to the other side? After all, any choice, no matter how improbable, is made in some timeline.

For that matter, what do other people do? Do they take him as a spy in some timelines? Do they reject his claims about gunpowder? Does one of the king's subjects conclude that he bewitched the king and kill him? Does his story about being sent here by a sorcerer spread? Do his enemies, the priests of Styphon, instantly realize the game is up and come clean?

Does the Paratime Patrol have to assassinate him to stop him? Do they succeed? Would they not logically fail in other timelines? Would they not spawn other timelines in which they failed? If all choices split times, how could there be anything except timelines where it was secret and those where it leaked out?

The proliferation of timelines that is made an issue in other Paratime works gets seriously downplayed here, for the obvious reason that it undermines choices and so undermines the story both aesthetically and philosophically.

Aesthetically, it removes the drama by making the choices unreal.

Philosophically, it removes the thought experiment by nullifying the choices' importance.

That is, if you think too hard about it. The thing is that pure philosophy can work with absurd examples to avoid superfluity cluttering up the question, but philosophically minded fiction (phil-fic?) still has to work as fiction, including not jolting readers out of the story. Ideally, not even after the reader has finished the story and gone to the frig to grab a soda, so a flaw that can be passed over is inferior to an unflawed technique.

Now, the other common method to produce an alternate history—a time traveler changes things—has a lot of other baggage. It does not even work as well as the splitting of universes, because it introduces elements that make the thought experiment about choices less clear, but it is conceivable to use the alternate history without the time traveler and his baggage, or the "all choices" issue.

The original idea stemmed from the Copenhagen multi-worlds theory of quantum decay, based on the decay of atoms, not on people's different choices. That, of course, would produce an endless array of trivially different worlds. Every time an atom could decay, it both would and would not.

If you state that the world dividing is driven by some quantum difference—choosing the rate based on how many worlds you want it —you can create as many alternate worlds as you want with no differences between them.

Then you can say that some people make same choices, and others make different ones. In the moment after the break, John Doe has a raspberry pastry AND a strawberry one in different worlds, and Richard Roe resolves in both worlds to take the job rather falsify his father's will, and James Poe, in both worlds, breaks into the jewelry shop.

Thus you get the intellectual exercise of contemplating different choices, and the dramatic satisfaction of real choices.

The Philosophy of The Always Evil Beings

Can this trope work?

Ah, that awful race of always evil beings!

Sometimes the Evil is comically used, to indicate what team the characters are on. The thing is, that gets into tension with the terms good and evil.

It's a major contributor to the confusion of alignment. I have heard descriptions of Evil saying that just because you're Evil doesn't mean you can't have friends. That is wrong. Insofar as you have real friends, you are not evil.

Then, most people are of mingled yarn, good and evil together.

But consider the Evil race where it's not just a label. The race is truly evil. Consider a race of dragons, all consumed with the deadly sin of Greed.

How does that come about?

Does that implicate metaphysical matters?

Only if you, as the writer, put down the truth. A world of people can philosophize about their nature without dragging the metaphysics on stage any more than it is in our world.

They could have all kinds of possible reasons. Such as:

The race lacks rational souls. They were actually animals, however clever, and couldn't fathom morality, at all.

True, if the world also had magic that worked specifically on animals, it might work on members of this race, thus settling the question. If it did not, they would have hypothesize why this race was not subject to animal-based magic. Perhaps their being clever might prevent it.

Another one would be that the race consisted of the insane. Perhaps sociopaths. Perhaps another form of insanity that allowed them to work together.

If the world has curative magic that works on insanity—well, no doubt there would soon cease to be such a race if it was at all feasible to apply it widely.

On the other hand, it might not work, and then there would be the question of whether this can be true then. There are possibilities for its failure. There would be the question of its working on personality disorders, and the possibility that it's a different form of disorder than the one the spells work on.

One notes that an artful sociopath would notice that it was very useful to have people believe him cured, just to complicate life.

(One also notes that a sufficiently angry and powerful wizard might cast a great spell that would cause people with personality disorders to assume a grotesque form. Which would lead to a world unlike many fantasy worlds, since monsters would be born to humans regularly.)

For these two reasons, characters adequately far from the race's depredations might philosophically ponder whether the race actually was evil, any more than a venomous snake was. Probably not those who suffered from their attacks, however far off.

On the other hand, the race might consist of beings who were fundamentally evil. Perhaps they were minor devils who took this form to be better plagues to mankind. Or perhaps they were damned souls given a corporeal form. They could not change because they were damned and so not affected by the passage of time as mankind is.

Would exorcism work? Perhaps the bodies are there to make it harder.

Or perhaps they are still living rational beings who had used magic to set themselves in that shape. And to set their wills in concrete. Let us suppose they were unjustly furious about something, and then used magic to ensure that their fury would last forever. Or whatever character flaw they refused to surrender. Pride. Greed. Envy. Perhaps dragons are the result of misers who slowly transformed from the desire to watch over their treasure.

What sort of anti-magic would work in such a world would be a crucial question. If the magic could be undone, characters would be hard at work to undo it as soon as it was feasible. Then, there might be an endless source feeding into it as people were tempted to try the magic. Perhaps the reversal would not work without their consent, and they had set their wills to never consent.

If you wanted the race to be born evil, a sorcerer, even in a world without reincarnation, could offer the deal to vengeful, or otherwise evil ghosts, to be born in his artificially created race, with sorcery to keep them concentrated on their aim without letting the flesh cause them to waver. The dead might be fixed in will, unable to repent.

All of these, with sufficient care by the writer, could be argued for without any character appearing to be a fool for holding his position, in a world with an evil race.

Metaphysics and the Powers That Be

Might and metaphysics

When wrestling with the world you build, monsters can give you issues.

Still worse awaits when you get into the entire question of the Powers That Be.

That is, polytheistic type gods, who are finite, contingent, caused, temporal in nature, and all the other limits, though they are actually also control the spheres of life they are gods of. If the god of death is imprisoned, people stop dying. (Otherwise they are just very powerful rational beings.)

Contrary to some claims, putting in Powers That Be does not establish the base metaphysics of a fantasy world. Beneath this multiplicity of forces lies the question of how they came about, and what puts them in order.

These beings are so different from the monotheistic Supreme Being that someone can be both a polytheist and a monotheist. Plato was.

There is still a range there, where the implications differ.

Sometimes it is the god's very nature to have that sphere. The god is born with a skull for a head, and the midwife keels over, and thus the god of death appears. That has metaphysical implications, starting with that no one died before that.

At the opposite end, the celestial bureaucracy slots in a new god of death to fill the post, and his underlings keep things going more or less until then. And that has metaphysical implications in that the world set up by a bureaucracy, and run by it, and will stop running if the bureaucracy stops. How did that come about? Who appointed them? Did they seize this power?

Or the three most powerful gods, being brothers who overthrew their father, throw lots to determine their order. Then they get to pick which sphere is his domain in the order determined by the lot. But once he picks one, it's his, and he is the master of its forces. Even their sisters, in their domains—why, one can, every year, stop growth for a season.

Whatever the means by which gods gain their spheres, whenever the author lends to the weight of his authority to their powers, there will be metaphysical implications brought with the gods.

Yet, most writers who bring the gods on stage do not consider this.

The gods generally turn into human beings with trivial differences, up to and including having higher powers of their own. (Turtles all the way up does not work any more than turtles all the way down.)

True, a god can be ignorant of much of the universe. He can also be pursuing his own purposes. The pagan philosophers who demoted them to daemons (not demons) thought they were evil in the same sense that men were evil, which makes them easier to characterize—if not *easy*.

Still, the god should be godly. Either sage or showing bad judgment in a way related to the sphere of power. And this, even if the gods were once humans beings. Apotheosis should change people.

Yes, many myths show the gods behaving badly. But not in the infantile manner that many writers think shows something besides how infantile the writer's concept of the divine is. These also shrink your world because these are the beings running it.

Fleeting appearances, brief acts, or merely signs expand the universe by putting things outside the work's scope. The most impressive gods, the most numinous ones, are the most mysterious ones. It's the act that could be coincidence, or natural, that can carry the authentic ring.

Their spheres of influence can help with the necessary numinous touch. Slowly realizing that the sweep of greenery on a hill before you is also the green skirt of the goddess of plants—which also helps explain why the visits have to be fugitive. (Perhaps the locations of her visits are lushly green forever after. Worse, the villain realizes it and scouts for those to look for his foes while they are still young.)

As an added bonus, fugitive visits help deal with the obvious problem of a literal *deus* even if the *machina* is still metaphorical. After all, the god either swamps the characters or forces them to match the god in power, if on stage for any long period of time. Brief appearances can dwarf the character and not derail the story, only add mystery and expand the world.

Putting the gods in disguise can help prolong their stay since it covers up many of the issues.

However.

Convincing disguises for gods take work. A lot of work. Enough work so that when the god stands revealed at the end—or even the protagonist stares after the old beggar as he ambles off, chortling over the comment that means he might, or might not, have been a god—it's convincing. Surprising, perhaps, in fact it's better writing when it's a surprise (if that's in character for the god), but convincing is more important.

At that, you need to use a god where taking the disguise and guiding the characters is convincing. If your plot is world-shaking, it may require direct divine guidance, and it takes little work to persuade readers that this is reasonable. (That it was *this* god, and that his actions were in character, takes more work.)

Lesser quests may require that you succeed in convey the inscrutable wisdom of the god, who, though finite, knows much and fathoms more than the characters he guides, so that it is believable that he had some purpose in his actions.

And that's even before you get into the questions of religion in the world.

Angels, Devils, and Metaphysics

Where the metal meets the metaphysics.

What happens when you bring devils or, worse, angels on the story stage?

What definitely happens is that metaphysics are implicated, as the very existence of these beings has implications for the world.

Furthermore, unlike the polytheistic gods, they are not plausibly ignorant of the world's metaphysics. The angels are ministers of the Supreme Being, and the devils were created as such.

The orthodox Christian view is that each angel, at the moment of creation, makes the decision between good and evil that mankind stretches out over time. A man can do right today, wrong tomorrow, lie all the time, be generous with charity—and it will calcify into a habit. But an angel is all or nothing.

This may be because they are not related to time in the same way as mankind is. The theory of aeviternity posits a state between temporal existence and fully-outside-of-time of eternity.

Writers who have them show up for a scene, or a still more fugitive appearance, can elide the issue of whether these are true.

But when they appear as regular characters, or even have viewpoints—well, these are hard to depict in fiction, but writers do not use either of these. The thing is, this invariably turns into turning the angel or devil, or both, into a human with a few tweaks. Sometimes all the way up to disconnecting the angels from Heaven.

This is even more pointless than having humans with pointy ears, which you call elves.

Particularly silly worlds generally ensue when you also include polytheistic gods. In my experience, these tend to be the rational being type, not the gods of spheres, but writers who plop them in do not consider the metaphysical questions.

It is possible to do well. John C. Wright has stories with both majestic, powerful gods as characters, and angels as fugitive appearances, far more numinous than the gods are. The metaphysics are past the gods. (One work includes a Greek god who converted to Christianity or, rather, Donatism.)

But it's not easy. All too many writers who put in both end up with two humans with superpowers and only the vaguest distinctions from each other. And the metaphysics gets cluttered.

Still, even if you wisely omit the gods and those confusions, you do have to consider your choices.

Then the question is: Is this angel *necessary*? What on earth are you gaining by introducing an angel?

Or, for that matter, this devil. It does have its aspects that make it a little simpler.

Starting with the obvious advantage that a devil, unlike an angel, does not take over the main characters' role in the story. As the antagonist, the devil makes a dangerous foe.

Furthermore, since the devil is a liar, a devil can appear in all sorts of manners, not only to serve his purpose, but to confuse his purpose. Which gives you a little more flexibility.

Still, even for a devil, you should not make them appear like a human being unless it's part of the purpose. (Angels, also, can appear in human guise. For a purpose.)

The disguise can be completely convincing, but in the end, when the truth is revealed—or hinted at—it needs to cast a backwards retrospective on everything the character did and said while in disguise. More so than if you reveal that the character was one of the Powers That Be, because the angel or devil knows more about the universe.

And because angels are always good, and devils are always evil—this is a grand opportunity to show off the depths of your shallowness. I advise forgoing it. There is grave danger of making them all too human, and the necessary moral judgments to depict them well are not easy. Above all else avoid using them to try to score points about moral views. Also, because of their powers, they would know more than the human characters, though the diabolical characters likely lie to themselves about some things.

The wisest route is to make their visits—particularly angelic ones—short, fleeting and mysterious. It helps to make them suggest a greater universe than the story could possibly contain. It also enables them to be good and evil in a more limited scope, thus limiting the chances to do it wrong.

Their necessary visits. No more.

In A Form You Are Comfortable With

Beings from beyond

It's a common trope, a being who descends from a plane past mortal comprehension to deal with mortals, but the implications of appearing in a toned-down form are not simple, especially when it's not in disguise—though making it a disguise is not a complete escape.

The hospitable Philemon and Baucis, as well as their hostile neighbors, were taken in by the appearance of Jupiter and Mercury, at first. At the end, when the couple became aware of whom they had given shelter to, they still did not suffer the full blast of encountering a god in godly form according to (some) Greek myths.

This does elide a lot of issues. The rhetorical most obviously, though you still have to deal with the viewpoint character's dawning awareness that the reason the goose ran to the guest was that the guest was a god. The concealment is part of the awed viewpoint and must be conveyed.

Still, before that, you must set up the form, and the thing is, the form the mortal can be comfortable with—or, at least, endure—has to be compatible with the being appearing in that form. It is not chance that Jupiter, the sovereign over hospitality, and Mercury, the god of travelers, appear in that myth.

This obviously is most difficult to handle with angels and devils.

An angel will adopt a less than terrifying form in order to render the characters comfortable enough for what is necessary. A conversation, perhaps. Perhaps to deceive those with inferior judgment, so that the wise and prudent realize whom they are talking with, while other characters continue on in their misjudgment. Still, the form does not prevent their speaking with wisdom and prudence beyond the measure of mankind.

A devil, on other hand, would have deceit at the heart of the guise. Nothing better than a false appearance to hide, though if the diabolical identity were known, he would probably lie about why he is taking the form. And altering it when caught would mean taking on another as false as the first. Perhaps the malice is not evident, but a prudent mortal will be all the more terrified by that.

More considerations come into play for powerful rational beings—whether you call them gods or not. Such beings have a personality, or at least a character, whether it can be fathomed by mortals, or not. (And if you want a character not fathomable by mortals, you have a rhetorical task before you that requires no little skill. Even in disguise, you must convey it.)

Give this character, the forms adopted by this rational being would turn on that.

The Powers That Be might be dominated by their sphere, but that would dictate their personality rather than eliminate it as a consideration. A mountain being would not adopt the form of a high-energy, continually moving, wiry mortal; a wind being would not adopt a slow, bulky and sedentary mortal.

A trickster would be happy donning all sorts of forms to advance his pranks or just for the glee of it. Even a crafty being would take on many, to advance his plans. Athena adopts a great many forms in the works of Homer to get things to happen—though there she is so devious and underhanded she might qualify as a trickster.

Other gods would be less pliable. A jovial being would be, more or less, jovial. Magisterial, maternal, saturnine, martial, regal—the true nature of the being would be evident in the pose chosen. Perhaps only after some consideration, perhaps even only after the truth is revealed. But the truth ought to cast light on the events of before. (Even the trickster is revealed by his mercurial nature.)

True, that might mean a false pose. If the beings appearing to a character act childish, it could mean a world-weary, cynical, decadent set of beings, playing games with the lives of the characters for something to do. But that sort of play-acting should tinge the story in its own way.

Or it could actually be childish characters in a powerful position. The thing to consider there is that they can't be running the world as the Powers That Be. If gravity, photosynthesis, combustion, and all the rest are ticking merrily along in good order, is it likely that these silly geese are actually running it? Either they are maintaining a pose, or these things are run by other means (including other beings). And if it's a pose, that plays back into the issue of what sort of personality would lead to such a pose.

It could be the fault of the mortal. Still, if the character requires such a silly and childish appearance to cope, that's a severe limit on the characterizations.

If, on the other hand, the beings misjudge the level that the mortal character can handle, that requires ticklish handling. True, the beings could be so far above the mortal plane that all humans, from the wisest to the most foolish, are much on a level to them. But if they are that much wiser, they should be wiser at making distinctions. It would have be carefully shown that these wise beings are chiefly concerned with other things than mortals, and even so show a degree of deliberation and judgment in their form.

Or, of course, it could be comic. When the setting, the plot, and the characters are all taken not too seriously, a foolish and frivolous being running the show is part of the joke. Then, it's a limit on the story. Even some comic tales can't be told in that frivolous a world.

A form you are comfortable with, however chosen, will still affect the entire set-up.

Metaphysics and Escalation

The plot vs metaphysics

There are many good reasons for shoving the fictional metaphysics of your fantasy world off-stage, but one of them is that your story may turn into a series. You may even want to make it last a long time. This requires episodic structure, and strictly limited escalation.

Now, it is possible pull off an episodic fantasy series where the stories have no necessary connection, and in which the dangers are greater and less in no particular order. Conan was running into demigods before he left the frozen north. While his adventures subsequently had varying dangers, it was not an upward slope.

But most series nowadays tend toward a climbing structure. The danger escalates in hopes of keeping people's interest.

If you already have brought metaphysical principles on stage, you have already started at a high level, and if you allow it to escalate, it has to reach higher and higher levels.

Even if you sensibly limited the first book to dealing with a sorcerer who summoned a demon, what can you do for a second? Three demons? Seven? An archdevil?

And what do the forces of evil do? Perhaps the demon was to kill a rival, but then what do you do with more? Raze a university? Conquer a city? Turn a kingdom into a desolation?

Sooner or later the Legions of Hell show up and threaten the world, and then you are out of places to escalate, or the series gets very silly, however unintentionally. (Other planes of existence, other worlds, created to be threatened in a larger scale, are obviously paper scenery.)

Nor does it help to use polytheistic gods. Here you help the god of a stream, then of a river, then of merchants, then of kings—once you reach the king of the gods, the lord of the lightning, master of all weather, you are running out of ways up. Perhaps the Fates? But then, once you have brought back the scissors to the Fates so they can continue to cut the threads of lives, so that mankind does not suffer endlessly from fatal injuries and illnesses, where do you go up?

Part of the problem is that the largest scale must encompass the whole fictional cosmos. A cosmos that can be stuffed into a novel is a pretty small cosmos. It doesn't help the novel to take place in such a tiny world.

Also a certain degree of confusion, clutter, and incoherence lends realism at a lower level—and allows characters to differ without one being an idiot—but breaks down as you get to higher levels of metaphysics.

"From the Way arose the ten thousand things"—whatever your basic principle is, it should be simple, though capable of producing great complexity.

Some try to add layers of abstraction on top so they can keep on climbing. The gods have higher gods, and then there are gods for those gods. It doesn't work. Turtles all the way up doesn't work any better than turtles all the way down. Best to show only a hint of the tortoise shell.

When generating new stories, it is wiser to vary the circumstances. Indeed, this works better than escalating, because a reader may not care that the storm giant in question can menace a province instead of a city—it is, after all, just another storm giant.

Also remember to never threaten the world. Kingdom, yes, you can scale up to kingdom, but once you threaten the world, you should bow out of the series.

Conan, mentioned before, goes from devil-summoning sorcerers to pirates, to denizens of a fallen city who threaten him with sheer force of numbers, to eldritch monstrosities. All have power to threaten him, many have ability to threaten regions, and none escalate the series to the point where the next story feels like anticlimax.

Manly Wade Wellman, with his Silver John stories and others with like heroes, frequently deals with demons among other evil magic and werewolves and ghosts, but he does not escalate. All problems are treated with the seriousness they merit without making them larger than the one before.

Indeed, when one of Wellman's heroes visits a friend of his who has a healing spring, a neighbor, the friend's love interest, visits with her bucket. She blushes a little to explain that the reason for the visit is her chickens, but the hero firmly states that sick chickens should get whatever they need, thus establishing he has the proper priorities.

Escalation is always a problem, but particularly with metaphysics. Much, much wiser to play up the importance of the problems to those who suffer them, rather than raise the stakes. And then the story is kept new, and the readers awake, by innovating new and different menaces.

Where'd He Go?

A metaphysical isekai issue

Some isekai drop the character in the new world as himself, perhaps with a character class. Others have the character suddenly remember his past life.

Still others have the character appear in the life of a character from a game or book, and have to cope with the hash the character had made of the life before them.

And what on earth happened to the person who was there before them? Whose body and life they have usurped, however involuntarily? I have only once seen it addressed, and if nothing else, the danger of this person would hang over the character's head. What if the person returned and ejected the character? Would the character end up a ghost? In a new body in another world? Back in his own body? Off to the afterlife?

Given that he's never sure how he got there, he doesn't know whether it can happen again. Without warning. (The one exception I mentioned above did address it, though unfortunately in a manner that didn't preclude its happening again except that would be hard on the plot.)

Perhaps the most logical explanation of the main character's situation is that the world was created at the moment that this character became aware of it.

Everything before that was backstory, and all the characters, and the setting, were created in this moment, fully formed, with the backstory they remember.

On the other hand, since the other characters remember that past when the main character doesn't, who are they? Or what are they?

Are they actually people, or no more so than cardboard cutouts? Do they have rational souls, or just appear as if they do? Is it suicide for the main character to sacrifice himself for their well-being, as it would be if they actually were cardboard cutouts?

If that were even a real question, I would expect it to be important in the plot, and if it got answered "cardboard cutouts" that would have vast importance in the plot, down to completely determining the main character's actions. (It would, at least, be an original plot for the genre.)

Hmm. Perhaps they are actors. Servants pressed into this job. Then, to be sure, their motives would revolve about doing a job and getting paid, or perhaps appeasing the being that gave them the job. That, also, would have plot consequences once discovered.

Alternatively—

Are the other characters in fact other souls brought into the world? This option is rarely used, perhaps because it would send the plot flying in all sorts of directions. If they came from the hero's world, do they remember it? Or anything? Do they react like the hero?

A world in which everyone started to let slip that they were immigrant souls—and it would slip unless there was a lot of *very careful* picking and choosing among the souls—would make an interesting plot, but somewhat limited in choices, because their reactions would dictate the plot, and tear up any plot they were bound to. (At least the plot would be original for the genre here, too.)

Even with carefully selected souls, with inhibited and traumatized souls whose defense mechanisms had them act with extreme caution, a few slips might bring the whole edifice down. Plus such defense mechanism would limit their acting ability.

No, for most plots, the necessity is for the other characters to be real people (to make them important considerations), living in their real world (to avoid their derailing the story to deal with their being sent there) and for their backgrounds and history to be real (to give weight to the actions of the world around them).

So what happens to the character you replace? A quest to rescue that soul, imprisoned somewhere while you take over the life, would also be limiting. If quite original.

Hmmm.

Perhaps the most logical explanation is that the beings that put you into the world have the power to retroactively create your character and the character's backstory, and put you in it. It helps there if you "remember" your backstory.

This does blur it with the character living life and remembering a past life. But your suddenly "remembering" that you're another person, not at all like the person you've been acting all those years, is also a jar. If you are the same person in different lives, why is your personality so different? What do you and the backstory have in common to make you the same person? The blurring makes that trope more of a metaphysical issue, not this one less.

No, the best explanation is the retroactive creation, and the being who did it created your backstory. Insofar as you don't elide the whole thing as a plot device.

Fantasy Religion Follies

Tropes that DO NOT WORK

Some blazing annoying tropes about fantasy religions reach absurd proportions, and are unfortunately common. In part because writers keep pushing the metaphysics on stage.

They often, though not always, come together.

One is that two mutually exclusive explanations of the universe can both be true for two characters.

This is not syncretism. When Julian the Apostate claimed, in the best *interpretatio romana* style, that the Romans also worshiped the god of the Jews under another name, when a Viking carved the cross of Christ and the hammer of Thor on opposite sides of a stone, when a Shinto oracle declared that Buddhist priests were the correct people to perform funerals—they were not changing their cosmology. Their cosmology, if never explicitly framed, was that the world was governed by various powerful but finite beings, whom mankind had to propitiate. They were just slotting in one more such being. If this contradicts what the other religion taught, well, they already disagreed with it.

No, this is where if three characters are raised as Catholics, two become Buddhists, and one reverts to Catholic, only the one who remained a Buddhist would reincarnate. The other two would go to heavenly judgment. Worlds where this is known to be a fact. (Thus demonstrating how shoving metaphysics off-stage is prudent.)

I have seen a work in which the possible destruction of one cosmology's afterlife had the viewpoint character pondering whether people would convert to another religion to escape to another afterlife, or perhaps to this one to know that they could thus escape another world's Hell.

I have also read a work in which the viewpoint character and an ally have to put down a resurgence of the Aztec worldview, which first appears as a sequence of brutal murders, because the point is to revive the sequence of human sacrifices. Yet, at the end, the viewpoint character professes that he will follow the Christian beliefs, which are fine for him, and without prejudice toward what other people choose to believe.

Including, oh, the Aztecs?

You can not be a Christian and regarded it as true (or even innocuous) that other people kill people to keep the sun rising. Or that the beings who demand these deaths are worthy of worship even beyond the question of false gods.

Closely related to this, and equally silly, is the notion that gods, and the very cosmology, are entirely created by belief, fed by belief, shaped by belief, and in the final recourse, entirely dependent on belief. (This does, indeed, provide a mechanism for the different rules, to be sure.)

Terry Pratchett used it in Discworld, with his merry declaration that it was important to shoot missionaries on sight because you will go to Hell if and only if *you* believe that you deserve it—your actual deserts meaning nothing—and so you want to remain ignorant of its very existence. Hur, hur, hur.

Then he introduced Vorbis, and if ever a man firmly believed that he deserved to be wafted to Heaven, and a high place in Heaven at that, by flights of angels, it was Vorbis. Suddenly the idea that your deserts matter actually applied.

Harry Turtledove also used it, in *The Case of the Toxic Spelldump*, where the hero is tasked, among other things, with figuring out whether certain gods of a Californian tribe had really gone extinct for the want of belief.

He claims to be a Jew. A practicing Jew. He can attend synagogue all he likes and still not be a Jew, because he literally and explicitly believes that God and all His angels are sustained, and gain their great power, from the belief of him and his co-religionists.

You can not believe that God made you if you believe that you made Him.

All the more in that the religions teach, and their practitioners believe, that God exists independently of them—and so too do the gods, down to the lowliest household god.

Some thought the gods needed religious rites for strength—Egyptian gods, like all other beings, needed their names pronounced for power, and Mesopotamian gods after the flood gathered around the survivor's sacrifice like flies—but not existence. Egyptian magicians would hunt down the names of forgotten gods because they would give more for having their names pronounced, but they had not vanished.

Among the Greeks and Romans, sacrifice was important only as the acknowledgment of divinity. It wasn't necessary for the gods.

At that, if belief makes and shapes the god, the belief that the god is independent of human belief should make the god independent of it.

And the only thing that could keep the clashing cosmologies both afloat would be the positive belief that they were both valid for whoever held them. Anyone who would believe that can not, at the same time, believe a specific one.

Not to mention that this clashing cosmology belief can not be privileged over all the rest by its own nature. It is the belief that all these other views are *valid*.

If you had some quasi-neoplatonic philosophers whose superior minds could enforce such a clashing cosmology, that these philosophers regard the cosmologies as inferior, for the riffraff, would affect the metaphysics of the world itself, making the others inferior, and would have to, given their superiority is what lets it work at all.

No, there's no real way to make it work.

Fictional Fictions And Metaphysics

Layers of fiction

One has a fictional world. In this world, a character reads a tale, or plays a game. Then the character is drawn into the world of this tale.

Some works have the world be the inspiration of many different in-universe works, but that is not this trope, because it is no more than the inspiration that anyone might get by visiting a location, and the inspirations hit the writers wildly differently.

Or even having one author having visited the world and come back to write its history and pass it off as fiction—that's not this trope.

This trope is a single in-universe work of fiction, intended as fiction by its writer, and a single in-universe fantasy world, clearly bound together—or several, but always one book/one world.

Some nineteenth century tales come close to this. Children sent back in history in one of Edgar Eager's tales, to land in the court of King Arthur, and the like. Even if the setting is meant to be historical, even if you regarded King Arthur as a historical figure, the children landed in a court that was a hodge-podge of anachronisms, starting with things such as the existence of Lancelot (who makes no appearances in the oldest tales of King Arthur).

The oldest clear variant of the trope I've seen is the Harold Shea tales, by L. Sprague de Camp and Fletcher Pratt (collected in *The Compleat Enchanter*). In that one, Harold Shea (and later his friends when they join him) do not need to have an explanation of why they went to the other world, because they did it themselves.

At one point, a character raises the question of whether these worlds were created when the writers created them, or whether the writers were taking down accounts of the other worlds without realizing it. Another character chuckles and dismisses the question as meaningless, and the other character's objection that it's meaningful does not result in its being settled.

It is indeed a question. And one past the usual lot of the metaphysics of other worlds.

Later, Harold Shea and other characters land in the world of Coleridge's *Kubala Khan*, and from the warnings of the experienced character to the new ones, he thinks it's dangerously unstable because it is incomplete. But at no point in the series does it explain when he came to that conclusion, let alone why.

I shudder to think what such a world would be, in which all sorts of things—history, people, settings—can vanish on a whim, or be utterly altered on a moment. Or do these things act retroactively?

What would really be absurd would be if worlds were created incompletely. Let us suppose that a sphinx asks a riddle to those who seek entrance to her library. If the answer is good enough, she tells them it was well thought out and lets them in—but she's done that for several characters who gave different answers. If she ever says that the answer is *right*, why, all sorts of things would happen.

However, the writer, having thought of this scenario, has not managed to puzzle out what riddle would be good, having a number of plausible but wrong answers, and a correct answer that would resonate with the themes and plot of the story. Being a turning point in the plot does require that the correct answer have more significance than a random piece of background, or even a minor event.

So, the world has—a sphinx both with and without a riddle?

Publication would provide some clarity as to what is the definitive version, but it could still be incomplete. And what if the drafts were published later?

Though, if it went the other way, if the world is what exists first, and the writer is picking up on it, there is the little issue of why drafts can be so radically different. Even when characters take on a life of their own, and the writer just chases after them trying to get it all down, there can be radically different drafts.

If it's just incorrect knowledge, a problem in communication, why is the end result so close to the world?

A better approach might be to have a book appear in this world with an author that's just a byline. It is a conscious manipulation by a being that can reach between the worlds. Especially if this being is using it as bait to find those to send over.

On the other hand, that requires skill in depicting how and why this being did that, or else the being being the main villain of the tale. (Once the matter is on-stage that much, brushing the matter aside as a plot device does not work that well.)

You could do that with an existing work, and thus make the precise mode of the work that the being used the setting of the world. And also explain any discrepancies as the being's choices—or possibly necessities, to paper over holes in the world-building.

Or you could leave it open, as long as the characters are indifferent enough, or else are willing to acknowledge the somewhat creepy nature of the question, since it touches on whether things are real.

Different Dualities

Possibilities

Good and Evil, despite earnest efforts from everyone from philosophers and sages to the makers of role-playing games, do not make a good duality, because they are not equal.

This does not mean you can not use a duality in your world. Even as a metaphysical principle, if you are thus moved. But you need to think about it.

The great dualities about presence and absence—light vs darkness, sound vs silence, active vs. passive—generally hit the problem with the absence being, well, not much. Too much light can blind, too much sound can deafen, but darkness and silence are harmless. You can do something with an ascent to enduring more and more, but it's not a conflict and so not a duality.

You can do something with heat vs cold, because excessive cold, like excessive heat, can kill. I worked with this in *Fever And Snow*, where, as in many dualities, the Golden Mean rules. It's the middle that is good, where the extremes are both bad.

I was thinking of this when I disliked the idea of the Positive Energy Plane and the Negative Energy Plane used in RPGs. And I bounced it against the idea of Form and Matter such as was used in the medieval times.

You could do a nice duality of Form vs. Energy. Form is absolutely rigid. Energy is absolutely fluid. When mixing in Form, Energy first becomes Fire, moving of its own nature but still having Form, which it endlessly shifts; then Air, which moves on its own but conforms to a shape it's given; Water, which does not move on its own, and while it conforms to a shape it does so without changing its size; Earth, which can be moved but does not move. (Or, if you view it the other way round, Form becomes Earth when Energy is mixed in, and so on the other way.)

Thus things become a question of whether the elements so mixed in the things as to create that the necessary balance.

One note that elemental spirits would be more likely to be evil in such a set up. Beneficent ones would be more mixed and equitable in their composition.

Then I ran across a description of the Negative Energy Plane about how it's the force that drags stuff out of the Positive Energy and is the reason why anything else exists besides the Positive Energy Plane.

Ooooh! How Neo-Platonic!

Well, not necessarily. It could easily be worked into that, though that would make it Good versus Evil. The Positive Energy Plane as the Absolute, absolutely Good, all wrapped up in its perfectly perfect perfection and needing nothing outside itself, somehow manages to emanate an inferior and Evil Demiurge that draws things out of the Absolute to make bad, inferior things. The only really Good thing is for these to get back to the Absolute.

But, of course, you do not have to run with that, especially since the plane is *energy* and not the absolute. One could do something, symbolically, like the Three Graces: the Positive Energy Plane is Beauty, the Negative Energy Plane is Desire, and the Material Planes, thus produced by Desire pulling out Beauty, are Delight. (A symbolism widely used in all sorts of allegories.)

Elegant. Definitely more elegant than the use of Law versus Chaos. In *Three Hearts and Three Lions*, Poul Anderson managed to use it as Good versus Evil—and not so much a duality. Michael Moorcock used it as a duality, and asserted that perfect order would be a flat featureless plain. Which is impossible. Logically impossible, even. You can only put elements in order; you can not put an element in an order because there is nothing else.

Simplification is as much as opponent of Law as Chaos is. Or Disorder, where everything is grouped but not by its nature. A farm in which the cows hunted the mice, the cats pulled the plow, the dogs barked at dawn, and the rooster cackled at intruders would be as much as against Law as one in which any given animal might be doing any given task.

So Law (or Order, if you prefer) is a Golden Mean thing, between the lack of order of Chaos, Disorder, and Simplification.

The Golden Mean really is a good thing to keep in mind.

Fiction And Philosophy of Good and Evil

Some groundwork

In a story, pushing ethics off the stage is not so wise as pushing metaphysics off. True, philosophy holds ethical complications, and ethical conundrums, and the best and the wisest have broken their hearts over them over the millennia.

Still, ethics are important in the forefront of the story. Starting with that it is a great aid to your main character's winning over the audience if the world actually will be better if he wins. (Nothing puts me off a story faster than the hearty wish that all the factions could lose—when that's clearly impossible—but not really caring is a close second.)

Then, ethics has all these conflicts and character arcs built in. The conflict between choosing the marvelous ruby the Sea of Wine and the wonderful emerald the Lake of Leaves is never so sharp as the conflict between choosing the ruby and the life of your companions—unless the ruby gives you unending wine, and the emerald lets you restore life to a wasteland, thus pushing it back to ethics.

It also reflects the other thing about ethics. You can easily stick to the elements with no real arguments. The character learns to tell the truth, or to refrain from gossip, or to avoid murdering people, and thus you have an arc where you don't have to stop and defend it with arguments.

This is good. Life is a comedy for those who think and a tragedy for those who feel—per Walpole—but I have already discussed the caveat that for a writer, it's not so much tragedy as drama. Even there, I put in that a quick revelation that a man's liminal status slid through the magical protections can be comic. This sort of quickness and clarity applies to moral questions, too. No one is going to laugh at the end of a long and careful reasoning coming to a conclusion, however sound.

One can smile at the boy whose doctor father died poor because people scorned paying him, and who became a superhero because he thought that would bring respect, only to learn that being a superhero is about doing what's right regardless of whether you were respected—as indeed, his doctor father did. But the fundamental precept— that good is good in itself, not as a tool to gain respect—is simple enough.

More in-depth thoughts on respect, on how the respect of those worthy of respect can be a guide and even an aid to keeping to the right thing—but how do you judge who is worthy of respect?—can be treated in fiction, but it does require careful judgment and juggling. For instance, any discussion between characters needs to be adequately motivated on their part.

For in-depth intensive thinking about complicated topics, there is non-fiction. For writing, and for reading. This non-fiction can be useful to get a broad picture, and steal things for your sage to say.

Still, if you consider these writings philosophically, you will notice that many treatments of ethics tend to oriented toward a certain condition of life. Which is all very well if you don't try to generalize it too far, and may be exactly what you need for a particular character, or set thereof. (What did knights think was obligatory? Consider *A Knight's Own Book of Chivalry* by Geoffroi De Charny Samurai? *Hagakure,* by Yamamoto Tsunetomo. Even if all the usual rules about primary sources apply.)

But I will fall back and regroup on a higher level, to be more general in the best philosophical manner.

Once you do that, you tend to notice that teachings in virtue tend to be rather grabbag in the level they teach. Courage, politeness, magnanimity, hospitality, concord, or patriotism—

There is some sense in that, in that teaching virtue generally is for children. It is far easier to teach children to not eat too much, to wait for what they want, to not prattle incessantly, to save money rather than squander it, and then, when they are more mature, teach them these are all subsumed under the virtue of temperance.

Still, even discussions for adults tend to wander in a way not conductive to sound philosophizing, and ordering of virtue.

To avoid this and philosophize, I shall start with the cardinal virtues.

> Wisdom teaches temperance, and prudence, and justice, and fortitude, which are such things as men can have nothing more profitable in life.

And so I begin on series on those virtues known as **cardinal** because they are pivotal, and their use in stories.

Prudence, The Cardinal Virtue

Mother of all virtue

Prudence is the ability to tell good from evil, not just in general, but in specific cases. It has long been defined as "right reason in action" and is closely related to Wisdom. Which is why it is called the mother of all virtue, and is the first of the cardinal virtues.

Whether to tell the truth or lie. Whether to omit a truth that the other person is not entitled to know. Whether to deceive to protect the innocent, and if so, whether it's better to lie outright or to mislead. Whether your judgment is sufficient to understand the matter before you, or you should consult a wiser head. All of these, and many more, fall under Prudence.

Now, I've already talked about how feeling, not thinking, is the stuff of drama, and how subtle and lengthy reasoning processes are not even comic. So what's a writer to do?

For a scene, perhaps, the wise king, the sagacious abbess, the perspicacious archmage, or any other authority figure can resolve a mildly complicated dilemma as a bit of characterization—but past that, prudence must be carefully deal with.

The stuff of drama lies in conflict.

So—for a character, if the problem lies in the arena of prudence, and is internal, what the character suffers is a temptation to delude himself. To want to decide for his friend over his enemy until he tries to delude himself that his friend is in the right when he isn't. To convince himself that it would be unfriendly to refuse just one more glass of wine. To tell himself that only a coward would avoid a fight. To call it mercy when he lets the bully off one more time, knowing that nothing has changed and the bully will go on beating up other people. To, in fact, cultivate ignorance—studied or affected ignorance, which aggravates guilt because of the hardness of heart involved.

Thus we have a dramatic struggle in which a character can win out to clear knowledge and act upon it. Or, perhaps not.

More commonly in fiction than in real life, the character does not succeed in deluding himself, but sets about the wrong action with full knowledge that what he does is wrong, but lacking the other virtues that would enable him to act on his knowledge. It's more dramatic that way.

Even the situation where the character persuades himself into ignorance is generally portrayed more dramatically than in real life. Habitual drunkards get that way through continually drinking with friends and blunting their judgment—in part because it would mean that they have to judge not only their future actions, but condemn their past ones.

Indeed, such conflicts are often dramatized fully. The character who wrestles with the knowledge that he should drink no more alcohol meets with characters who urge it on him, and characters who rebuke the very thought. These characters' reactions to his choice to know the truth or not can pull his internal conflict out onto the stage.

A frequent complication of this is that the other characters are often strong with a low prudence that uses the same talents and abilities to argue against whatever virtue is at stake. Deriding the notion of goodness, arguing for avarice and excessive safety, or lambasting the entire notion of prudence as cowardice.

For more drama, and indeed drama more like real life, there can be conflict over a prudential decision. Whether a patient who has received every tested treatment for a condition and is still dying should receive an experimental treatment. There's the chance of prolonging life and health, and the benefit to others of the knowledge gained by this treatment. On the other hand, there's the time and effort spent, and the chance of pain, suffering, and death.

Perhaps it may again be wisest to dramatize it with different characters in support. The patient's mother and father, perhaps. The mother tells him not to waste his final hours on earth chasing after life at all costs, when it's likely he will pay the price and not receive the goods, and the father tells him he should seize the chance and not just dully await death.

You will find people sneering at the conflict of good vs. good, insisting it must be weak tea. They are simply assuming that all good vs. good conflicts can be solved without real sacrifice. That is only true where there has been a misjudgment, a failure in prudence, and so the conflict is unreal.

These conflicts can be plenty real, where the prudential judgment must weigh the good things in question, and the problem is that something good must be sacrificed. Unlike evil vs. evil conflict, where the big problem is that it's impossible to care whether one side wins except insofar as you wish they could both lose.

And, of course, prudence can be in the background as the other virtues take center stage.

Temperance, The Cardinal Virtue

Mastering moderation

Temperance is the ability to master and moderate your appetites to keep them in the bounds of reason.

That's a technical term, by the way. As a cardinal virtue, temperance does not mean the intemperate denunciation of temperate drinking, as G. K. Chesterton so sagely put it.

This obviously is so basic a virtue that it's a rare story where mastering it takes center stage. All the heroes, and all the villains, need temperance in at least some of its elements to keep the plot going. (Including, yes, in drinking alcoholic beverages.)

Impulsive villains can not plot and plan because they will always be haring off after new ideas, making them at most a nuisance. Possibly a major nuisance if they happen to have some power, but still a nuisance. The self-control is necessary even to chase after goals that Prudence would order you to abjure.

As for impulsive heroes, they would get nowhere except against the most simple of battles. Always distracted, or slowed, by whatever they failed to control. And very likely incompetent without, by pure luck, happening to like whatever practice they need to keep their skills sharp.

This is why a hero may have an "informed flaw" where the reader is *told* he's a drunkard, and perhaps he's even found drunk, in a tavern that the other characters have to pry him out of, and then he suffers no further complications from the drinking. No DTs, no pink elephants, no smuggling hard spirits on the trip, no drunken folly on the way. . . . (They don't even explain that he's fine as long as he has something to do. That would require attention in the lulls when they have to wait.)

Intemperate drinking, and even simple laziness, can, of course, be useful to dispose of a logically necessary but inconvenient character. If the wizard in charge of the library is habitually drunk in his room, or simply doesn't bother to work, it gives his young assistant a freer hand than would be reasonable with a good boss, and lets the young adventurers do more. (It also indicates what the master wizards think of the library, giving another contrast between the groups of characters.) But that's more of a plot device than a characterization.

Other elements of the virtue are more useful, and feasible, for plots. Ill-temper, for instance. The Evil Overlord who kills servants when thwarted in anything shows his evil. (Though that does raise questions on how he manages to acquire any servants. They are often treated as a plot device, requiring no explanation.)

In milder doses, an ill temper can complicate all sorts of incidents for the hero, whether it's the hero or a companion that's ill-tempered. And form an excellent character arc.

It can also be a way to set up the ending. The villain blusters his way through all sorts of obstacles with his bursts of temper where the hero has to work his way through with courtesy, and then the ending turns on these characters remembering who was polite to them.

Controlling one's money is less used nowadays, though it has a lot of potential. Misers are not so much used as villains. As for prodigals who squander all their wealth, this seems to be used solely as a way to get heroes on the road again. The folly of not mastering your desires to soak up all your wealth until you are in actual want of what you need gets no play.

Then, careful budgeting does not seem dramatic. Lining up a friend to act as an accountant is the most I've seen.

Perhaps the most common issue that surfaces lies in modesty, and immodesty—the braggart.

The *miles gloriosus* is the classic form, combining endless boasting with a complete lack of Fortitude. Generally he gets to show his true colors only once because as an endless burden on the other characters—with his bragging alienating those he meets and his cowardice actively interfering with fights or other dangers—he neither moves the story forward nor amuses the readers.

So thoroughly engraved is this form that having a braggart turn out to be even mildly competent is a surprise, no matter how often it happens. Or very competent.

Or even better than he bragged.

One notes that in works where the braggart is good enough to be actually useful, the bragging tends to be regarded as a minor quirk, even being amusing. The important thing is that he controls himself enough to master the skills he needs.

Other than that, the only way where it works in a reoccurring character is for the braggart to be forced to acquire skills and courage to keep up the facade, until it is no longer one.

So vital is Temperance to the characters.

Fortitude, The Cardinal Virtue

The fortress

Fortitude is the ability to act with constancy and firmness in the face of difficulties. It is courage, not only steadfastness in the face of immediate danger, but in the face of troubles such as poverty and loss. It encompasses patience, for instance, and magnanimity.

This virtue is very common in fiction, for the obvious reason that in any action-and-adventure tale, the lack of courage in any number of characters would make the story—much shorter.

Even villains must have fortitude, or they will greatly simplify the task of defeating them. At the very least, a cowardly mastermind needs minions who will embody this virtue—though it is not unknown for an apparently courageous villain to fall apart on defeat or setback, revealing that what had appeared as fortitude had only been overconfidence.

It's more likely to differ between the true heroes and those who abandon the quest as simply too difficult, or too long, or too abstract for them. Or possibly because they panicked. You can give heroes moments of wrestling with fear, but those who fail at them can only rarely retrieve the situation. Perhaps running away when the goblins attack, only to return before the fray is over.

Lacking patience is also more likely if a contest is set in the story. The villain, or the other competitors, are more likely to cheat because they lack the patience and sometimes the courage to win through the the ordinary means.

On the whole, the chief character arc about courage is likely to be a hero learning that courage is not feeling no fear but instead overcoming fear.

But what about stories outside the action-and-adventure arena?

Well, where courage is not relevant, it does not come up. Admittedly, there are genres where the villain can more easily be cowardly, such as murder mysteries, but even there the hero has to be courageous. The villain's very cowardice leads to the danger of sneak attacks.

There may, of course, be the necessity of moral courage. All depends on the conflict. All sorts of doubts can be cast on the efforts of the hero. From well-meaning friends, often those who think the issue is too big for the characters—which is where magnanimity comes in—to villains deriding you as a fool.

Magnanimity is a big part of it, which is often underplayed. The hero and his party are on a quest to save the world! What a great-hearted deed!

Is it adequately motivated?

Yes, the world is in danger. That means that everyone is in danger. Not everyone is going on the quest. That means that more than the world's being in danger is required.

The great charm of the Chosen One plot device is that it removes the need to motivate the character, at least in the eyes of many authors. (All the more noteworthy in that they tend to entirely omit who the Chooser of the One is—and what *his* motives and purposes, and character, are.)

What is needed, of course, if you want to save the world—or even for many large goals that are less colossal (which may be wise)—is a magnanimous character, who will act on the behalf of others. A great-hearted hero who will set his intentions on great deeds. Who will not be turned aside by the peril, or the cost to himself of time and effort, or the derision of others.

Many writers skip this stage and just send the character on the quest.

True, there can be other motives involved. The love of danger—Bill Maudlin has a nice passage on this in *Up Front*, about soldiers who loved war. On the other hand, he makes it clear that these guys tend to be nuts. So that limits the types of characters you can use there. Even the types of characters who would be willing to associate with them, though the degree of danger may force it.

The revenge motive is, perhaps, overused, but then, it's very useful. A character can set out because the threat to the world injured him, personally, and only slowly develop the great-hearted motive to save the world.

Or, perhaps, remain the same petty soul, who evinces courage and patience, perhaps, but remains obsessed with nothing but his own petty concerns.

That may be better told from the viewpoint of a character who, perhaps, does less but has the Prudence to see the truth and the Fortitude to carry through, because he will be able to see what the main hero lacks even in his heroism.

But, at least, the world is saved, and the Fortitude that brought him to help save it will help him bear up under that knowledge.

Justice, The Cardinal Virtue

Order and fiction

Justice is the rendering of what is due, to the one to whom it is due.

Here is where the story pedal meets the virtuous metal. Peace has been described as the tranquility of order, and conflict can be usefully described as the commotion of disorder.

Guided by Prudence (or misguided by imprudence), founded on Temperance, strengthened by Fortitude, the character fares forth to collide with other characters, and work out the whole drama of the story to a new order, no matter how local or how universal.

Prudence, in fact, is vital, given the whole flurry of things that fall under Justice: patriotism, courtesy, filial piety, religion, friendship, concord, and so many more.

This, obviously, is where Prudence fails most often. Indeed, in the non-fiction discussions of virtue directed toward a particular condition that I mentioned up front, this is where *they* fail most often, pushing the duty of allegiance to one's overlord, obedience to one's parents, or respect to one's teacher, past bounds of reason, even to the point of excusing wrong-doing in obedience.

Fictionally, that is where the minions act, and perhaps the heroes have to surmount, but, of course, the central perpetrator of injustice is the main villain.

The number of villains who are selective about whom they give what is due, and whether they give what is due, or more than others are entitled to, is very high. The Evil Overlord who regards everything as due to himself, the evil tribe that treat everyone outside its border as not a person, the boss who favors the sweet-talking slacker over the socially awkward diligent worker, and fancies himself particularly kind every time that he makes the diligent worker's life more difficult—each of these villains does wrong.

Or, of course, the hero when he does the same. Or the other characters. Not only does natural inclination push us toward helping those closest to us, they are those most likely to have greater demands in justice on us. But not all consuming.

(Indeed, it is not unknown for the writer to play favorites that way, with the story justifying conduct toward other characters by the main character while viciously condemning it in other characters. The heroine's repeated bursts of ill temper—well, she was tired and under stress—while her classmates in the isekai are obviously villains for their bad moments, even if each of them had only one. I have heard of a villainess isekai where the main character realized that the game she was in was unduly partial to the heroine that way.)

Still, in a reasonable story, the villain is more likely to wrong people. That's what makes him the villain. He regards other people *solely* as tools to deploy toward his own ends.

Whether he realizes he is being unjust can not be determined without viewing the matter from his viewpoint, since an unjust villain will, of course, lie if it's useful to him.

Though, for drama, the villain may hold forth on his views in a manner with varying degrees of plausibility. Soliloquies are obviously more or less—staged.

Where there is more than one villain, depending on their exact nature, they may talk among themselves. *Frieren* manages this elegantly with the demons—and even manages to characterize them on top of their all being uniformly psychopathic.

More complicated is the issue of the hero's having a character arc. Usually, this entails his learning to extend justice further. This usually also makes the further off characters more sympathetic and the closer ones less because doing justice on behalf on the unsympathetic, and to the sympathetic, is hard to make satisfying.

This can lead to some unfortunate implications. When the rich girl the other girls were cruel to is revealed to be suffering parental neglect, and they repent—does that mean it is fine to be cruel to rich girls if their parents are good?

Writers can work at making suffering from injustice the cause of sympathy, and injustice the cause of alienating readers. It takes skill.

Some writers, alas, do not bother, and some readers follow them. You end up with works in which the importance of injustice is treated as a factor of how much it hurts the main characters, and how on-stage it is. A villain who exterminates a city off-stage is more forgivable than a villain who kills the hero's mother on-stage—even if, on top of the severity of the crimes, the mother's death stemmed from arguable self-defense, and the death of the city (and all its mothers, and fathers, and children) was gratuitous cruelty.

Complicating all this is the question of administering justice. The hero's killing the villain who exterminated a city is far more dramatic than his arresting him, bringing him to authorities, going through the rigmarole of a trial—and perhaps not even seeing him receive the death penalty he so richly merits. To be sure, lack of a justice system, war, and resisting arrest can lead to this more dramatic conclusion.

It takes careful work to make the just resolution work. It's worth it.

Super-Philosophy And Justice

Philosophy in story

Superheroes are a genre particularly well suited to thinking philosophically.

In one respect, the superhero genre generally does run philosophical thought experiments, even if not very thought-out either in detail or in quality. Perhaps not thought out at all.

This revolves around the way the heroes handle justice.

As vigilantes.

More or less. Differing over eras of comic books, of course. Sometimes the superheroes work so hand-in-glove with police forces that a lawyer would have no trouble arguing that they were governmental agents. Sometimes they actually work for the government.

Still, formal affiliation never stopped them from acting freely. Like vigilantes. (Except in some specialized stories within the enormous superhero universes, or in the hands of writers working outside it. This discussion does not apply to those stories.)

Now, philosophically, the only theoretical argument against vigilantism is from an absolutist position of political power. The government has the absolute right to administer justice, or injustice, as it sees fit, and it does not answer to its subjects—whether it's totalitarian and does not answer to anyone, or views itself as answerable only to God. Therefore anyone who acts as a vigilante is usurping the authority that only the government rightfully has.

(Even self-defense can be—interesting. One finds governments requiring that killing in self-defense be pardoned, even while admitting it merits a pardon, or people arguing that since the dead man committed a capital crime, the killer did the government a favor, and laws being passed on that basis.)

There are, however, a lot of practical arguments against vigilantism.

For one thing, vigilante justice tends to concentrate on crimes that personally offend the vigilantes. There is a degree of correlation between the severity of the offense and the degree of offense they take, but it is far from perfect. Crimes fall through that system more than in many others, even corrupt ones.

Also, vigilantism shades into private revenge, in that most vigilantes are personally concerned with the matter, with all the notorious effects that has on judgment, whether of guilt or of the justice of the punishment's severity.

As a side effect of that, vigilantes tend to concentrate on the wrongs of the popular and those connected to them, by those who are less popular. The awkward and unpopular can go whistle if they are victims of crime, and lucky. If unlucky, the popular may sacrifice them for being victims. Indeed, the popular criminals may use them as scapegoats.

After all, vigilantes have all the problems that a justice system has with evidence, plus some because of inferior ability to gather it and a shortened time frame. Many vigilantes act solely on mass hysteria.

Then, vigilantes have a limited set of punishments that are feasible to inflict. Furthermore, their personal connection to the victims, or personal reaction to the crime, mean they frequently punish disproportionately to the crime.

Do superheroes have any of these problems?

Of course not!

Even those who have no connection to the police force at all, even those who are repeatedly (for dramatic purposes) suspected of crimes, can solve the punishment issues by leaving the perps for the police. (That's the dull part, anyway.)

Evidence is also not an issue. The repeated appearance of popular supervillains turns on their escaping—whether from prison or a mental institution—not on how it's impossible to convict them with the chain of evidence so tainted. (Except occasionally, for dramatic purpose.)

Partly because the superheroes are amazingly accurate.

Then, stories are not so much about reasoning as sentiments, as C.S. Lewis described in *The Abolition of Man*. They can portray the triumph of the superhero as right and just, but in story, it is properly subordinate to the prime consideration of portraying the triumph as admirable and proper.

In this, the advantage of vigilantism is that instead of seeing the process drawn out for months in court and than the punishment dribbled out over years, justice is delivered in one KER-POW! punch.

The true philosophical problem with it is, of course, the monthly schedules and the aesthetic issues involved.

Having to produce a new story every single month, writers naturally had issues producing fresh, original ideas every single month. At least for villains. If they kept repeating the villains, they did not have to invent a new character as a villain every single month. Just give him a new gimmick.

The problem with this is that such revolving-door justice, where the law is manifestly unable or unwilling to hold nefarious murderers and restrain them from evil-doing—is historically the way to bring out vigilantes. The sort that resort to their own, rather permanent sort of justice.

And aesthetically, the satisfaction of seeing justice done is rather undermined when you know the villain will be back next month.

This, however, is the philosophical issue of aesthetics: there are only so many variations you can work on a theme, and so all series are ultimately limited.

It's not a problem with philosophy of comic-book justice, as such. It's just, well, just a problem with depicting philosophy in the comic book setting as currently sold. Such are the problems of aesthetics.

Super-Philosophy And Injustice

When the setting hates the supers

Vigilante justice has its points for superhero stories, and can even work philosophically.

Two other issues complicate the picture of justice in these stories.

One is the reaction of the public to superheroes. This tends to be very story-driven and not at all logical.

In some settings, the hero is highly regarded by the general population, which could be justified by that being in the background and so needing to draw little attention to itself. Except for stories where hatred is whipped up very easily and dissipated by the end of the story. (The plot device nature of it undermines the effect.)

This is seen on a larger scale in the superheroes whose background is hatred. No matter how often Spiderman exonerates himself when charged with a crime, everyone is ready to blame him again when the next allegation is made.

And with the X-men, it is not only constant, it is monolithic. No characters have degrees of mutant hatred, so they will argue that some acts are too much. No characters hate mutants in general but carve out exceptions for those they know personally. No characters express platitudes about mutants' humanity and then privately do everything to avoid them.

While this does have its advantages on the pure philosophical level, discussing virtue separate from fame, that shoves it more on the intellectual level.

On the level of emotions and sentiments, it does have its bite, in that we can all feel for an underdog, and we have all been in situations where people took against us for no reason that we could discern.

Still, at times, this became a nagging issue: is this really plausible?

Pile up the drama too high, and it becomes absurd. At points, comic-book persecution reaches an intensity at which it is a persecution complex projected outwards to justify it.

At that, it undercuts the theme of justice. You can't just leave the crooks for the police if the police think you are a monster. Then all the questions of how to administer punishment when you are only a vigilante with a limited set of powers, and whether you have all judgment necessary.

(It would explain why the villains are always back on the street within weeks or months, to be sure.)

And then there are the governments. The other issue where justice and injustice are not adeptly handled.

Governments trying to bring our vigilante superheroes in line are, of course, their opponents. This is—embraced with enthusiasm by superhero writers.

When it comes up. It doesn't always. The Justice League, for instance, tends to push all those issues to the background.

On the other hand, there's things like the way Thunderbolt Ross hunts for the Hulk. He would have gotten himself court-martialed, with the way he throws resources into trying to catch the Hulk.

Or the Accords in the Marvel Cinematic Universe, which turned anyone with superpowers into an object. If you resisted being deployed by the government, you could be detained forever without trial. When this was the same government that had, a few years before, been controlled by HYDRA. (That any effort to remove HYDRA members, or trials for their crimes, were off-stage, and not even mentioned, aggravates this.)

In these tales, in pursuit of conflict, the writers often drop the philosophical side of it. While the fights may be dramatic, even the fans of the works often observe that the government's side is made as idiotically as possible.

The thing is that there really is no point to pitting the superheroes against the government unless you want the political philosophy and ethics involved to become front and center. If you want a fight against a force mostly consisting of people armed with weaponry but with sheer mass of numbers, there's nothing wrong with a secret conspiracy.

Or perhaps the point of it is to split the team and have them willing to fight each other?

The thing with that is that unless you want to alienate the fans of half the characters, you have to give the superheroes a good, sound reason to fight. The strawman makes half your team look like idiots for falling for it.

"Anyone with superpowers must register with the government, or be imprisoned without trial, and then must use the superpowers on demand, and at no other time, or be imprisoned without trial" fails even the most pragmatic test. Machiavelli, who argued against disarming a conquered people (because they needed the weapons to defend themselves, and would be able to get weapons to revolt) would point out that anyone who has superpowers has no incentive to hold back in this scenario. For the mere crime of having powers, he faces life in prison or life as a slave. You can not punish him further for any additional crimes.

Find another excuse. A MacGuffin with trade-offs, perhaps. And then, if you want to tie it up neatly, with a bow, you reveal that the trade-offs are worse than expected, so the team can come together again.

Or make it a fight against a tyrannical government, so you don't have to split the team, and can even have characters argue that the claims the government puts forth are meant to be absurd, to humiliate those forced to repeat them.

Or, of course, make it an actually sound prudential judgment, so characters really could go either way. It's a choice, but it's also a challenge.

Such are the issues of dealing with philosophy in fiction.

Hero Of His Own Story?

The villainous viewpoint

I have run across one too many pieces of advice solemnly declaring that the villain is always the hero of his own story.

This is wrong, and obviously wrong on the face of it.

Yes, there is a place in fiction for a villain who thinks he is doing the right thing at great personal sacrifice. If such a villain serves the story. It is not the only option, and certainly its use is far more dramatic than realistic.

How often do *you* think of what you do as heroic?

Often, when we're caught doing something we ought not (even by ourselves), our reaction is to blame our circumstances. To treat ourselves not as heroes but as pawns of forces beyond our control. I was tired, he made me so angry, you misled me, and so on.

Criminals (and narcissists) do this all the time. In extreme cases, a murderer, serving a life sentence in prison, described the killing as "the knife went in." (Poor impulse control may be involved. This can work for a low-level villain, though many forms of villainy require impulse control.)

There does have to be some judgment about it because another factor is that the criminal (or narcissist) is often lying. Whenever they think they can get something by looking pathetic, they lie blatantly. Blaming external factors is one of the easiest and most convenient ways.

Sometimes this can be easily discerned by listening in the conversation when the lie will buy nothing. Sometimes the lie is discarded until the next time it might be useful.

Not always, thought, so it can be hard to tell. Bluntly saying that it's false, or even proving it, may shock them, but given that they are hardened liars, it may be nothing more than surprise that it didn't succeed this time.

When caught, the practiced liars drop their original lie for a new one, incompatible with it, so quickly that they are clearly aware of what they are doing.

Sometimes they even lie to themselves, expurgating their memory of such things as their agreement to what the other person proposed, or inventing agreement that hadn't occurred. Though (and this can be a bear) sometimes if the pressure is high enough, the person can be brought to admit that he's lying.

But the lying points to the other side of things.

The vast majority of decisions made by people are pragmatic. Even the most heroic of heroes chooses a route by which one gets him to his next destination more quickly, with perhaps (if there is enough time) some consideration for the scenery or ease of travel.

In criminals, this is vastly aggravated. People who get in their way are obstructions. A burglar explains his career solely in terms of his own gain; at most he dismisses his victims with the claim they are insured. A murderer blinks and justifies his killing his victim because he could have identified the murderer.

This, of course, lies behind the lying: why not claim to have been abused as a child, if it might be useful?

Insofar as there is any consideration, it's for not being a sucker. You have to be a smart guy. Suckers never get rich.

When they sit in prison, and will be broke when released, they laugh at the poor law-abiding suckers, who will never get rich.

When interviewed about why they engaged in a long-term fraud that required a lot of law-abiding and profitable conduct before the final fraud, instead of just keeping on with the law-abiding conduct, the criminals involved committed the fraud because they enjoyed tricking people. It makes them feel powerful, and they enjoy making people look like fools and hurting them. Insofar as they justified it, the people they defraud—including their own colleague—shouldn't have let themselves be defrauded.

Enjoying hurting people is, of course, another motive. Very few criminals act upon it, but they commit a disproportionate amount of the crime.

These motives can all be used in fiction as well. Of course, each particular one would vary in usefulness depending on how large-scale the villain is, and what the villainy is. Far easier to give the Evil Usurper the motive of wanting to push people around and feel powerful than for him to blame everything on circumstances that forced him to act. (The latter might work splendidly, it would just be tricky to pull off.)

But there is no need at all to make him the hero of his own story.

Morality Meters

This trope needs work to work

I reflect on a Gamelit tale, where the hero of the game—a major character in the story—has morality meters.

The first problem is that the meters are the Seven Lively Virtues wrested out of the framework where they function. Instead there is a god of strict order and goodness who, it is claimed, abandoned the world. (The beings running the world do not give high confidence in their judgment, and the Church, while having some admirable members, had some real issues.)

The second problem is that using them as meters is really, and for more than one reason, a philosophically unsound way of thinking of morality.

Even in the computer games. Players complain about them.

Sometimes, of course, the players complain that the only choices are stupid. Not a fault limited to morals! But when your dark-side choice in a *Star Wars* game is to pointlessly rob a woman for money you don't need, instead of, say, suggesting to her that she will owe you for what you are doing—the light-side choice being to help her freely—players can be annoyed that to be evil is to be stupid.

Then RPG players, less constrained by programming requirements, are free to take that route, and often do. Many a Game Master can tell tales of players who insisted on doing deeply idiotic and wildly counterproductive actions because the actions were Evil, and so as Evil characters, they had to do them.

(A good person is like a good ladder. A ladder is only good when all its rungs are sound. While it's possible it could still be useful with half of them not able to take weight, the right three being unsound could make it unusable—and any one being unsound could spell disaster at some point.)

Not that writers are necessarily wiser, though in practice they generally aren't so stupid. The time factor helps.

But even were the choices sensible, the meters still have philosophical problems.

The games suffer from the running-total aspect. If you gratuitously help four people, you get Light Side points. If you gratuitously harm four people, you get Dark Side points. If you gratuitously help two and gratuitously harm two, you—balance out?

Don't become some kind of lunatic buffoon?

Don't dissolve into an incoherent sequence of actions instead of forming an actual character?

It is not for nothing that Batman's foe Two-Face is depicted as a madman because he will refrain from, or engage in, evil at the coin's bidding.

Fictionally, it is more important that the character hang together to convince the readers. More so, even, than real-life people. The tallying up of virtues as check marks does not really depict the moral life; the development of the character's character does.

Even if you don't get into such prudential judgments on whether a severer or a more lenient punishment would work better with a given pupil, or such questions of casuistry as whether it's wrong to lie to stop a murder, it needs to hang together.

Putting the meters in a Gamelit may work, if they are clearly run by a finite being with its own rules. Like the rule for magical objects that one GM used, that the alignment requirements were set by the views of the person who made the object. Except that an object you can take or leave—or perhaps go on a grand quest to be rid of, even if it's just to find a wizard who can cast remove curse strongly enough.

Sticking a meter on a character, and having it have affect on his life as it would on game-play—hmmm—my first thought was that the character development would have to be rising above the meter and learning to reject its moral judgments as incorrect even at a price.

But it would be possible to have the character shaped by the meters, though it would have to entail rising above the carrot and the stick entailed, and realizing the wisdom behind it.

In either case, a truly convincing picture of a blinkered and obscured view of good and evil being superseded by a better one has to be drawn. That is the sort of thing that gives wise and prudent people qualms, with all the questions that wise and prudent people have broken their hearts over, over all the centuries, but some things are clearly to be avoided.

I have read a work in which people encountered a magic in the woods, and behaved badly, and a girl tried to pull free by thinking of what was better in mankind—but it was truly a weak, milquetoast vision of goodness, that aspired no higher than "nice" or "decent" and would be unable to tackle commonplace crime. Certainly not war.

A game (or Gamelit) is more likely to concentrate on the big heroic deeds—to the extent of forgetting that, actually, the quotidian goodness is the point of all this heroism. One slays the dragon because it menaces the town, thus to allow the life of the town to go on: cooking of meals, tending of gardens, children bearing messages for their parents or attending to their lessons, building of homes, mending of clothes, elderly grandmothers spinning thread and enchanting children with their tales, and all the things that make up a town worth defending.

You might get an interesting story about the character who landed in a Gamelit world and a sprite that manages his morality meters both learning to aspire higher than that. Just remember that you are tackling profound philosophical questions in the process.

Black And White, and Gray

Moral complexity

Some people will tell you that you introduce moral complexity into a story by turning everything into a mass of gray. Simply contemplating the metaphor shows the folly of that. The simplest drawing in black and white is more complex than a flat gray.

No, the simplest way to make your story more morally complex is to put people of the same caliber of morals on opposite sides, and of differing morals on the same side.

This requires choosing the issue with care. Should the king offer succor to the refugee queen mother and her children, the young king and his brothers and sisters?

On one hand, refugees. You can make the children young enough to be guiltless, to add to it.

On the other hand, those who deposed her husband may have an ambassador right there to argue that they would make trouble for the kingdom, and they have every right to take offense at the way this king is nurturing a lion to bite that kingdom.

And why was the queen's husband killed, so that his young son inherited? Was the king trying to concentrate power in his hands? Perhaps more important, was he doing to allow himself to tyrannize the land? Or to take power from the capricious and arbitrary nobles? Or both? A simple power-fight does not lend drama to the situation, let alone add to the moral quandary, but then, it doesn't remove any, either.

And was the queen innocent in all this? Or perhaps was her capricious conduct the trigger of the revolt? Or was she accused of capricious conduct so they could capture the king, make him put his queen in a convent, and restore the old ways without blaming the king for his conduct?

And with that as backstory—

Do you tell the queen to take her children and be out of the kingdom within a week? Hand them over to the ambassador as captives? Relegate them to a convent as prisoners, and send the young king to a seminary to take him out of the line of succession?

Or perhaps the queen and children aren't there to dramatize it. Perhaps ambassadors from either side of civil war, or just domestic strife, are there to ask you intervene in their city. Is the resentment you will gain as a foreign power throwing its weight around greater or less than the resentment you will get for failing to support them in their hour of need? Can you choose the side that will win—whether because you support them or not?

And what is the right and wrong of their strife, anyway? Is the merchant arguing that the nobles are oppressing them motivated by spite, inspired by his arrogance? Is he right anyway?

Are the nobles forcing the guilds to certify journeymen as masters when they aren't competent enough, thus depressing the reputation of the guild? Or are the masters concentrating the power in their hands and holding out the promise of a mastership to the journeymen to induce them to work, while in reality reserving the promotion for those with connections? Or both?

And what do the common folk think of it? Is one side arguing for something that will actually benefit all the dock workers? Or do they just want the fighting to stop, because they are being injured and killed in it?

Likewise in character. It may be more dramatic for actors on stage to fully embody one side or the other and go after each other with anything from barbed words to atomic weaponry, but in a work of fiction, you can put the conflict in a character.

You do not make the character morally complex by reducing his motives to defend the princess to the desire to get paid. You make him morally complex by making him want to protect the princess in particular because she is an innocent pawn in all this, to show up the knights who acted scornfully toward him, to—well, to get paid.

Play it up enough, and it can be a real pang to him when he realizes that her safety would be best secured by escorting her to a nearby stronghold, which will have knights enough to secure her safety. It will protect her, but it will minimize the knights' realization that he did the work where they failed. Perhaps only the realization that it's the reliable path to get the pay will tip the balance, and perhaps that will make him morose with the thought that he was willing to endanger her for glory.

Complexity requires differences, arranged in a complex manner. Moral complexity requires moral differences, arranged in a complex manner.

Morality Meters And Good Deeds

Ethics meets epistemology

So you have a world where something evaluates the character's character. Perhaps it's a magical object, perhaps it's a game stat.

Perhaps it was created by a wizard who invested it with his own judgment of what is good and what is evil, perhaps it is, by fiat of the writer, actually evaluating good and evil—but since I already harped on that, I write on another angle of it.

Namely, how is the evaluation being performed?

Can the object actually read his heart and mind to judge (according to its lights) his motives, his judgments, and his sentiments?

Or just his deeds?

Or what it can infer from his deeds?

Or what it *does* infer from his deeds, wisely or unwisely, justly or unjustly, reasonably or unreasonably?

At one extreme, perhaps a holy sword only works for a paragon whose heart is free from anger or desire for revenge.

At the other, a character, with the enchanted sword in hand, can openly gloat that with one more ogre slain, the sword will unleash its greater powers for him, and he'll be the greatest hero of the land and wallow in luxury, because the sword does not care whether he is arrogant, greedy, and selfish, only for his tally of killing dangerous monsters.

At that, when does an object evaluate his conduct? The game stat would be constant, presumably, but perhaps a sword only cares that he is honorable and courageous while wielding it, or carrying it. If he hangs it up at home, the sword does not care.

Other swords might care. One dings him for separations on the presumption that he was up to no good in those times, if it can't evaluate him without being present. Another simply does not work if the character separates from it, or at least resets to the beginning. Still a third can and does evaluate him at a distance, perhaps giving him extra if he acts well in its absence.

One that judged him by his heart would care all the time, effectively, since the evil motivations would be clear even during the noble deeds.

Judging solely by the deeds would, of course, allow a hypocrite free range, but one that requires constant presence requires consistency. A swordsman who defends the innocent with the edge of his sword and then lays it aside while exploiting them shamelessly after is a different sort of hypocrite from the one who defends the innocent, takes a modest reward for his necessities, and internally gloats over what a wonderful hero he is, because he truly does not care about anything but his own fame.

Which would have some interesting philosophical implications.

A truly deep philosophical question would be whether a sword that requires purity of heart to be unleashed could ever be unleashed by someone who knows it. After all, if you desired the power, the purity of heart is not being sought with a pure intention.

At the other extreme, what would really be philosophically incoherent would be if the evaluation is inconsistent.

If the sword rejects a character for insufficiently pure heart when he harbors resentment after betrayal, the character can not win it back by racking up sufficient good deeds without regard to intention. He certainly can not win it back by *setting up* a situation where he could do something heroic.

Philosophically, that is. If the sword is presented as thinking that unclearly, that would make sense, but still would produce eye rolls about how silly the sword is by those who notice. Assuming, of course, it's not used thematically as an example of imprudence, necessary to rise above.

Though with the meter, it is necessary to consider whether anyone else could consult it, and with the objects, how difficult it is to make them. It's one thing if the sword is a unique holy relic. Another if one wizard can make one sword every several centuries. Still another if the ability is commonplace.

After all, if any old wizard could make an object telling whether someone was honest, or courageous, or any virtue you please, the courts would have their jobs greatly simplified, and that would have world-building implications.

Even if it did also raise in-world questions of how, exactly, it was determining whether the character had the virtue.

At least that might give the character some useful guidance in dealing with it.

Magic

The wondrous plot device, the major issue, and pitfall, in fantasy world-building.

Curses!

What are curses?

Their own category of spell? Or just a spell that people don't like?

Probably there are other categories of spells if there are curses, but curses are a special case because people regard them differently from other spells, even when they aren't really.

They can be. If witches or wizards are needed to work other kinds of magic, but anyone can lay a dying curse, or another curse in revenge, obviously curses differ from any other kind of magic.

Can you detect a curse, as opposed to other kinds of magic? So that you can tell whether a situation is a curse, or some other misfortune? Perhaps another spell having an unexpected side effect?

Can you remove a curse by means that would remove no other spell? Do you have to work about other spells about while removing it? Do you have to carefully research a spell to remove it, and curses are no different?

Or can you remove other spells by ways that do not even perturb a curse?

Do curses require loopholes in a way no other spell does? That you can be woken up if the bite of apple is dislodged from your throat? Where the blessing that turns your kingdom into a prosperous and happy land doesn't need such a loophole? (It can, of course, which may be a convenient plot point for your characters to act, but it doesn't have to even though curses do, if that's more convenient.)

If you turn your fairy goddaughter into a bear to let her run away from the marriage to her father, do you have to use a different spell than when you turn your stepson into a bear to curse him for not marrying your daughter?

What happens when you turn your stepdaughter into a deer to punish her, and she runs away so you can't catch her again, and uses the way she can live in the woods to stay away from people? If someone just undoes it as a curse, what happens to her?

Is it possible for a curse to have beneficent effects? Can that be done with intent? Cursing the princess to sleeping could let her escape a war. Does that work only when your intent is malicious, and she accidentally benefits and leaves you gnashing your teeth? Or can you do it willfully?

Can you even work out how to cast the curse if you aren't doing it in the heat of passion? A vengeful ogress can curse a princess to have to disenchant a sleeping prince to ever marry, and so require a quest, but if the princess's fairy godmother realizes that her mother and father are spoiling her rotten, and they keep her out so she can have no influence on the girl's character, and there is a grave danger she will be a wicked and miserable queen, being a blight on the land until her subjects rise up and drive her out, at which point she will be lucky to be eaten by wild animals—can the fairy godmother devise a spell that will remove her from their influence quickly enough? Which, since neither she nor they want it, is going to look enough like a curse that it's quibbling to question whether it is. Still, do her good intentions make it a different and probably more difficult spell?

Some forms of curses are more ambiguous. When the young prince laughs at an ogress, and the ogress curses the prince to be unable to marry anyone but Rose-Red-Lily-White, she's acting as a plot device. The same effect can be achieved by having him dream of the lovely lady. Or go into a room of stained glass windows to pick his bride, and to curiously pull aside the curtain of the one covered window.

What if she just aroused his curiosity so much that he can't stand the idea of marrying a bride less marvelous in nature?

What if his father descends on his fairy godmother in a rage demanding that she remove the curse? And she can't persuade him that it's not a curse?

What, after all, is a curse?

Remove Curse

Considerations on what it means

Consider the *remove curse* spell. Popular in RPGs, and works based on RPGs.

One notes that the logic is that there exists a definite set of enchantments, whether cast or on an object, that are categorized as curses, and this will break that entire set of enchantments, and no others.

All a wizard has to do to evade it is to devise a spell that causes harm but does not fall in the category. A spell that forces people to tell the truth, perhaps, cast on a silver-tongued charmer. A spell normally cast to draw rats out of a building that is, instead, cast to draw them to a person. A healing spell that repairs limbs but in this case causes cancer. A translation spell that prevents you from accidentally speaking in your native tongue, but for a language that no one who hears you can understand.

Transformation spells have long gone both ways. Greek myth had Io turned into a heifer either by Zeus (in an attempt to hide her from Hera) or by Hera, but regardless of the perpetrator, she was trapped. Corone, on the other hand, cried for help while fleeing Poseidon, and Athena turned her into the crow, whereupon Corone entered her service.

So what's a wizard to do? Devise new spells that remove them one by one? Devise still more new spells to discern what, exactly, is the spell that curses without being a curse? Devise ways to interpret the spell as a curse? A new category?

Can you discern malice in the spell-slinger that laid the curse? But then it would follow that when a herb witch who cursed a thief in her garden into the form of a wolf, the ability of your spell to remove the curse would turn entirely on whether the herb witch intended only revenge, or regarded this as a salutary lesson to the thief. Or even a warning to her fellow man about the thief's character.

Conversely, consider petrification. A curse surely? Unless you are ill, or have been poisoned, or face a famine, or otherwise could desperately use the stasis of being stone. A wizard could have a nice livelihood turning people to stone. Or consider the value of guards who can't be seen because they stand among the statues. (Though petrifying people until you need their labor may start to turn back into an actual curse.)

Perhaps what should be considered is the attitude of the person under the spell. A man tearfully exclaims on the horrible effect of werewolfry on him, and a wizard whacks him with a *remove curse* and declares, "Nah, he likes it."

Or a spy who gulps down the cursed potion that causes him to stammer and stutter uncontrollably, to the point where he's unintelligible. At least you can figure out that he's a spy because he wants to go on stammering and stuttering uncontrollably.

But what if it's just a *very powerful* curse? A curse that can be knocked down by any hedge wizard is unlikely to satiate anyone's thirst for revenge, though some petty souls will not look far enough into the future to see the inevitable removal. But can a wizard tell the difference between the curse is just too strong, and the person under the spell wants it, thus voiding its cursed nature?

Then, consider the ramifications of charming someone. Bewitching someone. Enchanting someone. Being enamored of a person who wants you to keep the curse is a good way to ensure that you want to keep the curse. Other emotions might include magically inculcated loyalty, and even fear—the cursed character wants to keep the curse because as long as it is on, the cursing character will seek no further retribution.

Perhaps what would be needed is a spell that targets all emotional control spells, regardless of what the enspelled character thinks.

But, of course, they need not all be curses. An emotional-control spell on a character who suffers insane bursts of rage could easily be a disaster to remove.

The elegant simplicity of curses vs. other spells has a lot going for it if you don't want to get into all these weeds, of course.

Removing The Problem

Curses and ghosts

How hard is it to remove a curse? Or, for that matter, to remove ghost haunting a castle?

This may be the root of your decision to make curses hard to break, and even hard to detect—or, of course vice versa.

It may even affect the metaphysics of the world, for the ghost. If the religion holds that the clergy, or the pious, can exorcise ghosts or demonic infestations, whether it's right may be a question, and the plot will dictate the very metaphysics of the setting.

On the other hand, of course, the characters may be casually secular, and so the question of metaphysics doesn't arise, or perhaps the religious friend can arrive as the cavalry to save the day.

Perhaps only a philosopher can exorcise a ghost, with his wisdom and his indifference to worldly things, or perhaps by being calm and measured, and so (at the time when less wise souls panic) observing the ghost and gleaning from the sight what binds the ghost to the place it haunts. (What is keeping it there is, of course, a metaphysical issue. If you must find the murdered body and bury it, that implies a great deal about funeral rites and their effect on the very soul.)

Or perhaps a ghost can be fought like any other creature.

But from your viewpoint—as long as you haven't painted yourself into a corner by earlier works in the series—the question is how long it needs to take in order to serve the story. Everything else turns on that.

If the curse or ghost was the bait to draw the character to where the villain wants him, a way for them to establish their good faith to the strangers, or just an introduction to the characters, to start them in action, it can and should be dealt with briefly to get on with the story, having established the characters and all the rest.

If the curse or ghost is the central problem and conflict of the story, it must be hard to deal with. How hard determines the length of the story; a novel needs more conflict, and more complex conflict, than a short story.

Whether the conflict is working out what to do, or actually doing it, is also a major factor.

I note it takes a deft hand to make discovering what to do difficult, and then actually doing it also difficult, since they are, in effect, two different conflicts. Though it does give your story a sharp swerve, which helps give it shape, you do have to have a story long enough to bear the weight.

A deft hand can also, sometimes, in a series, escape having painted itself into a corner. Discover the differences in nature in this story from the last one where something like this happened.

Perhaps the priest can easily dispel ghosts as such, but this ghost is a wizard, and what looks like ordinary haunting is in fact magical workings. These workings, not being directly powered by the ghost, are not so easy to dispel, and the ghost can not be easily reached through them.

Perhaps a magical object drives the curse, not just laid on the stones of the castle, and until you dig out the object and destroy it, the curse can not be laid. (And perhaps it was put under the cornerstone, so that removing it will destroy the castle. Some things come at a price.)

Or, if the ghost requires a funeral for its body to be laid, perhaps the body is harder to retrieve. Or else there are specific requirements for the funeral that will require deciphering the objects found with the bones so that you know who to call upon.

The great trick is avoiding making the precise level of difficulty look like a plot device. Especially because it is one.

Foreshadow with care. If it's in a series, remember that while earlier installments may paint you into a corner, they make bad foreshadowing because you do not know whether the readers have read them.

Character reactions are also important. Grumbles about how the better they get, the harder the cases that are assigned to them. Raucous betting pools about what the problem will be this time. Arguments about whether applying the basic removal is the best way to test whether this is a simple case.

Then, since the question is central, just about every element of the story can be artfully aimed to support the matter, which helps. Even the elements that are used to conceal the matter are part of supporting it.

Which is just the gentle art of writing, in one form it takes.

Calibrating Magic, Briefly

How do they know?

Here's a magical object right out of chivalric romance. Two gates, one for knights, and the other for their ladies. How closely you can approach shows what a true lover you are. When the hero arrives, he not only reaches the gate, but flowers fall on his head, and the little statue of a child trumpeter blows a fanfare announcing him.

My character stands there and thinks, "How did they calibrate that?"

A pearl that turns white in the presence of truth, and black in the presence of lies, is simple enough. You'd probably want to test it with someone known to be delusional to test whether it judges subjective or objective truth, but it's reasonably easy to establish.

Other evaluations of character are more—iffy.

Or, of course, you can just decree that the spells work and there's no need to calibrate. You don't draw attention to the question, and it's unlikely the reader will think of it, even after the work.

Especially given its wonderful plot device purposes. It will validate who is good and who is bad. Let the hero draw the sword that decrees it can be only drawn by those of noble worth, and he has proven how he has grown since his days as a callow boy who tried it and suffered for his presumption.

On the other hand, if you want to give your hero from another world, or risen from the commoners, a trick to make him stand out, questioning calibration may be it. Especially if he embarrasses someone by proving that a spell doesn't work, or doesn't always work, and thus sets off the story.

Fantasy Diagnostics, Or Not

What has he got?

Fantasy healing magic tends to be blandly generic, as befits a plot device that remains in the background, keeping the world from being too unpleasantly historically accurate.

Dungeons & Dragons was both an example and an influence toward this. (An additional influence, the tendency did predate them. Aragorn diagnosed in the Houses of Healing, but the herb treated all the cases.)

Consider the limited problems you can have in D&D, depending on edition: wounds, blindness, deafness, paralysis, poisoned (now that poison isn't instant kill), and disease.

Occasionally, there would be various kinds of disease, but given that except in rare cases, you slapped a *cure disease* on it and were done, it wasn't made much of.

The described ones were generally infectious diseases, too, and that's another thing where fantasy novels follow the same tendency.

Did people suffer from nutritional deficiency? Would *cure disease* fix scurvy, beriberi, pellagra, or anemia? And how long would it last? Would the disease immediately reoccur, albeit with the usual slowness in development, as the diet remains deficient?

What about birth defects? There are *restoration* spells, but if you are born with a club foot, or spina bifida, or congenital blindness, can the spell *restore* what you did not originally have?

How about genetic disease? Would a single spell, curing all infectious diseases, also cure sickle cell anemia, cystic fibrosis, or hemophilia? If so, do you remain a carrier, and all your children carriers? Or does it cure down to the gene?

All of which may seem knowledge usefully hazed over because of its immense tedium, and probable irrelevance to the plot. Even a quest to find a cure need only give a reason why a particular disease is unusually hard to cure.

On the other hand, an ounce of protection is worth a pound of cure.

Even if they misattribute the problem to the bad air (*mal-airia*), and wrongly reason that the incense wards off the air rather than frightening off the mosquitoes (because it smells funny), they will cut down on the amount of magic they have to spend on curing disease.

The other side of this is that diagnosis is hard. Even nowadays, diagnoses may be made after saying, it's *this*—no, the treatment for *this* isn't working—it's *that*—no, the treatment for *that* isn't working—it's *the other thing*—yippee, the treatment's working. Maybe.

Even when we get a clear, concise account of symptoms from yesteryear, it's generally enough to rule out some diseases and not others. There are, for instance, great debates about the plagues of Galen and Cyprian—whether they were the first outbreaks of smallpox and measles, and if so, which one was which—even though Galen and Cyprian described the symptoms.

On the other hand, perhaps there are magical protections that are as broad as the cure spells. Perhaps every wedding has a blessing on the couple to heal them of any genetic incompatibility. Perhaps the grace on meals has a charm to fortify the food. Perhaps houses are built with charms in the rafters.

Or perhaps the spellcraft does not work as it does in many a fantasy novel. Healers might have to diagnose with all the same wearisome labor as modern day doctors and then apply the right herb or jewel with the correct incantation.

Then, of course, you could have two schools of magic. One just blasts with healing; one diagnoses and treats specifically. The first one is wasteful; the second one leaves people suffering for too long. Etc. There's lots of room for two schools of magical medicine.

And if those schools overflow into other aspects of magical practice, it can have some interesting effects, if that's what's desired.

If what's really desired is to shove it all off-stage, there can be a kingdom-wide spell to bestow health generally. Or just a lot of happenstance such that that's not an issue on stage.

How Do The Wizards Know That?

Magic and knowledge

Calibration is only one problem with knowledge, and diagnostics is only one of the others. Especially magical knowledge.

The ancient tomes inscribed with hidden lore—where did they learn that? How was it known? How were new spells devised? Were they ever devised? How were they tested? How can wizards trust the wizards who went before? They are justly notorious for writing their magical knowledge in codes, after all.

And even if the spells are not hidden, but as open as engineering—how do they find out things? How does a mending spell know what is the tear, and what is supposed to open? How does the truth spell discern the truth? If it detects manipulation, can it tell the difference between deception by false suggestion and deliberately selecting only the relevant portions because the irrelevant ones should be suppressed lest they do injury to the innocent? How does the sword that demands that it slay a man before it is sheathed again determine that what it struck was a man, and that he died?

There is a reason why epistemology is an entire branch of philosophy. Not all of which apply to magic, but a good number do.

When the sorcerer of Sword & Sorcery was evil, he was naturally seldom the viewpoint character. Still enough the stories were clear that he would search for spells, not devise them.

It was enough to raise the real-life questions about *magia*. True, it was not *goetia*, it did not traffic with evil spirits, but those hidden if natural attributes? How did you learn about them, and how they worked, and how to apply them? Perhaps the original person to learn them was a sorcerer given them by a devil. And you could be quite certain that the devil meant no good by them.

At that, given that the attributes are, indeed, hidden, how could you *know* that it's not a signal to a devil? St. Augustine wrote that if you didn't know how a thing worked, the prudent thing to do would be to use it only when you were very certain of your good intentions.

In fantasy, however, all sorts of plot devices and magic are a means to bypass epistemological issues. You don't want to deal with coinage issues? Force the money to be full value. You want your courts to move briskly? Use spells to discern the truth. Your sword will work only for a noble paladin? It can just tell what sort of man holds it. Court must rule justly? There's a truth spell on the courtroom, and even the judge must truthfully tell what he judged.

The spells have it even more. If you cast a spell on a man to treat his gunpowder wound, you do not aggravate it.

In reality, one reason a good many historical magical treatments "worked" was that they kept people too busy running around doing the thing to go poking at the wound or the sick person, thus giving nature a reasonable chance to heal the injury or illness.

Also in reality, the first attempts to treat gunpowder wound regarded the contaminated flesh as dangerous. The aggressive treatment killed many of the wounded. When one doctor could not do the aggressive treatment for lack of resources, and found the patients were more likely to recover, the other doctors—did not receive the news well.

Can a healing spell restore health even if you have no idea what is wrong? Scurvy, tuberculosis, cancer—very different diseases. If your spell-slinger just knows they are ill, does the spell do all the work of figuring what the illness is, and how to cure it?

How do we know this quest will find the way to purify the Holy Spring?

How do we know the loophole in the Evil Overlord's magical protection?

Ah, the wonders of fantasy in clearing up the questions of epistemology and knowledge, so we can get on with the quest!

Two Kinds of Magic

A different slice

A common trope in fantasy is the two types of spell-slinger. Not based on what model they use, but on whether they use models at all.

These are the learned scholar types, with towers and universities, and the village herb witch or hedge wizard types, with cottages and cottage gardens (and presumably an apprenticeship, possibly self-taught).

This is often treated as a matter of tone, with hedge wizard simply being an inferior sort of wizard. In spite of the obvious effects that the differences in education would bring.

Not always. Herb witches, in particular, tend to be associated with not only using herbs in their magic but with the sorts of curative spells that nearby peasants might want. (Not so much others. Locating objects was another big business for cunning women—and men—historically.)

Oddly enough, despite their lack of instruction, the hedge wizards tend to be perfectly sound with such spells as they have. It's not unknown for a hedge wizard to be running a con, but it's not common. At an extreme, you have things like Master Sean in the *Lord Darcy* story lamenting the people would rather go to unlicensed wizard who will go and treat heart disease with foxglove of all things.

In reality, treatments for diseases have been found unreliable, or even detrimental, even when tested by science and used for decades.

Folk remedies are still worse. Such remedies can have an actual pharmaceutical basis. They are much more likely to cure through placebo effect, through reversion to mean (because most diseases will end in time), and through distracting people from doing more harm. (An atheist doctor recounted the most successful medieval treatment for a wound: get the weapon that inflicted it, pray over it, and destroy it. He had no doubt that it worked because doing all that kept the people too busy to keep poking at the wound, thus giving it a chance to heal.)

Reality, of course, has the disadvantage of being undramatic. Most magic is effective in fantasy because having it be non-functional does not move the story forward.

One work where a good distinction is drawn is in *Frieren,* where Frieren is searching for all the odd-ball folk magic. If you want her to do something, you must pay, but you can secure her help with a grimoire for a trivial spell, to flip pancakes, to avoid getting egg shells in cracked eggs, and the like.

One wonders why folk magic turns up such spells. Perhaps it pursued the interests of the hedge wizards rather than the purposes of those in power.

I drew another distinction in my own *Spells in Secret*. What were called spells (without modifier)—at least from the viewpoint of the student wizards—were mastered in your field of study. You learned the principles, produced the spells, and could even work out how to generate new spells.

They also mastered rote spells. Everyone, even master wizards, did some of the time. You got a spell that you wanted to cast (if you could), you memorized the incantation, you mastered the wand motions, and you cast the spell. If it was an advanced spell in your own field, perhaps one day you would realize how it fit in.

That is, for the wizards.

There were other spell-slingers. Indeed, there were those who took on jobs of casting spells that they learned by rote. They might spend all day casting spells without having learned a thing of the theory.

As a consequence, they had a large number of spells that could be brought to bear on different problems that they faced. There were entire groups of spells that had no common root but were regarded as a common field, because people would learn them all by rote to deal with the problems of a situation.

This is why even master wizards learned spells by rote. This is why virtually everyone learned them. They were useful, and you could not hope to master theory in every field. And some people were effectively hedge wizards—I did not use the term—because they concentrated their magic on selecting for practical use, not for theoretical knowledge.

The reason why master wizards, and those aspiring to be master wizards, learned anything else included that only with the theory behind you could you hope to devise a new spell.

Thus the distinction survived.

Sorcerer's Specialties

Wizards' ways

In many a work of fantasy, you have the herb witch in her hut with her potions, and the wizard on the battlefield throwing fireballs.

If they have innate gifts to work magic, and furthermore those gifts are more specific than "magic," obviously it can required to work that way. But in a world where anyone can learn wizardry by study, or in which you require a gift, but it's a simple, binary "can work magic" gift, specialization is more in the air.

At one extreme, there's the utility wizard, who can blast fire bolts, cure wounds, locate the enemy, and many other useful things.

At the other extreme, one could make it as specialized as modern life, where the technicians who run the X-ray machine can't repair it, and the pulmonary doctors who look at it want to send the image to the doctor who's specialized in tuberculosis because they aren't certain.

Could, but don't. There is a certain comedy in arriving at the wizards' university and tracking down the specialist in Uttian curses only to be told that he can only do so much because he specialized in the delta curses, mostly, where the cities were, and obviously this man was subjected to a curse from the hill-folk, where they were less regular. It's probably weaker, he can grant you that, because the hill-folk were less learned, but it's generally different enough that they are harder to remove, especially since the hill folk were known to put surprises in—

But a work composed of such running around to find the exact expert needed—would have to turn on that joke, because there's no time for anything else.

It could be pushed to the backdrop, a magical technology, but that merely makes it a convincing technology, and limits both its usefulness as a plot device and its differences from technology.

And really, if it's too much like technology, what's the point? Where's the fun?

There is, however, a whole range of possibilities. At one extreme, the wizard can simply teach the witch a fireball spell the night before the battle. Even if it is by rote.

Then there's the possibility of study of the subject matter.

One notes that the accumulation of knowledge has forced specialization. In the Renaissance, or earlier, or for some time later, a man could learn everything there was to be known about many fields. That was because there was little to be known. Nowadays, the very accumulation of knowledge that allows all the technical wonders and marvels causes there to be technicians who can repair the X-ray machine, and those who can read its images, and overlap is little.

If you want your wizards to be able to do a wider variety of things while still being able to do as much, magic needs to be more unified than technology for that to work in a fantasy tale.

Perhaps the technique is more important than the object. An enchanter must chant the spell. A herb witch must use the right herbs and make a potion or possibly a posset. A wizard must draw the right sigils. (Perhaps tying into models.)

At an extreme, there is the exclusion possibility in a way that is not really possible with technology. Someone who studied astrophysics to the point of doctoral degrees can throw it all away and study axolotls instead with no constraints except the shortness of life.

You don't have to allow that in fantasy.

Perhaps the principles can be a few simple rules, such as those who have slain rational beings can not cast healing spells, and perhaps food spells as well.

Perhaps the effects can be a backwash from the magic. The more fire spells you use, the more fiery you grow, and so the less watery you are, and the fewer the water spells you can cast. Likewise with water spells repelling fire.

Perhaps elementalists who carefully balance earth, air, fire, and water spells to leave themselves human are less powerful but less warped than those who throw themselves into the working of one element. Letting you make your heroes less powerful than the villains in a way that they can't fix with a tweak. (Even a magical object concentrating on the element could be dangerous.)

There are a lot of possibilities out there, and it's one way to differentiate your magic from technology.

What Shall We Call The Wizard?

Inventing some terms

Have you ever heard of the Far-Eastern movie with a necromancer? I know nothing of it but what I learned from a meme: the translator didn't know the term, so the subtitles talked about the "zombie wrangler."

How wonderful!

I did something like this in *Spells In Secret* where Kenneth and the other pupils are in the tower for stonework, though they are not called stone-workers.

If the magic the wizard uses has a settled core, one can call the spell-slinger after it. Fire, stars, wind, healing—and then one can run amok on the verbs. Fire-flinger, star-dreamer, wind-dancer, heal-hand.

Logically, of course, presuming that magic is a technology that evolves like any other form of technology, some will grow to be inaccurate. Originally, the chief job of a fire-flinger was to throw fireballs in battle. Nowadays, with all the steampunk technology, it is to monitor and control the boilers. A fire-flinger spends more time keeping fire from flinging itself far than he does flinging it.

Or perhaps he spends less time with fire than you might think. After all, it could evolve into a whole system of magic from the roots of flinging fire.

The problem is, of course, that such vivid terms wear their origins on the sleeve in a way the standard terms don't. How many people will complain that a sorcerer never casts lots? Or even fastidiously avoids games of chance despite the very meaning of his job is *sortarius*, one who tells fortunes by lot?

Necromancer is still close enough that people will sometimes complain that "-mancy" means *divination*, and a necromancer should be someone who talks to the dead to divine things.

Perhaps the wisest route would be to let the term mutate once the origin was lost, but then—what is the point? A vivid and unique term is merely a piece of verbiage that the reader has to memorize once it means nothing owing to semantic drift. Unless the terms are very few, and their origin actually comes up, and probably becomes relevant, it's probably just strangeness for its own sake. Better to use the classic terms to sort them out.

On the other hand, as long as the term is still reliable, there's no reason not to use them. It does indicate what sort of magic the world has, but that can be useful as well as limiting.

There are various ways a writer could handle the verb. Perhaps there are all sorts of verbs, and really, only the noun clues you into significant knowledge. A wind-weaver does not need a loom; a heal-singer may hum, but may not; a water-breaker may not even divide water up.

Perhaps the verb is deeply significant. Those who are "singers" do in fact chant their spells, and those who are "dancers" do in fact enspell things by their rhythmic motions. (Hmm—to music? If you have fire-singers, fire-drummers, and fire-dancers, you could get up a quite complex set-up. Possibly with a circle-scriber to lay out the dance floor beforehand.)

This creates a certain degree of specialization. The noun, of course, dictates what your spell-slinger slings in the way of spells. You need a fire-flinger to deal with your child's fever. You need a water-weaver to counteract the dehydration. Etc. As these examples show, the noun can be treated as narrower or broader, but if it does not define, there's no point in not just calling them a wizard unless you go digging very deep.

If you use the verb as technique, not result, you may get no more narrowing from that. But depending on how you work it, you may need either a fire-singer or a fire-dancer for some things.

This sort of specialization has its costs, of course. Are there any hedge wizards and herb witches who pick and choose spells from many schools? Getting scorned by the purists who can only support themselves in large cities because of the narrowness of their specialties? Do people pick up spells here and there, just because the powerful wizards are hard to get to, at least the ones you need?

Everything has its world-building price. Even amusing yourself with the names you bestow on wizards.

Sorcery and Subtlety

A range of spells

A beautiful young woman is sent to a distant castle in the countryside. She hears tales about a curse laid on it, and watches the members of the family succumb to mysterious accidents, and survives only because her beloved arrives and carries her off.

Ah, a Gothic novel, the reader knows at once. A fantasy? Much harder to tell. While any fantastical element not justified by appeal to the authority of science makes the work fantasy, there is a borderline of things where the magic is hinted at, but possibly not present. (Some ill-conditioned souls interpret fantastical elements as symbols or signs of insanity at the drop of a hat, but there really are works in which they are intentionally ambiguous.)

Or, perhaps, a band of intrepid adventurers arrive at the distant castle, jeer at the story that a kidnapped damsel cursed the castle before her death because she didn't have a character class let alone a spell-slinging one, detect magic on the castle, and cast a remove curse, clearing up that little problem.

Ah, a Gamelit novel. Obviously fantasy, obviously run by RPG rules, possibly including characters brought into the world from another, with clear magic, down to the very clear rules by which it runs.

Which encompasses a great range that fantasy can fall between. All the more in that you don't actually have to pick one. A fantasy work can have a utility wizard who can find wedding rings and purify wells while the castle looming over all is a desolate ruin because it was cursed.

Perhaps the wizard can even explain that such subtle spells take a long time to unravel, and the breaking fits the curse like a key to a lock, so it's of little use once you have it—and it can take a year and a day, seven years, or even a lifetime to work out the spell that will break it.

Hence, breaking it tend to fall into the laps of those who are not wizards. The ones who do all the tedious work of investigating what went wrong, and how to set it right.

Like casting it. Perhaps the gift of wizardry only means that you can use simpler and more economical means than the age-old art of subtle magic. Which can, indeed, be cast in short times, but only by those deeply passionate about a matter. So that when the lord abducted a village maiden, and her beloved rescued her only for the lord to have her shot with arrows as they fled, his curse could fall on the castle though he was no wizard.

It doesn't have to be curses. Wizards may mutter how about the hedge wizards shouldn't be able to increase crops without leaving visible magical traces, but they can't deny that they do.

A wise-guy writer can have one fulminate that the hedge wizard advises planting a field in clover and using it as pasture for a year. Or if you have a field with yellow-flowered weeds that aren't that yellow, and other plants are putting forth new leaves that are yellowish, the hedge wizard tells you to treat it with a mixture he gives—a mixture containing *brimstone* no less! (Yellow wildflowers grow less yellow, and new leaves yellow, when the soil is sulfur deficient.)

If, however, you want the hedge wizard to be actual magic rather than secret science, you can have him offer charmed metal plates to be buried in the field, or beads like blue eyes, and the wizards have to concede that while neither show any sign of magic, the crops grow better with the plates, and misfortunes said to be caused by the Evil Eye are less common when people wear those beads.

It is wise to note that subtle magic is either a background element or the main matter of a plot—or at least a subplot. If a hedge wizard is handing out the plates in the spring, this can be background color. But if a mysterious man shows up and offers charms to farmers, and the king sends our heroes off to investigate whether he is a fraud, or possibly causing the ills he purports to alleviate, the nature of this man and his charms are front and center, and until you get to the bottom of it, the story is not over, and it's hard to distract from.

Such is the nature of mysteries, involving magic or not. If you want to use magic as a plot device, make it as subtle as a sledgehammer.

The Quack Conjurer

Fantasy fakes

At the fair, between the dancing bear and the tent offering a glimpse of the unicorn, a wagon displays glass bottles gleaming like jewels, and a man stands before it boasting of the finest healing potions known to man.

The adventurers limp into town, and the inn-keeper immediately points them to the hut at the edge of it, surrounded by a vast, enchanted garden. The herb wife there can patch them right up. Except that only the size of the garden gives away which cottage is meant. The wizard sees at a glance that the garden bears no enchantment, and none of the plants are suitable anyway.

The traveling show trundles into town, and the young man goes forth with his mandolin to sing of their wonders and pull fresh flowers out of the oddest places. The show's wizards, no matter how closely they watch, can't see the legerdemain that he has openly told them that he is practicing, but it saves their spells and advertises the show.

Over a range of farmland, mysterious clay objects appear by farmhouses. Everyone knows to send for the cunning woman, to come and remove the curse. Everyone knows how she moved to the region shortly after the clay objects started to appear, and how those who plant them use invisibility to hide. Which is only too true, as the royal wizard blasts invisibility and reveals the cunning woman did have an invisibility cloak, though no other magic, and planted the objects.

A master of pest control promises to keep mice and rats from your pantry. He does not stint to cheat you. He wears red while casting the spell (which has no effect), insists on casting the full seven circles instead of cheating you with three (which is overkill and wasteful), and using the best cheese (which is counterproductive because the hard cheese he uses isn't very attractive to mice)—but whenever you cast a truth spell on him, he passes with his complete sincerity, because he believes his own superstitions.

In a fantasy world, it's improbable that no quack wizards will prey on the gullible—or be the gullible, since many quacks have sincerely believed in their nostrums. In a world where hedge witches learn their spells by rote, superfluous steps may be passed down. Or even rank superstition, working (if at all) by distracting anyone from doing anything harmful and letting things revert to mean.

The degree of subtlety in a fantasy world has a great deal of effect. When everyone knows that spells produce auras of colorful light, a quack is helpless unless he masters a light spell—or convinces people that this is a true innovation, the light was a *waste*, all *his* power goes into the workings of the spell. But if spellcraft is subtle, the quack can take the money, warn that the spell takes time to work, and wait for reversion to mean. As the patient slowly recovers, he takes credit for the cure; as the victim suffers random misfortune, he assures the person who bought the curse that this is the curse coming to fruition.

In a full-blown magic-as-technology, his options are more limited, but (looks about at modern quackery) far from non-existent.

One can count on many quacks using the jargon of high wizardry, or even pieces of high wizardry, in their claims or in their works. *Agatha Heterodyne, Girl Genius*, taking place in a universe of *Mad Science!*, had Mistress Olga in the traveling Heterodyne show, the Mistress of the Science of Telluricomnivisualization, instead of claiming to peer into a crystal ball.

Others may decry high wizardry as soulless, dry, or what-have-you, and conspicuously invoke counter-claims. Since they are quacks, they have the advantage that what is dramatic, colorful, and artistic is never hindered by whether it works. The quack seller of potions may loudly praise the clarity of his potions where the genuine compounder of potions knows that the elements must be so mixed that the result is neither clear, nor colorful, nor tasty.

One can, of course, simply use real science. The old hedge wizard treats minor scraps with honey, and the wizard rolls her eyes about the inapplicability of it. In reality, honey can keep injuries from infection, just as making jam of fruit helps preserve it. The downsides of this technique remain: it relies on the reader's knowledge because the characters don't know, it's rather limited, and it carries a whiff of the comic about it.

Whether quacks should appear in a tale is, of course, a grave question.

It's possible to use them just as background color: the young man in the group uses legerdemain to pick pockets and steal documents in pursuit of their aims, and to conjure flowers as a hobby, or someone points out Madame Rosalba's Enchanting Perfumery only to be told that it's a fraud, and they let it stand because it attracts frivolous, empty-headed girls and keeps from them from seeking out worse things.

Other than that, most quacks dominate the story they appear in. It's harder than you think to debunk one, but fictitiously, most use hidden means that could be revealed. Serious quacks, who laugh off the objection that no magic can be detected with the counterpoint that they *said* it was a different kind, and who would have reversion to mean if nothing else to help them, would be hard to debunk. This rain-making wizard took four tries to bring rain? Well, he said it looked like a hard case, and no one is thinking that it would have rained sooner or later.

Indeed, one who claimed that the wizards treat the world as soulless and is revealed in the end to be ignorantly trafficking with demons, or one whose potions turn out to prevent scurvy because of the lemon juice, are easier to work with in fiction because they have a definite core that could be reached. Most quackery is too thin to be grasped that definitively.

It's probable that they exist. But consider them well before you deploy one.

The Guild Of Wizards

Does this trope work?

Once I read an article about a role-playing game where the writer proposed that the wizards' guild would work like a Renaissance guild, the great mass of wizards being relentlessly exploited by the master wizards, who hold out the bait of a mastership when one opens up, and who then ensure that any open mastership actually went to one of their own relatives, or at least someone with connections.

Wizards without such connections grind their lives away working minor spells, all they are allowed, until they die of old age, still journeymen. The masters enjoy all the power and perks and their role in the government of the city.

This was proposed in spite of the way to grow in power in a RPG being to go adventuring, slaying dragons and goblins and all between, taking their gold and their magical objects, in places far from the city and the guild.

(Does *that* trope work? To adventure and grow powerful? It's possible to contrive an explanation that would fit a world—fighting magical beings frees up their "mana" so you absorb it instead and grow more powerful, the god of magic gave magic to fight monsters and rewards those who fight them, the dungeons are actually otherworldly Underworlds where nothing necessarily works as it does in mundane circumstances, and the gain in magical power is part and parcel—but it's impossible to contrive one that doesn't shout to someone familiar with the gaming trope that this is a way to put the trope into the story. Moot point. Where it's used, it's incompatible with historical guilds.)

At that, game spells are overwhelmingly useful in an adventuring context, and not for other purposes. Not so much as the adventurers finding, as part of their loot, a grimoire filled with agricultural magic. This gives wizards' guild even less clout.

What if it were a more sane world? Where not everything is set up to enable RPGs?

Assuming, of course, a world where wizards are wizards, and other people aren't. If just about anyone picks up some useful spells, wizards are more likely to be in guilds by how they apply their magic, and the spells serve as trade secrets.

But in a world where wizards are wizards, and other people aren't, if they live in a world with a wizards' guild, and where a wizard who studies in his tower and practices in an abandoned quarry grew in knowledge and power, perhaps more than the wizard who fought relentlessly in the king's army—what then?

The problem there lies in the work they do. A wizard useful in the king's army means that the guild is a direct threat to his kingdom if they throttle the magic like that. Kings granted charters to cities, allowing them liberties, and in particular for their guilds, because that would encourage their trade, but never for something this crucial to his kingdom.

The guild would have to train wizards to fight, at least, or face his wrath—or being conquered by another kingdom where the wizards were more cooperative, for whatever reason.

If they did decide to face his wrath, why, they might conquer the kingdom. Then, even before you factor in the other problems of governance, the wizards face the little problem of keeping themselves in power.

They would have to train wizards to fight in their own armies.

Furthermore, they have spells that are useful for spies and scouts, if they have typical RPG spells. They would have to train wizards who could use this magic to steal grimoires from them. Or sneak in on secret training sessions for those with connections.

Or they would be conquered by those about them who were less chary in training wizards.

Mind you, they do have a point if they are less than willing to train other wizards, even without the danger of spies. Their power rests on their magic. The more they train, the more rivals they have within their country. Hence their lives would be a balancing act between keeping their country strong enough to hold off all comers, against keeping themselves safe against their own countrymen.

In fine, they would be, quite possibly, worse off in keeping their magic limited than if they had trained wizards for the king.

All in all, a simple transference of a guild system to wizards does not work. A lot of development needs to go into it.

Wizardry For The Compleat Idiot

How smart does a wizard have to be?

All those books, all that study—how smart does someone have to be to master magic?

Well, we do have the Danish fairy tale *Master And Pupil* where the answer is "smart enough to lie about being able to read after having been rejected once."

On the other hand, learning to read was not that common a skill once upon a time. And the widespread tale of the sorcerer's apprentice shows the difference between a smattering and full knowledge. Or possibly learning and wisdom. Though he still had to be able to read.

Even the sort of witch who lived in a cottage in the village, or near it, required wits.

Where magic really can unfurl its abilities is in objects that can be used by anyone. Even if the wizard can set them to be used by only people of a certain character and can even determine their character, what about their wits, and their knowledge?

This is not quite so important as how easy it is to make them, provided that the ability to use them is somewhat common.

Old-school sword and sorcery, to be sure, often filled the sorcerer's tower with crystal balls and magical wands that only the sorcerer himself could use. Or, at least, that only the sorcerer *did* use.

Still, it had magical things like boots and cloaks and ropes useful to the thief. And if their means of manufacture was such that only a knave would use them, the heroes of sword and sorcery were notoriously less than heroic.

But if the mighty sorceress creates a wand that any old hedge witch can use to lob fireballs at the enemy, all the king needs to do is recruit hedge witches, and his only problem is that since he's giving her the ability to lob fireballs, he has to keep her happy.

He might, as a consequence, prefer that it require more study. Perhaps enough so that the aspiring wand-wielder would have to spend several years in dedicated study. That would give the student a stake already in society, without the king's having to give him anything. Probably more would be wise, there's only so much that you can demand from duty, and besides, rewards encourage others to do the same. But it would be less costly.

Or maybe it can't be curbed like that. Maybe you need locks and bolts and thick doors and heavy chests, and spells that scream whenever someone unauthorized tries to get at the object. Stone dogs—or lions—that come to life and savage the intruder. Spells that paralyze, or petrify, or trap in spider webs of astounding strength.

And, of course, ways to identify yourself, by password or by appearance, because otherwise, there's no point to creating the object in the first place. (Barring accidents while creating. Given that the number of badly made magical objects in fantasy is quite small—and it's a trope unknown in the source material—that would take some work on its own.)

Maybe you need a powerful spell to dissolve magic all about your tower, because with all the problems it brings, it's the only way to keep some utter idiot from getting in and asking stupid questions of the enchanted brass head that answers questions—and worse, listening stupidly to them, because it does tend to talk in a subtle, abstruse manner, full of many fine distinctions.

The great nightmare, of course, is for a fool to inherit such objects. Whether lacking in intelligence or not. What is required is sufficient judgment to tell whether you can use the object wisely.

The dread of a wizard may be the royal order to make something for the fool of a crown prince. The brass head may speak in a subtle, abstruse manner, full of many fine distinctions, in hopes that it will not enable the prince's notable follies, because, as Machiavelli so sagely observed, a prince who is not himself wise can not be wisely counseled.

The order for a fireball wand, on the other hand, may require evasion. Or simply running away. After all, if the kingdom burns up in fireballs, the wizard would have to leave anyway.

Such are the problems with magical objects.

Magic And Marvels And Monsters, O My!

What's a monster to the world?

Rational beings aside—an intelligent dragon would inspire some thoughts in mankind, but an unthinking wyrm would inspire different thoughts.

And consider the many marvels that could be wandering the mountains and hills, the plains and the forest, swimming in the sea depths, or flying among the clouds.

Gryphons. Unicorns. Wolpertigers. Sea horses. Basilisks. Nuckelavees. Manticores. Winged horses. Firebirds. Kraken.

There's always the possibility of just making them beasts and birds and fish. What the reader thinks of them is of no import to the world-building. Perhaps they are as anomalous as the duck-billed platypus, but no more—and possibly somewhat less.

When they are, or some of them are, magical, this would make no real difference because many real animals are apt to be magical in fantasy worlds. White or golden deer that can lead the hunter astray in the forest, perhaps. Kingfishers that build their nests on the sea during the halcyon days. Scrawny little colts that can outrace all the fine stallions in the witch's stable, which is why it is wise for the prince to ask for it in return for his labors.

Especially since the characters are apt to divide them up more by their traits than the magic of them. A basilisk lives in a desert because wherever it goes, it poisons the ground and air. This is not fundamentally different from a venomous snake making a place dangerous. (And various fantasy creatures can bridge the gap. Snakes that poison at a touch, perhaps.)

If a gryphon and a dragon, after the lore, hoard gold, that does not fundamentally make them different from a magpie or a packrat.

On the other hand, they could be the original monsters: portents. When a white stag, or a manticore, roams the forest, everyone knows that trouble is coming.

A monster could be a portent in a much more particular manner. More magical beasts could indicate a more magical region. When a prince rides in the forest and sees a firebird, he realizes that he has reached the lands where ogres and witches may be.

At that, the apparition could combine those two: the gryphon or the unicorn or even the golden stag appearing in the forest shows that an eruption of magic is about to happen in that forest.

Much depends on the nature of magical eruptions in the world.

Perhaps they are horrible incursions of death, destruction, and famine.

Perhaps they are difficult to navigate but still marvels and wonders, which you want to harvest for the future.

Perhaps the monster really is a portent, such that a manticore has you sending your fastest messenger to the king's court for his knights, and you yourself packing what you can to flee, and a unicorn has you sending word to all the wizardly universities and making preparations to give shelter to all the wizards (and fleece them for every coin you can).

Or perhaps the monsters are made. Perhaps wizards cross-breed animals to produce the gryphon and the winged horse and the hippogriff. It is, after all, said in the folklore that the wolpertiger has no one shape, because it springs from the cross-breeding of animals and takes after its parents—whatever they are.

The monsters might be conjured, at that. A wizard who can pull a rabbit out of a hat might pull a jackalope instead. If he thinks of it merely as a creature of a far-off nation, he may not even realize that he made a new species as well as a new creature.

It would take a good number of creatures, by either method, to make a stable breeding population. Perhaps that explains why they are so rare and fugitive. They never really exist except in the immediate vicinity of a wizard, and die out because they do not have a sustainable number.

Which would not preclude their living quite long lives, at that, and thus lingering and filling the place with wonder for a long time. Giving the characters all sorts of thoughts.

The Sorcerer's Superstitions

World-building fantasy superstitions

What are the superstitions in your high fantasy world, where magic is real, and runs—well, not so much wild as rampant?

If it runs wild, there will still be superstitions, but they will be hard to unravel from the background of lore. Just as it's hard to sort out the willow-bark from the headache treatment, and the caffeine as well, it can be hard to sort out what really works in the magic.

It frequently takes full-blown experiments to nail down what works, and what really doesn't. If all else fails, reversion to mean happens. If you perform enough rain-making spells, it will rain, because the weather patterns changed.

Experiments are not always required. Around the end of the nineteenth century, a meteorologist studied weather proverbs and concluded that all proverbs that name a specific day as having unusual significance were unreliable—the first twelve days of the year did not predict the weather for the twelve months—but the other ones were as reliable as the best meteorological forecasts of the day.

This points to a major factor in determining your fantasy superstitions: you need to determine what does and does not work in your system. *Are* days and times of particular significance in your magic system? Or systems? Do the fire wizards ape the enchanters in using liminal times, even though they aren't actually significant to the fire wizardry, only enchantment?

That's the sort of thing that requires experiment to establish. And, of course, no one is going to risk it. If you are desperate to counter the enchanted singing of the witchbird, which lures children into the forest, and the enchanter's enchantment cast at dawn worked the best, everyone will cast it at dawn because the children are in danger.

It would take a prosperous and secure enchanter, cold-blooded to the point of evil or highly confident in other means of restraining the children, to experiment and establish that time of day made no difference; that actually, noon worked better than dawn, though the chief element was the details of the enchantment; or that all that mattered was sunlight, preferably direct, and so morning mists meant that dawn was the worst time in the day—but better than the night.

This level of complexity is probably why most fantasy works that use superstition have it with hedge wizards using foxglove to treat heart patients, bread mold for wounds, and willow bark for headaches, despite these herbs have no proper magical connection to the conditions. (The Doctrine of Signatures alone should tell you, fulminate the properly trained wizards.)

The problem with that is that it turns on your readers' knowledge of science, that it is always touched with comedy, and that it's really quite limited in what you can do.

More useful is investigating real-life superstitions, and inventing your own. People see patterns where no patterns are, in reality, and so they will invent things from wearing red leading to bloodshed, to warding the spell-casting chamber with iron in each window, to inventing sprites that like to mess up the ingredients in pantry or wizard's store room. (The last can help morale issues, by giving people something to blame besides each other.)

The first and most obvious is that if the ability to work magic is distributed randomly, people will have superstitions. Oh my they will have superstitions. For good or for evil. The degree to which the mother, or the father, or someone else entirely, will be blamed for failure (which way you make failure is up to you) can range from mild grumbling to lethally dangerous.

Perhaps wizards, or serious scholars of wizardry, can grumble that it doesn't work like that even if they don't know how it works.

Some superstitions can be eliminated entirely without knowing the truth. That is, eliminated as reasonable beliefs. Not even definitively establishing how something works will eliminate the superstition as such. That turns on the usual moods and fads of belief.

But all sorts of superstitions are likely. This is good luck. That is bad luck. You want to avoid the shadows of wizards' towers before you take the test for mastery. You want to avoid meat three days before you wrestle during the fair. White goose feathers make arrows weak.

Ribbons in your hair should be put in in even numbers, or the maid will never marry; only a widow who has resolved to never remarry should wear an odd number, and it is deemed unlucky to wear an odd number while in mourning, because it may trap you in grief.

Perfectly ordinary customs will pick up significance. Brides carry daisies because they are in bloom after the planting, when most weddings are held. That village will tell you they must be made into a daisy chain at the feast in order to link the bride and bridegroom for life. This village will tell you they are a sign of purity and will wilt in the hand of an unworthy bride, and she must hand them to her bridegroom to test him. They may even tell you that was how a witch warned Fair Elise to do that, and so discovered that her bridegroom was a werewolf and robber, and thus the custom was instituted. If you dig into the records, you will find that even though Fair Elise existed, the trial records of her bridegroom mention nothing of such a revelation, and the daisies at weddings were certainly older than that time.

And it should not be easy to see through their superstitious character.

White goose feathers may seem vindicated by the selective memory of people. It's a lot easier to remember things in correlation, so white goose feathers and a bad arrow are more striking than either white good feathers or a bad arrow alone. Likewise, withering daisies and a bad marriage, as opposed to one alone.

A widow who wears only one ribbon, or three, or seven, scares off wooers, while one with an even number leaves hope for those who think she may marry again.

Avoiding the towers is a conscientious act, and conscientiousness always helps in matters where diligence and details matter. Conscientious people who follow the rules will do better than those who do not, even if a number of the rules are superstitious. (As long as the useless and even counter-productive rules are not too many.)

Finally, of course, you can decree that some of them really work. Perhaps a wizard of long-ago turned into a wolf, and his eyebrows joined together in the middle, and he cast an enormous curse such that all people with eyebrows that join in the middle will turn into wolves periodically.

And then the wizards will sigh over how the superstition lingers after the curse is broken. Such is the nature of superstition.

Where Are The Wizards?

Time and place

If you have the ability to do magic distributed among people, and they don't know the rhyme or reason of it, there will be superstitions.

If the ability is unevenly distributed over space and time, there really will be superstitions. Even if it's a distribution of different abilities, a la Ursula Vernon's *Castle Hangnail*. This place has a glut of Necromancers and no Alchemists, that place has a lone Enchantress and a surfeit of Sorceresses, and the other place an abundance of Wizards and a want of Mages.

If the wizards have to learn from other wizards, this gets aggravated, because the schools will congregate where the pupils are most easily obtained, and then the wizards from regions where they are rare will congregate where they can be taught, and then people who want their skills will go there to find them.

At which point, it is regarded as a regional trait. Just as northerners are red-haired, and southerners swarthy, the shore-folk good fishermen, the mountain-folk skilled at dyes, the archers of Thusand-such are better than anyone else, and all the rest.

(With all the fun and games of such spell-slingers being foreigners, or regarded as foreigners, wherever else they go. Not to mention suspicions about the rare one born in an unusual place.)

And then there are all the issues if it also changes over time. *This* is the age of Alchemists, soon it will be the age of Sorcerers, once it was the age of Wizards.

Or, perhaps, they rise and fall in waves, so the regions changes.

If it takes long enough and is gradual enough—a matter of decades or perhaps centuries—only those with educations will notice. Peasants will tell tales of the days of wizards, but scoff at the notion that they were anything but tales—either in general, or because everyone knows that wizards are three kingdoms over.

Still, those with education will notice. And look for patterns, and perhaps find them. They may even be indicative of reality. But then, the knowledge may be of no use unless the lord of the land starts alluring spell-slingers from other lands, or no use at all if the drought is world-wide.

A lord who knows the peril probably would be wisest to encourage the manufacture of magical objects. Many of them. This will create the small problem that they will work with the knowledge that they have then. And for the purposes they had then. Every wizard in the land goes to glorify the city of wizards with wonders, and courts of justice that establish the truth, and hospitals that cure everything, and curse-breaking springs.

Then the wizards' city falls because it lacks the wizards to defend itself, and it was designed for magical defense. Thus it becomes a place for desperate quests.

It might be best for people in general if magical objects are portable, but those in a position to influence the decision are likely to want them stationary, so as to continue to bring power and influence to the place, even if they don't foresee the object's being the only reason anyone would come there.

And then let a man who made the journey to the wizards' ruined city father a child who turns out to be a wizard. Watch the superstitions infest the land. Perhaps even the way may be made easy, or easier, as people trek there.

Plus of course all the usual array. Children born while the church bells are ringing. Children born during twilight. Children conceived at either time. And so on, and so on.

Meanwhile, you, the writer, wanting actually random stuff, had drawn it all up by rolling dice, and you know enough statistics to tell that if things don't cluster, that's stronger evidence of tampering than many clusters.

Such is statistics.

Dragons' Superstitions

And elves and dwarves and ogres

What would a dragon be superstitious about?

Pattern matching is so vital a skill, and the patterns of the world are so hard to winkle out, that it's likely that any intelligent beings would have mistakes.

Indeed, I have heard that it is possible to induce superstitions in ducks by having a lever that *sometimes* dispenses a food pellet if pushed. (I am reminded of Hal Clement's *Still River*, where the woman notes that all the beings she is working with have a term for "luck.")

First, of course, you have to determine what actually works. Or maybe not. You can decide on what superstitions you want, and then work back to what really works.

Dragons superstitiously prefer bullion to coins. The reality is that they need gold, and coins are so constantly debased that they think bullion is what is needed.

Or perhaps they just need the treasure, and the accident of one dragon falling ill with more coins than bullion spooked them all.

Or perhaps they told each other stories that the more gold you had, the longer you lived, until they started to half-believe it and grew worried with every missing coins, because, who knew, it might be true. (Thus making it easier to lure them from their lairs, and slay them, because they think a missing coin is dangerous.)

If dragons are long-lived, this decreases the chances, because they remember the actual causes for longer. If they don't talk together much, that will also decrease the chances, because things have less chance to get muddled through the grape vine.

On the other hand, the more isolated the dragons are, the more time they have to develop personal superstitions—lack of chances to compare experience, and less fear of being laughed down—so that *this* dragon will not let his emeralds and rubies mix, *that* one thinks it dangerous to have any pile of a single color of jewel or metal, and *the other one* refuses to have pearls because they make the cavern flood.

Other species would work likewise. Particularly those that work in high-risk situations. For dwarves to believe in knockers might help with morale, as it is believed that gremlins helped with aviator morale during World War II: deflecting blame from your co-workers.

On the other hand, what would they think knockers were? Outlaw dwarves who ran into deep magic? Merely lost dwarves who did the same? The ghosts of miners, human or dwarven? Another race entirely?

In a world filled with rational beings, in what would probably be the biggest difference in a high fantasy world, it's likely that some will have superstitions about others, and that those superstitions will transform themselves over time.

The knockers are responsible for bad luck in a mine, you will be assured by the miners, both dwarven and human, even if they occasionally lead to good seams as well. They add that they are miners' ghosts, which is where agreement ends. Drunken arguments ensue over which is is worse, human knockers or dwarven ones. Only a sagacious historian, with access to good records, can determine that, at the root, the knockers were the other race, blended into a common creature with all the local and far-flung divergence that a creature only in folklore acquires.

If that seems improbable, the rakshasa of Indian epics, the foes of the devas, may be translated "ogres" but they are far more formidable. And the Indo-European root also went down the European branch to become "ursus" and "arctos."

Formidable though bears are—so formidable that northern languages refer to them by euphemisms, the Germanic usually "the brown one", the Slavonic usually "the honey eater", and the Baltic usually "the shaggy one"—they are not quite up to epic standards.

Then, the very divergence may make them less harmful than other superstitions.

Real beings may acquire a few fictional traits, which remain fully cemented to the real beings. Theoden said, "they do little, and avoid the sight of men, being able to vanish in a twinkling; and they can change their voice to resemble the piping of birds." Who knows? Perhaps some hobbits imitated bird cries, and the Riders of Rohan did not know how few of them did it. Or perhaps it crept into the tales after they lost contact with hobbits.

That is still harmless. But consider the superstition that all wood elves turn into ravening panthers. Perhaps some did—perhaps some turned to defending panthers, mistaken for evil because they were, well, panthers, or else because they defended the forest from the other side—perhaps because some tamed panthers—perhaps for no discernible reason.

Which is not, actually, purely fantasy, alas. There are Far East tales of rebutting the foreign Buddhist by turning him back into a camel.

The possibilities are unbounded. Indeed, the sagacious writer remembers that the "super-" in superstition does indeed indicate excess, and trim down superstitions to such as serve the story, whether adding a trifle of local color, complicating getting the wood elves through gnome territory, or making it feasible to slay the dragon.

Sorcerers Versus Superstition

Better knowledge may win.

Wizards may have superstitions about lucky colors and numbers. But what they may also have is more knowledge about magic than the common crowd, and so a hearty contempt for the superstitions they hear bandied about.

They may very well be joined by philosophers and clergy who maintain that such beliefs are obviously against the order of the universe. (For clergy, you need a religion with a defined theology to pull this off.)

This can cover a whole range. Granting a logical reason for the characters to talk about the matter, it gives you enormous scope to define how magic works by defining how it doesn't. Or even having wizards argue about whether something is superstition with all the chances to build your world involved.

This can range from a wizard huffing about how the newspaper includes "your lucky numbers!" to one bringing the authority (and if necessary, force) of the crown to bear on a village to insist that a peril be properly warded against and not hedged about with daisies. Or rowan trees. Especially not with rowan trees planted close enough that their roots will tear up the wards.

(In part, of course, because superstitious views can range from absolutely conviction to not being absolutely certain it doesn't work. One man has a panic attack on realizing that he slept the night in a house that has no daisies in the garden. Another idly thinks he might as well have daisies planted, they would do no harm—and perhaps is a little surprised at how much planting them calms him. A third doesn't believe a word of it and suffers no harm, but plants them to calm the silly.)

One notes that the wizards do not have to have advanced very far into making magic technology to hit on at least some objections to popular beliefs.

The treatise "On the Sacred Disease" may not actually be by Hippocrates, but it was indeed ancient and contains

> I am about to discuss the disease called 'sacred.' It is not, in my opinion, any more divine or more sacred than other diseases, but has a natural cause, and its supposed divine origin is due to men's inexperience and to their wonder at its peculiar character.

On the other hand, while this was unquestionably a correct diagnosis of epilepsy, there are far later clashes.

Such as a Renaissance doctor decrying the work of witches because they *always* neglect the important element of astrology, and pay no heed to conjunctions.

In a still later era, John Keats deplored the ignorance that prevented him from selling his carriage, because all those peasants are firmly convinced that consumption is contagious when all educated people know it's hereditary.

So you have a lot of leeway here.

Consider it well. You may, after all, paint yourself into a corner. If your wizard ridicules the notion that specific days are of importance, you can not have a plot twist dependent on waiting for a specific day for magical reasons unless you can go back and revise that out—possibly impossible for a series—or devise some reason why he was wrong. Or work around it. (It is, after all, conceivable that he was hired to cast the spells, and the contract specifies the days. Then the ridicule is foreshadowing.)

On the other hand, there is the question of scope. If you have a full blown magic system, models by which it works for different schools of magic, a historical development of magic, and superstitions of varying degrees of belief, accuracy, and populations who believe, you have—probably too much for a single work. Especially since you have to worry about what is crucial to the work, and what is necessary to make the world feel real and keep the crucial parts from advertising their plot device status.

Maybe a series. But keep what serves the story.

The Discovery of Wizardry

The young wizard

How do you learn you're a wizard?

Obviously, a world where wizardry means study has it happen any other academic matter: someone notices your talent, sets up your studies, and when you reach a certain point, you're deemed a wizard.

Even if there's a point at which your master turns you into a dog on a ice floe in the process.

But for that favorite, the wizardry as a special gift, how do you discover it?

Assuming, of course, that it doesn't get elided as irrelevant. If the character launches as a competent wizard, it doesn't matter. Even if, a la role-playing games, he launches as a competent sorcerer—that is, someone with inherent, innate, if somewhat limited magical powers—no one gets into the business of how this emerges, which could really complicate the past.

The *Lord Darcy* series had a story where a toy made a world-building appearance. It consists of a wand, a tray with indentations, and some colored balls, all with a simple enchantment, such that the child could move the balls into the right indentation with the wand.

Except that the enchantment would wear off after a few months, but the process of playing would teach the child how to cast the spell. It came with an explanatory pamphlet that if their child was still interested in the game and still able to make it work in half a year, the parents should have the child tested for magical ability.

This was in a highly magic-as-technology setting, well-ordered, where the study of wizardry was organized and licensed.

Harry Potter of course has a magical means of detecting them—but, then, it also has children spontaneously manifesting magic before the letter arrives, even if they have Muggle parents.

Such spontaneous manifestations create a great deal of problems. For the characters, of course, but also for the writer if they would divert the story.

Not to mention that having such manifestations among children but nowhere else is rather blatantly a plot device.

True, it's likely that training them out of that would be the first thing a wizard would undertake for apprentices. But how could that work so absolutely?

Do the powers manifest spontaneously when a character suffers fever? Brain damage? Grows senile? Or, for that matter, loses his temper?

It would take a fearful amount of training to drill control into you in such a manner that even medical reasons would not break it. (Such training would, of course, not be optional for wizards. Perhaps that rupture—between those who can not work magic, and those who must study far off, in a location where their original lack of control can contained until they master it—is the first inkling of the masquerade.)

Perhaps there is a magical way to contain it. As soon as you get a good and proper magical wand, there is a magical burst of power, and you are linked.

Never ever again will you be able to work magic without your wand.

Or some sealing ceremony.

The problem with that is, of course, that it's a transparent plot device to allow you to have uncontrollable power as a child, and then never again. Even with the obvious motives to do just that, it's still a transparent plot device.

Unless you figure out some way to complicate it so it doesn't just work, it has side effects and consequences. Such is the art of disguise.

Writing

Eventually, the writer has to sit down and write.

A Mistaken Viewpoint

The importance of the choice

There's one work which I keep recurring to as the prime example of the importance of choosing your viewpoint character correctly. This is because the writer choose the wrong character.

Mark Twain, in writing *A Connecticut Yankee In King Arthur's Court,* intended to blast chivalry. I have read people who read it exactly for the chivalry (ignoring the satire) and never once read anyone who thought its satire was effective.

Indeed, when it was assigned reading in the school, we thought it was a satire on the Yankee, who merited it.

The work opens with the problem in the paragraph where the narrator introduces himself and accurately depicts his character.

> So I am a Yankee of the Yankees—and practical; yes, and nearly barren of sentiment, I suppose—or poetry, in other words.

In fine, he declares himself exactly the sort of clod who would be blind to the most picture-perfect Camelot in all its glory, exactly the way the most star-eyed dreamer dreamed about it. Drop him in it, and he would play a vulgar and insensible lout.

The only exception to his boorishness is how he regards his wife and baby, at the end of the story. There, his intensity does not match his actions in the rest of the tale. (It might be more plausible were it not for its obvious plot device use.)

No, if you are to satirize chivalry, you have to provide someone who can see it, and then see through it. A sensitive and honorable man who enjoys tales of chivalry and is insufficiently critical of them—and if that wasn't feasible, a Miniver Cheevy, born too late, or at least, a stupid dreaming lunkhead who views the past in a rosy haze.

In fine, someone who would have seen the wonders of a truly wonderful Camelot, and so can be disillusioned by a reality. Not someone who can't even rise to the height of the illusion.

At that, his loutishness also comes across in his want of courtesy. He tries to explain to some peasants that their higher wages are more than off-set by the prices they pay, relatively higher than their wages, and fails. It does not help that he does not do with grace, and a reader is not so convinced that it's the peasants' stupidity.

This, of course, is not helped by his world-building. When you openly admit that your historical research has been sloppy—when you write—

> The ungentle laws and customs touched upon in this tale are historical, and the episodes which are used to illustrate them are also historical. It is not pretended that these laws and customs existed in England in the sixth century; no, it is only pretended that inasmuch as they existed in the English and other civilizations of far later times, it is safe to consider that it is no libel upon the sixth century to suppose them to have been in practice in that day also. One is quite justified in inferring that whatever one of these laws or customs was lacking in that remote time, its place was competently filled by a worse one.

you can't be taken seriously. History is chock-full of countries taking up evil customs after not practicing them.

And what is worse, Twain imputed a number that he took from the Deep South. It is one thing to blame Sir Walter Scott for southern culture. It is another for it to be aesthetically sound to make southern culture part of Camelot.

This detracts from his showing the evils of the land, because the hand of the author is too evident in setting them up.

(I mean, you could do a fantasy world where chivalry reigns openly, and the hero realizes that some nasty things from a different era were going on to support it, but he would also realize it wasn't a historical era. Possibly even a fantasy world created by the delusions?)

I suspect the work would be a historical curiosity except for the luster reflected by his other works. Let it serve as an example of the importance of viewpoint.

Uncovering The Villain's Plot

What does the hero know, and when does he know it?

The plot thickens.

The villains conspire.

The writer sympathizes with every writer who has, in the past, had the villain spill the entire plan in the last scene for inadequate motive.

The last point is important. Who, watching *The Incredibles,* thinks of Syndrome's speech to Mr. Incredible as "monologuing" until he calls it such? The point of Syndrome's plot is revenge. Merely killing Mr. Incredible while he's in ignorance—why, he would just think of it as the tragic but heroic ending to his life. Mr. Incredible has to be told he's to blame, which requires the whole story.

That is the perfect use of it, but other villains clearly show that they do not merely want to triumph, they want to be appreciated for their genius in pulling off such a triumph.

On the other hand, I have read stories in which the villain reels off his plot for no other reason that the heroes have found a flaw in it. When the motive for the villainy did not turn in any way, shape, or form, on the genius of the tale being known. Not a good story, but it happens.

Much depends on how complex the villain's plot is, since a simpler one can also be more easily inferred.

More depends on whether the story turns on dramatic irony or identification and discovery.

There's a certain artistry in watching a character, dreading what he does next and pitying him for it, knowing it's the wisest thing he can do in his situation, with his knowledge, and yet will bring disaster.

There's a certain artistry in feeling the character's dread, doubt, and bafflement, and feeling the surprise as the character finds new revelations, where the reader identifies with the character and is as mystified.

Mind you, there's a certain complication in that if the foreshadowing and clues are laid out, some readers will reach the right conclusion before the character, and thus what is dramatic irony to some will be a mystery to others. (Plus, of course, the effect of re-reading where you remember some or all of the plot.)

Obviously, for dramatic irony, you can just give the villain a viewpoint scene, or two, provided you are willing to either tell *all*—a viewpoint character should not have unrevealed thoughts—or establish that he's rather batty.

I have known writers who argued that it was conceivable that the character might not be thinking of the things the writer wants to keep a mystery during the scene, but conceivable doesn't cut it. It has to be very plausible indeed. The only ones where I have seen it succeed is when the viewpoint character is clearly batty.

(I once read a work where we had the villainess thinking about her scheme coming to fruition in a vague and dreamy way that suggested she was batty, only for her to reveal her motive in the climax. It was stupid, childish, and profoundly selfish and evil—but it was within normal human reasoning.)

If you have more than one villain, even if one is a henchman, you can unfold elements in dialog—provided you have a viewpoint character to listen in. Henchmen sometimes make good viewpoint characters.

You can sometimes get away with a scene where the viewpoint is completely objective, describing the conversation without giving anyone's viewpoint on it, but this can be hard to juggle.

But, if you can't provide any scenes from the villain's viewpoint, you have to provide the clues.

Conversations with villains, of any grade, are the simplest way, though you do have to motivate the talk. The villain wanting to be admired, or to intimidate into avoiding resistance, the henchman wanting to be protected—these things are often neglected.

Without them, there is nothing else to do but study patterns and infer practices. Which can get tedious.

It is not for nothing that it's common for the hero to arrive on the scene after others have amassed the evidence, for him to give a glance and point out a pattern they missed for being so deep in the weeds.

The writer sighs and is glad that the heroine both learns a lot of it from those who gathered it and has much to do while gathering the rest, to enliven it.

Flaws, Memes, and Situations

In which I argue with a meme

I've run across a meme where someone asserts that, as taught by an English professor, that tragedies are not about some kind of "flaw" but about the character being wrong for a situation.

To which I respond: what do you think a fatal flaw *is*?

Aristotle was the first to single the flaw as a necessity. He observed that if the main character was just bad, the audience would just rejoice at his downfall; if just good, his downfall would anger as well as grieve the audience; but if a basically good but flawed character falls, the audience can grieve over it, but see how the character brought his fate on himself.

True, it does depend on situation.

If you put Hamlet in Macbeth's place, he would figure that everything was all set up, and he just had to wait and let the crown fall into his lap. Lady Macbeth's arguments would be tossed aside, because if the witches had gotten him the throne, he didn't need to do anything, and if they had lied, trying to implement it was folly.

To get a story, you would have to have Banquo betray him, accidentally or intentionally revealing the witches, and then have other characters react badly to the news. Macbeth/Hamlet might have to take the throne in self-defense. Indeed, given his hesitation, it might even end tragically because he does not take it with sufficient force and determination.

On the other hand, if you put Macbeth in Hamlet's place, he would head down from the ramparts with sword in hand to lop off Claudius's head—assuming he actually needed to be prompted by the ghost.

To get a story, you would need to have Claudius realize that his stepson was dangerous. (Not a great leap, there.) Perhaps he would surround himself with bodyguards. Hamlet/Macbeth would have to figure out a way to get by them alive, at least hale enough to kill Claudius before he died.

Perhaps if Ophelia still went mad, he could figure out that if he feigned madness, the bodyguards and Claudius alike might conclude that he was harmless. (I have heard there was an older, pre-Shakespeare form of *Hamlet* where he resorted to just such a pretense for just that reason.) Though it would be difficult for Macbeth to pull off the necessary acting.

A flaw that only appears in some situations shows that the character is indeed a good but flawed character. It may even be part of the tragedy that you reflect that if only he had avoided that particular situation, he, and everyone about him, could have lived to a happy old age.

Of course, in stories with a happy ending, you have less need to make the character's fall be the character's fault. The readers can forgive a great deal of bad luck because the character will rise again.

But, if you want a character arc, you have to start with a flaw. After all, he has to be worse off if he is to grow to be better.

Possibly even something that wasn't a flaw before, but is now, because of the new situation he's in. He has to learn to adapt to his new situation.

He fails, and fails again, because of this flaw of his.

Then, finally, he gathers his wits and steels his resolution, and tries for the third time and succeeds, thus overcoming his flaw.

The important thing to remember, whether it ends tragically or happily, is what the plot function of the fatal flaw is, and work with that rather than with abstractions of it.

Love Triangles, and What They Need

And what will break them

I have seen a meme asking for a love triangle where the two guys are not bitter rivals but cheerful, friendly, and willing to let the other guy win.

This is not a good idea.

The first problem is larger, simpler in essence, but more difficult to create good art from it: if they don't care whether they get her, are either of them worthy of her?

The second problem, which could possibly be finessed if the guys cared, still has many more ramifications. The love triangle is best used symbolically, to represent a real choice.

I still remember the novel that ended with the heroine in jail. One man comes to her and explains to her that if she is meek and humble when examined, she may get out of this with a mild punishment. A few years behaving circumspectly will restore her reputation enough that they can marry without difficulty. Given his status, continued good behavior would make her a respected matron of the community.

Then his brother shows up, jeers at this offer as timorous, and tells the heroine that his ship is ready to sail on the tide. It will mean that neither he nor she can ever return to the port they are in, but he has a house elsewhere, where they can live.

Her choice of the ship therefore picks not only her husband but the theme of the story and determines her fate.

Likewise, in a commedia dell'arte scenario, there are generally two pairs of *innamorati*, but the rival of each *innamorato* is not usually the other. It is rather an older man with distinctly more money—sometimes his own father.

The guy torn between the *femme fatale* and the girl next door—the girl star-struck by the *miles gloriosus* until a fight reveals the quiet guy is the one who is not a coward—some of the foils so necessary to give a love triangle significance are so commonplace as to be cliches.

And not just in the pure romantic love triangle. There's many a Mad Scientist's Beautiful Daughter whose filial love combats her romantic love for the hero. It is not so much the romantic vs. daughterly aspect as the madness vs. heroism. The tale would change if a heroic father came to drag his daughter from the mad scientist who beguiled her—you might, for instance, have to give the father a supporting hero who loves the heroine—but the thematic change would be less.

One notes that both characters must be on stage, and vividly drawn, to give weight to the conflict. Their real, objective nature forms the core of the matter. It is perhaps worse when the writer drops the charming, affectionate rogue for the stolid citizen, flatter than a pancake—especially when the rogue did nothing actually wrong—but I have also seen a love triangle where the woman's current and very respectable fiance was depicted almost entirely through what she said about him, and that, too, did not convince. If one of her choices is not real, there is no real conflict.

Though the symbolism can be flipped with the Mad Scientist's Beautiful Daughter and the like, and often is. Then, it can be flipped with a purely romantic love triangle, in some conditions.

A flipped triangle occurs when the characters are not merely foils and thematic opposites and embodiment of the choosing character's choice. It occurs the main conflict of the story is between the two rivals.

The character who chooses is then the symbolic one, indicating the victory. Indeed, this character may symbolize the entire society that they dispute the leadership of.

She also, like the rivals mentioned above, needs to be a fully dramatized and objective character. If the rivalry is romantic, she has to be vivid enough to convince us that they would want to win her, and if it's not, she has to be vivid enough to ensure we regard her choice as important, and wise, and prudent, to fulfill her symbolism. Unless it's tragic, in which case we have to see how stupid it is.

Though, of course, it can get complex. A particularly memorable Doctor Who episode had an agricultural colony with a level-headed leader, who had a daughter, and a hot-head pushing for more aggressive approach and in love with the daughter.

When the colony survived owing the level-headed leader's heroic self-sacrifice, the hot-head was sobered by the experience and talked in a level-headed manner with the Doctor, the daughter clinging to his arm at the time.

Then, it can be simplified. If the heroine can accept or reject the hero's offer of marriage, it conveys her choice. Still, it helps if she positively rejects something else instead of merely accepting him.

Tone And Tale

Variations and range

Some tales are light-hearted, some are grim, and none of them longer than a short-short can maintain the same tone over the length of a story—and even short-shorts, or lyric poems, often have a twist.

It keeps the readers awake and the story from growing monotonous.

The problem arises when this creates discords. In mild cases, this breaks the story's mood, and in grave cases, it can ruin the world-building.

A light-hearted caper concluded with a death, and what's worse, the death of an important character whom the readers are attached to.

Grim adventure being broken by a silly episode—not an episode of silly and frivolous creatures, who could be regarded as simply heartless, but one where the story whole-heartedly supports the silliness.

This is a delicate matter, because, of course, mood whiplash is a powerful tool. Contrast sharpens things.

Uneven though *Mulan* is, the scene where the singing soldiers (even singing a plausible if Disneyfied soldiers' song) stumble into the scene of massacre greatly deepens the horror of the massacre.

Conversely, the scene in *Snow White And The Seven Dwarfs* where she sees those mysterious, monstrous eyes in the forest and flees until terror until she collapses, unable to escape as the eyes inch forward, and the delicate, harmless creatures of the forest emerge in a moment of enchantment. It is the mood whiplash of the monster-to-innocence that lends that moment its wonder. (C.S. Lewis thought the film very uneven, but singled that moment out as an example of being good and original.)

It's very hard to juggle. Some writers can manage a whole variety of moods, a world filled with them. Others end up undercutting the gravity of their serious scenes and the charm of their light-hearted ones even though their range of moods is very much narrower.

sigh. It's enough to make one remember Wayne C. Booth's wise observation in *The Rhetoric of Fiction* that it's really hard to make rules about things, past that if you use this technique badly, the results will be bad.

Sometimes it seems simple, as when Hamlet complains "Has this fellow no feeling of his business? He sings at grave- making," only to accept Horatio's observation that the grave-digger is used to it, and the following byplay about death is comic all right, but plays into the theme of death that *Hamlet* has, more than even Shakespeare's other tragedies.

But then, consider *Macbeth*. The knocking at the door scene—well, the jokes about Hell and being a porter there might fit in well with the horrors of the murder scene, just before, but what about all that joking about drunkenness? The mood whiplash gives a break from the horror of before before introducing the horror of after, when the murder is discovered.

It's hard to juggle.

One thing I find is commonly a problem is being *silly*, especially in world-building elements. Powerful people who are silly are a danger to everyone in hailing range. If you make them powerful enough, to whole world. Silliness that the story treats as harmless when it wouldn't be undermines the danger that produces conflict.

It's also wise to remember that while comic relief can bring highfalutin' ideals down to earth, the hero can wake up with his hair a mess and want orange marmalade for breakfast. Hegel's dictum applies: "No man is a hero to his valet. This is not because the hero is not a hero, but because the valet is a valet." If the purported hero actually behaves badly in private, that's one thing, though even there one has to consider that a hero is a man and therefore flawed. It's quite another thing if quirks, habits, and preferences are used to undermine the hero. (Though I note that petty souls who take it as such can actually build up the hero by showing what he suffers.)

In particular, sacrifices. If a character makes a sacrifice that, in his best judgment, was the right thing to do, other characters may treat it as something to jeer at, but the story should not.

Which is about all the useful advice I have, except that you want to watch your tonal shifts, and see to it that they harmonize rather than clash. There is no general solution, only wrestling out a particular one in a particular tale.

I Know Something You Don't Know

Irony and issues

When talking about point of view, I mentioned how important it was, when switching, to keep the characters distinctive so as to avoid confusing the readers.

One big aspect of that is dramatic irony.

From one angle, dramatic irony is the sole reason for having more than one viewpoint. The only reason to show something from a different viewpoint is to let the readers in on something that the first viewpoint didn't know.

Frequently, this is only to let the readers know it clearly and in more detail than the character who wasn't there. The main (or other) viewpoint character will know all the significant details for the plot, but given that we can not actually feel the hero's attachment to the family home, watching it vividly burn down may bring some of the reaction that he gets just on hearing the news. This greatly simplifies the issues.

But past that, there is the dramatic irony hanging over all uses of it. We know for a fact that the man the hero is confiding in is the spy of the villain, and the hero doesn't.

This is where stylistically distinctive points of view is important, because the reader needs to keep track of which things are known to which character. I once read a mystery novel where two detectives were involved in what would prove to be a single case, seldom met, and didn't talk about it, but I was annoyed at the folly of a detective, because they sounded so much alike that it was easy to forget that he didn't know what the other one had been told.

This is easier in a visual medium, where the actors or drawn characters are distinctive in themselves, but a writer has to work with the medium he works with.

Oddly enough, more writers manage more happily the situation where the reader reasonably infers things that the clueless viewpoint character misses, and so watches in an agony of suspense, or with gales of laughter, as the character blunders around.

The flashback story, which opens *in media res*, and then gives a large portion in flashback, is a bit less happy. The problem is that since the readers know the ending, they can't think themselves back into the ignorance of before. True, they may forget, which may improve the story, but on the whole, it's better to devise a hook that is in the right temporal order. A plot device that works better when it is forgotten is weak.

The case where the writers are weakest is in cases of amnesia.

Not the situation where a character wakes up in the story with amnesia. Then, there is no irony, only identification, as the reader discovers things with the character. It is overused as a way to info-dump, because it is an excellent way to do so.

No, I am thinking of the situation where the character knows something and has that knowledge taken away. This is hard to juggle because the reader has to remember all the time that the character no longer knows it.

The same problem as when you start with the ending and have to work your way back, except that not only you, but also the reader is in the privileged position.

That means, among other things, that you have to have situations of dramatic irony. If you destroy the memory of a character, and put him in situations where his former knowledge does not come into play, then you have deprived the amnesia of significance. You might as well drop it.

I have only done this once, and only in a short story. In *The Princess Goes Into The Forest*. Which is my portal fantasy that throws away all the advantages of a portal fantasy. Well, almost all of them. The heroine does remember some knowledge, though she does not remember how she learned it. It affects two situations in the story, in the foreground, and in the background. It was a trick to pull off.

Viewpoint And Patterns

How to portray point of view

When you choose your viewpoint characters, your work is not done. You need choose their pattern, too.

You have a lot of flexibility in the opening, because you are establishing the pattern. Only a third of the way in will it start to bug the readers if you do not deliver on it, but by half way, it's settled.

If you have chosen a single viewpoint, third or first person, you have chosen it for the work. You can not slip into another viewpoint for just one scene.

Well, except for epistolary. You can slap in an obviously relevant document as a scene. Other viewpoints are harder to avoid jarring.

If you want to give enormous chunks in a single point of view, it may succeed if you divide the work into parts larger than a chapter, and then conspicuously label them by the name of the viewpoint character, so that even with the first sentence, the reader is aware that the opening is Esmeralda, with Eglantine and Ermentrude coming up, you can set the pattern that way.

If we see the three or four major characters all having scenes, interwoven, we will not need labels, but we will expect to see these characters to all have scenes throughout the work. Indeed, if it shifts in an orderly manner from character A to B to C back to A, shifting in another order can be jarring. (Don't jar your reader out of the story.)

If you need to skip to whichever viewpoint is necessary at any time, you need to not set a pattern.

This is particularly important because it may make it clear to the reader that you veered from the pattern in order to hide something from us.

I once read a work, a romance, in which we got interchanging viewpoints from the hero and the heroine, *except* for one crucial scene, where we got only the heroine's. What was worse, the story was set up so he had two possible motives for his actions in that scene, obeying the orders of a superior and regard for the heroine, and we never learn which one it was. (Or what the mix of them was. It would have been quite plausible for him to take the orders with relief because it meant he had to do what he was realizing he owed the heroine, but we don't get that.)

Do not do that. If we ever get a character's viewpoint, we expect to get all his significant thoughts. (Worst being a book where a murderer's viewpoint, moments after the murder, omitted that he had done it.) Set up the pattern to allow for that.

If we see the main character having scenes peppered with viewpoint scenes from characters who will never get another or perhaps never again appear in the work, we expect that. If the main character is viewed by an endless succession of minor characters who leave after their scenes, and never from his own viewpoint, we expect that.

There's some leeway. Omniscient viewpoints can drift into tighter and looser views of the characters, from a camera view that shows nothing not clearly visible to the eye, to a tight view of one character's thoughts. Drifting does tend to be required, so that it glides onward without jolts.

Frequently, in fact, in a single work, the number of viewpoints declines, and the time spent in viewpoints increases, because the conflict is tightening, and the earlier viewpoints have served their info-dumping purposes. This also allows the identification with those viewpoint characters who are left to deepen. But this has to be done with a subtle hand to avoid jarring the reader. If the opening of the book was all sorts of viewpoints, and the second half is all one viewpoint, it is likely to jar.

Indeed, you may be setting a pattern for a series. It's possible for a series, to flip between first-person in one work, and third-person with many viewpoints in another, but if you use a common pattern, you may have to make a new pattern very clear, very early in the work.

So thoroughly is this expected that in a series with only a few viewpoints, a new viewpoint character in a new book may instantly tell the readers that the hero is going to get married, because this woman has viewpoint scenes.

Patterns can work like that.

Why Do You Feel That Way?

Characters and the objective correlative

T.S. Eliot came up with the term, which is how we ended up with a mouthful like "objective correlative," but it's a useful idea.

When characters react to things, there has to be an objective reality, in the story, that they react to. And their reaction has to be reasonable.

In the sense that we would reasonably expect that the depicted character to act that way. A hard-code cynic reacting to a noble paladin with poisonous distrust and resentment is a reasonable reaction, provided the paladin is noble enough to explain why he gets more than a twist of the mouth that the cynic bestows on other people.

Oddly enough in my current reading, the Macguffin, if an object, seldom lacks sufficient reason. You could, of course, substitute things without more than tweaking the plot, but despite the arbitrary nature of the object, the characters' reactions are justified.

You could substitute a marvelous ruby for the Maltese Falcon, to be found among costume jewelry. Your biggest problem would be giving it a suitably glamorous name to serve as the book's title, because its vast monetary value gives an objective reason for people to connive over its ownership. (A fraught history helps increase the value and so the motive, of course. Plus making it unique, so that it can't be replaced, which helps explain why people don't just go for something else. But fraught histories are many.)

On the other hand, when the Macguffin is a person, writers don't put in as much effort.

I'm off to rescue my sister! Yes—but why? If you love her, you seem strangely indifferent to what she may suffer in the meantime. If your parents will make your life miserable if you fail, why do you feel no resentment? If you regard it as a basic duty because of familial loyalty—or general benevolence—why doesn't that stern sense of duty overflow into other actions?

Still, more strangely, I've seen writers neglect to do this in cases of love.

I mentioned this in the case of love triangles. The two rivals must both represent a real choice, a convincing choice, and thus be objectively good, or at least convincingly attractive.

Also, the love interests have to be on stage. Actual present attractiveness is what the readers know. Even if the readers saw and remember the other person in the triangle, what is present is likely to trump that.

Witness that *The Lord of the Rings*, even, has an issue in that Arwen is not so vivid as Eowyn, and we are startled by Aragorn's approaching wedding.

But it matters past that.

Love interests who are off-stage are unconvincing in general. A soldier talking about the girl he left behind may work, but only if the talk is quite good. (Though war stories tend to accept that they love the love interests as a plot device.)

Not to mention that falling out of love can be as important.

I read a book in which a treacherous break-up—a character sets up a meeting at a place and time in order to ensure that the other character is out of the way while moving out, and only gives the reason "I can't take this any more"—where we never see the couple together, never really get any account of "this," and never get enough to tell whether it was treachery or desperation to escape someone too arrogant to listen.

The most aggravated is the prequel that explains how the couple got married after their miserable union is shown in the earlier published works of the series. I have yet to see one that really convinced me that the couple got married. Even in a book where the woman clearly exploited her leverage over the man to pressure him into the union, it did not convince.

As for the love matches—forget it.

It is, of course, tricky to portray a passion that everyone knows will end in disaster, or at least dreariness, but by the same token, it is unwise to write something that you can't pull off. Leave things that don't work as story in the backstory.

When something is in the story, it needs to justify the reactions it gets.

How Do You Feel About That?

Characters and the subjective correlative.

When you put in a plot device, you have to *carry through* to disguise its nature. Give it consequences.

One of those consequences is the reaction of the characters. T.S. Eliot missed this while discussing the objective correlative. Then, he was talking about stage, and this is one trope where the medium makes a big difference.

On stage, in a movie, and even in a comic-book format, you can depict your objective correlative. Give us a reaction shot of the character. Let us impute the emotional reaction. Indeed the reaction shot can be a blank canvas on which we can develop all sorts of reactions.

(It's not necessary, as we can all see in Hamlet's soliloquies, but that is just a matter of techniques being useful in different situations.)

In writing, you can get something of this by not making the character with the reactions the viewpoint character for that scene.

On the other hand, this will color it with the viewpoint character's own reactions, which is to say that the reader will not be left entirely free to impute his own imaginations, but get that character's.

And if, whenever something dramatic happens, you cut away from the viewpoint of all characters who have, or ought to have, strong reactions to the event, the reader is apt to notice that.

All the more in that reactions can differ strongly. If a young man brings a new song to his family, and they go to sing it of an evening, his younger brother may be delighted at the prospect of a new song, or frightened at the prospect of showing how badly he reads music before his older brother and parents. Either being plausible, one must be shown, or both if his reaction is complex.

Some writers just omit the reactions. This is unwise. I have read a story in which a character is going to meet a friend—his only friend in the setting, and he had not had many before landing there—and found him murdered.

All of his thoughts were about how to make a safe get-away.

Now this was a rational thought. Discovering the body means you can not be certain that the murderer is not nearby, and may not dispose of you, too. It is also dangerous in that you can be implicated—and, in fact, in this case, he had been framed. He knew his friendship with the man was not common knowledge, and that framing was possible.

But at the very least, some shock and grief would complicate the cold-blooded thoughts necessary to survive. Not to mention that his first reaction should have been surprise, and it was not shown.

It came across as very cold, and undermined the depiction of friendship.

At least he was concerned about his own life.

I have read a story where a woman is told that the man sponsoring her education was arrested for high treason. Now, this could bring a lot of reactions to his arrest as such: grief at his fall, glee at how his folly brought him down, surprise that she had known so little of him, or distant indifference because she had known that she was a pawn to him and cared no more for him than he for her. (Though I would expect her to at least have an opinion about the possibility of his guilt, even if it was that she could hardly tell at this distance.)

But what did this mean for her? She is told when she hears the news that her tuition had been paid for the semester, but she does not worry in the slightest about what it will mean for her. Being associated with a traitor might be perilous for her.

Instead she is swept up by another powerful man as a protegee, and goes on with her new life, learning more about high life since the new man expects her to move in Society. This makes its plot device quite evident, and helps shove it off stage.

Still a reader might wonder if her new sponsor had something to do with her old sponsor's fall. A less personal reason for her might have improved the story. Perhaps the scholarship fund had some legal issues, or a bad investment, or an embezzling clerk.

But a dramatic cause calls for a dramatic reaction.

Bridging Conflict

A question of beginnings

What do you do when your story needs a slow-burn start? With everyone urging you to start with a bang? With the awareness that people will read *maybe* the first page of your story to give you a chance?

What you need is bridging conflict. Whether you call it by that or some other term, what is needed is a short-term conflict to hold interest while the real problem is set up.

Sometimes as simple as Watson going to a place to do something short and simple only to find that Holmes is already there, so Watson does it, and then joins Holmes.

Sometimes as complex as an elderly hobbit, mysteriously looking years younger, having a birthday party before deeper implications are revealed—and even those only bit by bit.

Sometimes this effectively occurs while the real problem is progressing, but slowly. In many urban fantasy books, a slow-burn romance progresses throughout a series while every book revolves about a caper, a mystery, or something else to bridge the significant moments in the romance with action.

This can be tricky. You do not want to mislead the readers about the genre, or the relative importance of the elements, or the thematic elements of the story. Whether the bridging problem is entirely wrapped up as the real problem is introduced, or demoted to subplot, the reader should not be frustrated at the way that plot is dropped or decreased, or that the new plot moves in. (This can also mean shifting the importance of the characters, which raises the peril still higher.)

Sometimes, of course, the plot itself reveals new depths to the original conflict, and these revelations radically change it, effectively making it a new conflict. Jill is murdered, and Jack tracks down her murderers, but while finding one, he learns that the murder was a move in a much larger plot by wizards. Eagerly, he joins in opposing the plot in general, and helps bring the whole thing down. This requires far more complexity than locating and killing the murderers.

Other times, unfolding depths does not work. The new plot takes off in a new direction. Johannes desperately looks for a new master wizard so he can complete his apprenticeship after his master's death, only to learn that the other master wizards murdered his master to hide their evil plots, and he must flee with an appropriated grimoire. He hopes to educate himself as much to fight as to become a master wizard, because they will not let him go off and live in peace, not with what he knows.

A story in which Johannes continues his search for a master wizard to complete his apprenticeship after learning of the masters' corruption would not work in the same way, if it worked at all. Or a story in which he knew of the corruption from the beginning, because that underplays the secrecy, which is the most dastardly part.

At that, the connection can be even more tenuous. The change is not even a sharp turn in the plot, while keeping the same elements in play. Jack and Johannes fight an ogre that attacked a caravan, revealing that Jack keeps the enemy at bay long enough for Johannes to cast a fireball, they take their pay at the caravan's destination, and they walk off to talk to the locals in hopes of learning more about wizards, and thus start their main story.

A frequent technique, when the protagonist's job allows it, is to introduce the character *in media res* on one short and simple job. Then the character wraps that one up, and then gets the next, longer assignment, which serves as the main plot. Jack and Johannes take down the ogre and then are told the bandits have a wizard.

This set-up is useful for planting Chekhov's guns. It is, in fact, so useful for that that you have to use an artful hand, because the reader will be on a look-out for things.

Indeed, an important point is to remember that it's a plot device, and consequently needs art to conceal that, to lend it significance within the course of the subsequent events.

There is always the possibility that it will take over the story and the original plotline it was to lead up to gets demoted or even vanishes. Such is the writing life.

Wide Is The World

World-building as a trap

We've all heard of a would-be writer who started with world-building and after months, or years, or decades, was no closer to writing a novel because he hasn't been looking for a plot, or even characters.

This can be a problem even when you are dealing with an incident or other moment in the story, and working out a story for it. You have to build up the world to deal with it.

This is especially true when you're ripping off an idea. If it's from another story, you want to file off the serial numbers, but even if not, you need to fit it into whatever setting you want to put it, you want to fix any gaping plot holes (particularly if you ripped it off from history), you want to set the moral valances the way you want to. . . .

An innocent man is unjustly condemned by the officials of a city republic, in political conflict with his powerful father, in hopes of using him as leverage, and they force his father to sign the sentence of exile. When evidence of his innocence surfaces, he's already dead.

You need the city, you need the details of its government, you need the infighting that caused it, you need its justice system, you need the charges and to know what evidence is necessary to make the trial more or less of a farce according to the needs of the story, you need the father powerful enough that they want to have a hold over him and weak enough (or principled enough) that he doesn't just throw them off. You need the victim's death to either be directly caused by the opponents or someone else involved in the infighting, or else be plausible as a natural death. (Well, more or less natural. Most justice systems can give you reason to suspect his treatment gave him a little assistance toward the grave.)

Or you could read a melodramatic tale about a war captive being prepared for death by torture when a kindly and noble maiden of his captors decides to save him.

You consider the war, the sides, the setting. The motives for the war, the claims each side makes. What sort of skirmish saw him captured, and whether he was at fault—or someone else was. Why this side tortures its captives to death, and what authority she has to save him.

You wonder if perhaps you could place it in a land where, say, a curse was broken so that no one had claim to it, and both sides are moving in. Perhaps the captive's side were the ones who broke it? Or perhaps you think of the chivalric romances, and how often a captive knight was rescued from durance vile by the beautiful Saracen princess, and then brought her back to his own country and married her, and wonder whether the torture was necessary. As with justice systems, most historical systems put prisoners of war in danger of death without even any intention to do so, and it simplifies her rescue, since she can sneak about.

The last point at least hauls the tale back to the characters. It is oddly easy, sometimes, to go haring off after background details that don't forward the story, and distract from it with clutter. Some ideas are more likely to do this than others, but it's always a peril.

Perhaps the world-building leads to another story, but it's always a peril to the original one, in that you are building up scaffolding without building the original structure.

At that, the wisest place to put the most interesting things in the world-building is in the foreground of the story. Let the wizards work out their apprenticeships, or attend the college, and take up with them as they use their fire powers to float zeppelins over the sea too infested with sea serpents to cross on ships.

Whether carrying an innocent convict to a horrible prison island, or finding a cursed land that they hope to free for human habitation.

At which point, the sage writer starts to consider the original idea. Perhaps the father—or his son—was associated with the zeppelins. Perhaps the infighting stems from the prudent fear that the zeppelins allow too much escape for their power to continue. Perhaps those officials who condemned him did not realize that the innocent convict has the character that the other convicts lack, and is the first educated man to be sent there. Perhaps he cracks the curse, and then the people from a nearby land flood in, claiming it for their own, though they did not break the curse. Perhaps they lived there before, and cursed the land in a war. Or perhaps they did not live there before, and had laid the curse in the course of a war, thinking it would break earlier and let them claim the land after slaughtering all those who lived there.

Perhaps this innocent convict, or his son, is captured by the people from the other land.

Because you always have to keep dragging it back to the story if you want a story out of it. True, a large frame of history gives you plenty of time to situate all sorts of stories—but only if you look for stories in the frame.

Bait And Switch

Follow the conflict

The conflict posed in the beginning of the story has to be resolved in the ending.

You'd think that would be the simplest thing in the world, to remember what story you are telling.

But, no. I have seen published stories (traditionally published no less) where this failed.

It can happen in various ways.

Once I read a romance in which the hero had forced the heroine to marry him because she was an heiress, there was a war, and her lands lay in crucial regions. All right then, there's your conflict. The marriage traps them together, and there is no happy ending as long as she is a pawn in the war.

Then, at the end of the book, he puts himself at considerable risk of death, and suffers grave injuries, getting her back from the other side.

No.

The problem that your wife is a pawn to you is not resolved by your proving that she is a *very valuable* pawn. You have to show that you do not regard her as a pawn.

And I have read a YA novel in which the heroine has trouble in her home town, partly because everyone knows she's not her mother's husband's child, and halfway through it, this conflict is dropped entirely, to drag her off to a secret movement of those who, like her, have magical fathers and are doing Great Things in the land, so she has adventures among her fellows.

That did not work either, because the conflict changed entirely. The first part of the story and the second part of the story were different stories.

It wasn't bridging conflict, either, to bear us through learning the essential aspects of her and her world, so that we could *care* in the second half.

Unless bridging conflict is extremely brief, it must contain hints of the future conflict, foreshadow the difficulties either that resolving the bridging conflict won't resolve, or that will make the bridging conflict impossible to resolve without looking at a larger picture, and transition cleanly to the main conflict. (And even very brief bridging conflict is better if it does these things.)

The heroine had to show her magical abilities earlier, possibly with some difficulties that showed she needed training.

The problems in the town needed to be enmeshed in the kingdom's larger troubles.

The movement had to be hinted at earlier, perhaps through grumbles in the market, perhaps through calls from the authorities for knowledge of them, perhaps through a blaze of colorful fire burning on the horizon.

Some bridging conflict leads on easily enough: I must kill the murderers of my beloved! oh, that was part of a grander conspiracy? I must kill the evil conspirators who sacrificed my beloved to their nefarious plans!

Other occasions of it, less so. If the hero labors to guard the caravan to the city, is there a particular reason why he would hare off to take down the Evil Overlord? Those need to be woven together. The hero is looking for money, money, money—a purpose will help sharpen it, and also put in a deadline.

Or, of course, it could serve as a *bildungsroman*, where the hero learns from his blundering attempts to build his life as a wandering swordsman. He makes it to the city, discovers that there are no caravans leaving, learns that all his pay would not cover the cost to leave, concludes that the evil sorcerer that everyone curses probably has treasure enough to support him, investigates what he needs. . . perhaps he finds the companions who will support him the rest of the story, perhaps the sorcerer learns of him and recruits him to deal with the bands inspired by the city's slander of him.

That requires its being tied together by the character arc of the hero, always a delicate and ticklish operation. In particular, it requires several episodes in the life, because two or three are not convincing as completing the process of growing up.

Merely throwing together episodes does not a story create, either as a unified conflict and its resolution, or as a *bildungsroman.* So when a story could appear disjointed, art is needed with unusual care to handle the matter.

Speaking Of Secrets

The use of a plot device

Two characters—who are not necessarily on the same side, but where neither one is evil—are keeping secrets from each other. This causes misunderstanding and consequently conflict.

Secrets, as a plot device, require some careful handling.

And you can't please everyone. I have read some reviews where the reader dinged the book because the characters didn't just *talk*, without even brushing on the way they had powerful reasons to not talk to each other. Alas, such ill-conditioned souls must simply be written off as not part of your target audience.

Still, even people who accept reasonable motives justly require some reason for the secrets.

For examples—romance novels frequently set up secrets as a central problem. In modern times, one common plot device for this is that her sister and his brother had a child and then died, and so the hero and heroine are locked in conflict over the child's custody. In historical ones, a common plot device is that the hero and heroine are on the opposite sides from each other in a historical conflict.

Thus, in neither case do the characters want to reveal anything that can be used against them if they are wrong in trusting the other character.

Frequently, in both situations, one or the other has a background that gives them unusual reason to be mistrustful, either in general or toward this particular character.

Those are not the only causes of mistrust, wariness, and secrecy. There are many other justifications—particularly out of that genre—but most writers give *some*.

The first problem with justifying the secrecy is making the reason, and the mistrust, strong enough. Even if it's very likely that a character doesn't tell a secret in a situation where he might, the more times he's in the situation, the more likely it is that *this* one will be the odd time out. All the more in that the other character generally gives indications of trustworthiness along the way.

For this conflict to continue to be plausible, it has to be a very powerful reason for the character to hold his tongue.

On the other hand, one work I read did bring to bear how weak the reasons generally were. The hero and the heroine had immense reasons to keep their secrets, much more than writers generally bring to bear.

This did make it plausible, but it stirred up another problem. To have the characters' conflicts stem from a misunderstanding stemming from a secret led to a rather static conflict. They kept thrashing over the same things without any serious change.

A one-note plot doesn't have structure. It needs some swerves or changes.

One thing I found more effective, and used myself in *A Diabolical Bargain*, was when the character keeping a secret finds the pressure escalating. At first, the character thinks that it's not much of a problem to keep this secret. As the character realizes more and more what a problem it is in itself, and how important it is to the other character, he also realizes that every time he fails to reveal the secret, he makes himself look worse when it finally comes out.

Another trick, compatible with the first, is to have it finally come out long before the story ends. Generally, it is best to not have it come out by the character's finally screwing his courage to the sticking point and admitting it, because the other character's reaction will trigger the conflict for the rest of the story. But some other means of revealing it will send the story off in a new direction, quite sharply, which gives the story more structure.

Screwing his courage to the sticking point can work well as an ending trope. It often turns out that the other character had an inkling, or even full knowledge, but is astounded by this confidence, when he had thought this would have to go on. But this technique works best when the secret emerged in the middle of the story as a consequence of earlier conflict. A boy is taken on as a student, blunders, lies to buy himself time to fix it, fails to fix it, and goes to the teacher to confess all. The teacher is pleased and surprised, and explains that he fixed it himself, and then thought he would have to work on the boy to get him to admit it. In this story, the blunder and lie are the sharp swerve, and thus give it new structure.

Motives and structure. Those are the two important considerations when you give your characters a secret to keep.

Plot Devices, And Places

A brief note on deployment

If you put in a plot device, especially one you have to downplay because otherwise it would dictate the plot, it's better the earlier in the story you put it.

As a rule. If you put it in the opening line, you will have to ensure it does not catch the reader's eye in the wrong way, and all the rest of the art of downplaying it.

But—if a red-haired woman, with mismatched eyes, colorful full skirts, and a purple shawl, appears out of nowhere and offers the hero a key, so that shortly after, he faces a peril, realizes that the door beside him has a lock very like that key, and ends up in another world—that works fine as an opening, even an opening line.

If the people he meets in the other world dismiss her as a whimsical soul who is unlikely to ever concern herself with his fate, let alone his well-being, ever again, the story can roll on without returning to her, though that depends on the character's temperament. Some characters should at least muse on whether she meant him to play the role he's playing, or she was just being whimsical.

That's not something just happening to happen to the main character of the story, it's how something happened to someone, and thus he became the main character of the story.

This would not be so fine as an escape on the last page from the Evil Overlord whom he's offended.

Even as a cliff-hanger, that's lacking. Assuming, of course, that there's no mention of her earlier, or appearances by her or others like her, or discussions of their capricious choices. And certainly of the other worlds.

As an actual resolution it's deeply aesthetically flawed. The infamous *deus ex machina.*

Even if she had appeared in the opening line, something is needed to tie the beginning and the ending together. Perhaps she dumps him back in the peril, where he can cope, but he's made all new friends and a new life, and wants to return the world she first dumped him in.

But if she did not appear in the opening line, or earlier in the story—allusions might be enough if they were frequent enough, and told enough—she does not work in the ending as she can in the opening.

Where Do We Go From Here?

In the middle

When you are telling a story, you are wise to follow Mark Twain's dictum

> A tale shall accomplish something and arrive somewhere.

A finer point in that, in the middle of the tale, your reader should have some notion of what constitutes an accomplishment and a destination.

A character standing by a crossroads with no signs and a dozen different roads leading off is frustrating. A character where we don't know which destination he wants to end up leaves us with no forward motion.

Even a character whose reaction to what he envisions being in ten years is to complain that he's just trying to get to Friday should give the idea whether he'd be happy in any secure job that lets him hang out with his friends and not worry about money too much, or only in a high-status job with high wages.

Or, for that matter, whether he wants to escape the monster-ridden borderland with a nest egg, or would be happy with just some enchanted armor and weaponry to make the fighting so much easier and more profitable.

No amount of heaping up of adventures compensates for the awareness that it means nothing—though, of course, it is better than a slow portrayal of ordinary life without even the compensation of excitement to mitigate the awareness that it means nothing.

Episodic adventures do not have this problem. Provided that each one has a beginning, a middle, and an ending, each adventure has its own meaning. Even slice-of-life stories can have their own little episodes. Comics may make each comic strip its own unified thing.

True, if the tales are dramatic, not slice-of-life, you do have to juggle why he keeps on adventuring.

I have read a story about a heroine dropped into an isekai fantasy world, where she ended up fighting by the hero, and I was wondering what the end game was.

Neither one showed any signs of wanting to adventure forever. While there was an arguable way to end their battles, neither one showed any indication of thinking that if they just got rid of the central problem, they could happily settle down. Or found an adventurers' school. Or keep on hunting monsters after they dealt with the big one. So where was it going to go?

A character could, of course, fool himself, but in that case, the story has to foreshadow that, so we can see either the unhappy ending where he gets what he doesn't really want, or the happy ending where he works through that and gets the ending he does really want.

No matter how surprising the actual destination is, it has to fit in with hindsight.

If there is no real destination, if the hero has only a nominal goal—one that is transparently a means to move the character about so that he can have more episodic adventures—that may in fact hit problems in that the readers may want to see progress toward this goal and be frustrated at how it never appears closer.

A string of adventures that do have an actual goal needs to show progress at points. Furthermore, it has to feel like real progress. If the hero overcomes a string of obstacles, we have to see his goal approaching. And other characters should react as if something real was happening.

One handy way to ratchet up the tension is to have the mounting success draw more and more attention from the villains, for instance, which also has the handy effect that the readers realize that the more the villains react, the more clearly the hero poses a real danger to them.

The real problem appears when you land the hero in an intentional tangle. In Byzantine court politics, with a love tangle complicating the issues, with mysterious magical spells or objects moving about, whom can the hero trust? How will all these machinations turn out?

Or, obviously, a mystery. All these clues and red herrings? Do they add up at all? As the detective and any associates pile them up do they merely lead to bafflement?

This is one reason why red herrings are often dramatically cleared up. Rhetorically, it is wise to frame it as dashing the detective's hopes, but it still offers a glimpse of light in the gloom.

Then, mysteries have an innate advantage in that everyone knows what the end game is: deduce who the murderer is, and reveal it. Or conclude it should be concealed, sometimes.

In the Byzantine court politics, there frequently is a question of what the main character wants, even before the question of whether any faction would give him it, and if so, for what.

This can land the character in a maze where the reader has no notion whether the character's actions are for good or for ill. It drains tension while draining the work of significance.

It can be a difficult thing to juggle, but you need to keep up the reader's interest by giving him something to latch onto.

Series And Escalation

How to accidentally end an unending series

If you have carefully set up your series to last forever, so that the main character does not change and will want to adventure forever, there is one grave danger.

Escalation.

Romance series are in little danger of it. At most, a late entry in the series spends so much time calling back to the earlier series that the main story doesn't get as much attention as it merits. Not a peril limited to romance, but not actually escalation.

Mysteries do not face much more risk of it, but there is the possibility of demanding rising stakes.

If at first you detect the death of a city employee, then a city official, then a higher ranking official then a city mayor, then the mayor of a larger city, the effect will be an expectation that you will have higher and higher implications for each murder, where each murder has larger and larger consequences. A number of Sherlock Holmes stories make much of the noble, even royal, families, whose troubles he calmed by discovering the truth, and more than one states that if he fails, war is likely to result.

The problem is that after you investigate the murder of the head of state and thereby defuse an incipient world war, what are you going to escalate to? Even if you stick to that level—and how many heads of states can you kill, and how many wars can you stop without overloading credibility—your readers expect rising stakes.

Then, mysteries normally do not have this problem. Since the difficulty of determining the true culprit is the heart of it, it is perfectly normal to go from detecting the murder of a financier to the murder of farmer or even a vagabond. This may be awkward when the drama of implications is played up, but it can also be a deep theme of murder being murder. Let the detective talk about how the day laborer on a farm values his life as much as the head of state, and philosophize.

Or perhaps have the detective talk about how this murder is much more challenging the one before.

In fantasy, however, there's the problem that great challenges for the hero often escalate. First you fight a goblin, then an ogre, then a giant, then a dragon—and then where do you escalate to?

SF does not have quite so much a problem, but still, there are series that go from a conflict over a planet, to a stellar system, to a stellar cluster, to a galaxy.

It is, however, in the superhero genre where this sort of thing gets out of hand entirely. Fight a war, fight an international conspiracy that controls the governments, fight an interstellar invasion, in your search for allies against the next invasion fight an intergalactic invasion, fight an extradimensional invader who wants to destroy the universe, fight him again as he destroys other universes—

The advantage of mysteries is that you can't really escalate highly enough to make the universe they occur in look like cardboard. In superhero stories, conjuring up entire universes in order to destroy them does not make the villain look more evil. It makes the world more flimsy.

Thus, you run out of ways to escalate. If you destroyed a million worlds, their flimsy unreality. existing only to be destroyed, means you haven't really escalated.

Much wiser, whether fantasy, or SF, or superheroes, to keep the stories varied by making the dangers and foes different rather than strictly more powerful, and using such tools as settings to make the heroes' work more difficult.

Series And The Sequence

Reading order and aesthetics

When you set out to read a series for the first time, my recommendation is read in publication order.

Always.

Even if the author recommends another order.

It is not always an aesthetic improvement over any other order, but it's impossible to know that without reading them through. I've never known a series to improve by a different order, and you never have a second chance to read them through the first time.

The thing is that that as the writer writes along, he makes decisions that define the world. Even if he spent decades world-building before knuckling down to creating stories, the stories will influence the world.

This applies with special force for series with continuing characters.

If John Doe and Richard Roe are taking on the world in volume two, and you go back to read volume one, where John Doe, Richard Roe, and James Poe are taking on the world—well, volume one was not written with an eye to the reader wondering what will befall James Poe to keep him out of volume two. It was written with the death/imprisonment/whatever of James Poe being a plot twist, or a dramatic point.

Furthermore, what John Doe and Richard Roe were doing in volume two will give many clues to the reader, and volume one was not written to be read in light of those clues. If they are trying to raise a ransom, or find a wizard to disenchant a statue, the reader can see the twist coming. If they make no mention of James Poe, the reader can see that the fate is final.

Things that are mysteries in the earlier stories turn into dramatic irony in the later ones. For instance, a magical sword made by the villain is an aid to the heroes. They can wonder about it. Later, in a prequel, it is revealed that the villain made it able to cope with different foes according to its use. In the next book, we can appreciate the dramatic irony of how the heroes don't realize that. (Though some writers foolishly let the heroes know just because the readers do. Avoid that.)

The thing is that, although a writer can make something work as either dramatic irony or mystery, it generally works better one way. No matter how much the writer reminds himself, or his beta readers remind him, he can't really work himself back into the frame of mind that doesn't know what he knows. (Re-reading produces a different effect, of course, which is why the first time is important.)

This goes with double force for prequels. We already know how it will turn out, if we've read the prior books. A prequel can not be written both for people who know and for people who don't. And since the writer is one of those who know, it's very hard for him to write a prequel for those who don't.

If the main timeline series saw John Doe and Richard Roe taking on the world, and mentioned James Poe, that means the prequel volume, featuring James Poe, *is* written with an eye to the reader wondering what will befall James Poe to keep him out of volume one and the rest, and those to whom the death/imprisonment/whatever of James Poe comes as a shock are not getting the intended effect.

This is mitigated the further back in time, farther away in distance, and more distant the connection between the characters. Still, it matters.

I once read a book, and then another set in the same setting—thousands of miles away and centuries earlier. Still, given the clues given in the first book, I knew that the hero of the second book would go much further than the book bore him. That, in fact, he was bound on a path that would affect things, with visible and overt effects in other stories, for centuries and possibly millennia to come.

It was still a tale of adventure without it, and at that, I wax philosophical.

A work of art requires that it contain no unnecessary parts, and that its parts fit together so you can't switch them around at random. Is it better aesthetically that a series have a more artistically perfect reading order?

That's a question for the ages, for philosophy of art.

Meanwhile, it's wiser to read series in publication order.

Color By Numbers Series

The unending series and its problems

Vital though it is to have a way to keep the character from changing in a way that makes having more adventures either implausible or unsatisfying—vital though it is to avoid escalating the series until it's silly—the most vital thing for a series is to have new ideas.

This does not mean a new villain in a new setting.

It means a new plot.

Especially in the reveals. If the first two books have an Obviously Guilty Person who is not the villain, the third Obviously Guilty Person will fool no one. If a bit of procedure is explained for mildly contrived circumstances in the opening of the first three books, and proves relevant later, every reader will know it is Significant. But that is merely the aggravated case.

Tracking down the red dragon in the mountain lair and the green dragon in the forest lair and the white dragon in the snowy north lair only works if the different aspects alter the story. If the rocks and cliffs, the thickets of the forest, and the snow and ice do not change the effort of getting in, they are not actual changes. The dragons then have to differ in how to fight them, and how they fight, so as to require new plans.

In particular, you should make large alterations, early, in anything you do not want to keep forever.

This is because you are setting expectations for the series. The charm of a series, causing reader to pick up the book beyond the expectation that the writer is good, is to see variations within the pattern of the series.

If a wizard is sent out to discover what caused a magical problem, and for the first four books, she detects the wizard behind it, neutralizes the problem, and brings the wizard to justice, when the fifth book turned out to be that the migration of the fire lions stirring up the other magical beasts, or even a magical object that has started to act, you have a problem. (Throwing in someone profiting off it does not fix the problem.)

This is like throwing a haiku in a sonnet sequence. The world's most excellent haiku does not fit in a sonnet sequence. A mixed series of different lyric structure, or even a sequence of interchanging haiku and sonnets could work, but it has to be set up from the start.

For the same reason, it is far better to have, from the beginning, a mix-up of different problems in different stories, so that the wizard must detect the cause, deduce how to fix the problem, and determine whether there is a culprit, and what relationship if any the culprit has to the problem, before bringing any culprit to justice.

This is not to say that it is impossible to change and keep going. I have seen a series change like that. One where the character was assigned to a new task and immediately observed she had been promoted to tasks of greater responsibility. But this raises the specter of character change for the main character *and* of escalation, both of which threaten the series with inability to go on forever. Also, it can lose its charm for the reader.

So it can be pulled off once or maybe twice in an unending series.

Or, of course, it could remain a series of unmasking villainous wizards. That requires an endless stream of inventive new ways for wizards to cause trouble, and new and different ways for the protagonists to determine what they are doing, and stop them.

Within the parameters set by the series. Lord Darcy had a good long run in which you could reliably tell that, despite the presence of functional magic, that the murder would never turn out to be magically performed. The trick was novel ways to perform the murder, and novel ways to detect it, including by magic.

Repeating an obviously useful spell, say to detect whether the wizard is using fire magic, or whatever, is one thing. But the knowledge should sometimes be clear, sometimes misleading, sometimes absent. (And our intrepid wizard talks of how spells can be used to manipulate other things, leading to no traces where the eventual effect occurs.)

Likewise a trick that works one time should be repeated only rarely, and it's best if it works only with reworking, and that reworking is not merely doing the same thing only more. The characters have to twist it.

Or, of course, they could fail through overconfidence in it. Possibly even realizing what twist they should have used, after the fact, when the first use burned that possibility.

Even that, despite the series' parameters, needs to be rare if the series is to be kept fresh.

The Series As A Work Of Art

The series as a lump

We've all seen it.

When reading a fix-up where the stories had all been published separately first.

When reading a series in a weekend instead of with the months (if not years) between the installments of books.

Even when reading a collected serial.

Usually the works can, and must, be read as entire pieces of art in themselves (though not the serial), but when read in a single gulp, the series can be taken in as a single work, and often its flaws are evident as such.

There's the inconsistencies. A character changes a major interest between one story and the next, but the series acts as if he always was consistent. Two characters rub badly together, and this is dropped between one story and the next. Characters reconcile their differences several times without any explanation of why the differences came back between stories. A love interest who appeared in several stories vanishes without any of the characters, even the lover, remembering her existence.

This perhaps is forced by an inability to revise what went before, it having been already published, but still inconsistencies are artistic flaws. The explanation does not remove the flaws. (There's a reason why writers sometimes "fix up" the stories before gathering them into the book as a fix-up.)

There's the info-dumping because the series was written with an eye to be read in parts, and thus each piece needed to give all the knowledge necessary. Awkward dialogues between people who all already know everything they say and have no motive to say it again, or unreflective people over-thinking how they got there, or flat out chunks of "What Has Gone Before."

This can lack charm in the individual work. In the series as a whole, it gets amazingly repetitive because whether it is backstory to the whole series, or the prior story being re-told to move this story forward, after you had *just* read it in the prior story. It can reach truly absurd levels in serials, where the installments are so short that the repetition is like hammer blows.

Or, worse, the info-dumping where the writer wants to put in the denouement for the previous books as an Easter egg. When it's read as a series, this is clearer, since you just read about these characters just did, so there is no bafflement, but the clumsiness tends to be worse.

Then, there is the series that worked because when the parts were read far enough apart, you didn't notice the plot similarities. When read thus rapidly, you can't help but notice that the deciding clue in the murder mystery is always the blood splashes. For no good, in-universe reason.

Or that the villainesses are always gorgeous brunettes and the love interests pretty blonds.

Or the common thread of snakes. Or ancient coins. Or obscure poisons.

Repeating motifs is, alas, the great bane of series: the writer running out of fresh ideas. Or perhaps carelessness, where a writer's favorite motifs get reused without an eye to putting a fresh turn on them. (Gaps between writing books can help cause this, by forgetfulness.)

This, of course, clashes with the great charm of series: the readers knowing they will get what got before. Albeit in a fresh, new arrangement. If the charm of your werewolf forensic expert is his ability to work with bloodstains and glean knowledge that no one else can, it would take real art to pull off a story where bloodstains do not feature.

This is why the final limit to an unlimited series is not theoretical but practical. Can the writer keep on coming up with fresh ideas to write about within the series' scope?

Reading it all in a single batch heightens the issue, because it makes the freshness, or lack, clear, by making it a single unified thing.

Sequel Hooks

Setting up sequel stories

A different kind of hook. One you can hang things on. Namely, sequels.

This is not for the sequel that is actually just the next volume, because the story sprawls over several books. There, you just need the dramatic cliff-hanger to draw the readers on to the next book.

No, when you are doing episodic tales, so that resolution rounds out this tale, but you want to do another. Or realize you might. (Depends on the genre, of course. Mysteries do not need sequel hooks. Fantasy and other adventure tales often do. Depends on how final the resolutions are.)

What you need is horizons and vistas. Suggestions that the world is larger than this tale.

This requires a delicate touch. You can not suggest that they are important in the story, or the reader will expect something to be made of them. This is particularly important when the thing is a problem. It must counterbalance the awareness that something is wrong with the focus that it is not what the characters are dealing with, because they must fix *this*.

Furthermore, you must set them up in the middle.

If you bring down the Evil Wizard of Fire, mentioning in the denouement that he was one of seven evil overlords both damages the resolution and draws attention to the Sequel Hook! nature of it. Much better to mention the seven during the course of the story. Ideally, first mentioning the seven and then that this one is the problem, but the story, of course, has other demands.

Likewise, if the next story is to be about trying to restore the dragon's looted hoard to its owners, after it ravaged half the kingdom, this gets mentioned in the course of the story of hunting down the dragon and killing it. Conveniently enough, you can give the hook, in this story, as a reason to kill, and only have it dawn on the characters later what it will mean.

This sort of set-up is one reason why threatening the world is a bad idea—on top of the need to establish its reality and so the stakes before threatening it, on top of having no way to escalate the danger, it makes it difficult to give scope to the world past the threat.

Not impossible. If the characters are rushing to save the world, and the viewpoint character gets glimpses of things that he can not linger to learn about, it can be suggested, with sufficient rhetorical skill. One might even manage to use saving the world as the start of the series and make the rest of it about restoring the damage done by the threat and by the saving.

This would naturally give the viewpoint character motives to move about. It would also help give the world solidity. The mobile viewpoint character who keeps going to new places can keep the story going indefinitely, but you do want to avoid his appearing to walk on, stage right, and walk off, stage left, in each individual story. You can do such a series, it's just weaker.

Hinting at places beyond the horizon is a weak sequel hook. It gives you places to go with the new story, but you would have to motivate characters to seek them out. Which, from another point of view, means you have not constrained yourself so severely, and also that it's easier to resolve this story without the readers' being bothered by the loose thread.

People and problems have more potential to constrain, but then, also to motivate.

They both work at different levels. For instance, if you outwitted the fae peddler when he got up to his tricks, you may face him again in the future. At some point. He may attempt to remove you from where you might interfere again, or just go up against you again, or even present you to the fae queen as the solution to her problems because you're so much more clever than he is that it would be folly for her to rely on him instead.

Or perhaps he could be obsessed with showing you up and appear again and again and again. It may even turn into the series of how the character is plagued by this self-important fae peddler.

Problems work much the same way. If you dealt with a curse that changed people's forms, you may discover the same sort of magic in later stories, once or twice.

Or perhaps you have defined the series as dealing with this kind of magic. Your character has the reputation now, and draws those with those problems.

Such is the juggling act.

Series And Backstory

Another way to end a series you don't want to end

There's a temptation in a series, if you work with a character of mysterious origins.

You do not absolutely require a character of mysterious origins, but it's a far graver temptation if you do.

It is a particular danger if you emphasize that he's of mysterious origins.

Let your wandering minstrel travel through the mountains, stopping at villages to play his tunes and hear any tales of wicked witches, vicious werewolves, or dangerous ghosts, and dispel the evil if it proves true.

If everyone treats the matter of a minstrel as a matter of fact—there are minstrels, they do wander—there's less danger.

But if they start to whisper to each other than he's a nobleman hunting down the werewolf that killed the king, or a heart-broken lover of a ghost whom he had to dispel, the peril looms.

Partly because readers regard this as a Chekhov's Gun, which you must fire at some point. Especially the werewolf that killed the king, which is a series ending matter.

Partly because you can deepen the stakes for the character by making it personal. You do not actually have to be so blatant as to force him to face another ghost very like his beloved. Perhaps a werewolf that escaped his first fight with it, perhaps a giant that tricked him into being on the other side of a river and then tore down the bridge—anything from the past that adds a pang to the story.

Partly because that, in itself, is an aesthetic win for the story, it may make the next story flat if it's just another day's duty. Thus, the life may be drained from the series.

But you don't have to remove that, you may think. You can keep on making it personal.

Ah, but then time questions come up. And coherence issues.

Have you given the character more backstory than he has life to have lived it in? And have you kept that backstory straight?

Keeping it straight can come into play for any sort of backstory, but is particularly keen when dealing with origins, which have to be limited in time and place. You can only have one experience that made you a wandering minstrel to fight monsters, even if you have many that keep you going.

This is far more of an issue when many writers works on a theme. Even in the Matter of Britain, you end up with the wholly human Morgan le Fay. The comic-book universes shows the full horror though, with conflicting visions on top of the endless need to churn out stories.

Especially given that a writer can't just ignore that story told him before him. If he wishes to clean it up, he would have to tell a story to explain it away, and such stories are notoriously weak. (After a time, writers may ignore it, but that introduces contradictions.)

Granted, some characters can manage a welter of back-stories because it is clear that none of them have sufficient evidence to be established as truth, but that has to fit the character. A madcap peddler who keeps selling the party things that help, but only after greatly embarrassing them, or some other trickster.

You have to remember to keep them in suspension.

And if you have another writer working on the world, you may find it taken out of your hands. The problem of shared worlds.

Also remember that readers often take rumors as fact. The unsubtle use of them to dump knowledge is, alas, a known trope, and it takes skill to convince readers that the rumors are rumors.

Contradictions help, but you obviously can not use the technique of introducing rumors that the readers know are wrong, because the point of these character is that their background is not known.

One notes that doling out the contradictions over the series is more likely to convince readers that you are contradicting yourself than that the rumors are wild. At least the first time, several impossible rumors should be given.

Such is the burden of keeping the backstory from dragging down the series to its end.

The Series And The Ret-Con

When you do revise the series

I have talked about the problems with inability to revise series once published.

Now I shall talk about the problems when you do.

In one sense, this is as old as we can trace. Any situation where we have a mass of legends and can follow their development, we can watch things get elided and rewritten.

King Arthur picks up a mass of knights who were always there. Sir Gawain loses his magical strength in the morning. Morgan Le Fey keeps the name but becomes fully human.

Robin Hood turns from the outlaw such that a rumor that he's coming to Nottingham causes the populace to flee in terror—even crippled old women hobbled away on their crutches, as fast as they could—to the beloved hero who aided the poor, eliding the terror of old. Will S- splinters into two or three characters with different last names that begin with s. The era they live in slides about from king to king.

This is aided by the way such matters were not treated as a work of art. If you didn't like *Robin Hood and the Prince of Aragon*—in which a woman on horseback tells Robin Hood, Little John, and Will Scadlock that London is menaced by the prince, who is demanding the princess, and two giants; the three go to London and defeat the prince and giants, and then Will Scadlock marries the princess—you just ignored it. You didn't explain it away.

One consequence, of course, was that the matter was not a work of art in itself. This is why such works as Malory's *Le Morte d'Arthur* and Howard Pyle's *The Merry Adventures of Robin Hood*, where someone pares down the mess and produces a unified, coherent work, achieve such acclaim. They make a work of art out of the matter.

(To be sure, sometimes the odder elements, the ones that can't fit, can be good inspiration. For instance, the change of Bizarro in the reworked Superman to being attempts to replicate Superman that always work out badly, so that he dies within a day, during which he is good-hearted and stupid so that Superman must keep him from doing harm. If you did a story of Robin Hood and his Merry Men acting out the story of the prince as mummers, to get into a place, that could fit in.)

Now, with a single writer (or even a small group) producing a single series, your readers expect a single work of art from the word go. Or, at least, dislike inconsistencies.

Well, not always. L. Frank Baum seemed to get more demands to go on with Oz than complaints, and he couldn't keep the world consistent in two books. *The Wonderful Wizard of Oz* ends with Glinda's sending the Scarecrow back to the Emerald City, to be their king, and *The Land of Oz* has the Scarecrow appealing to Glinda for help regaining the throne and being refused because he had no right to it.

No explanation is offered.

And it is the explanation that changes things from glitches into ret-cons or, for the full length, *retroactive continuity*.

The temptation is that sometimes it works with ease and elegance. Let us suppose that we recast the scene. The Scarecrow asks for her help. Glinda, looking perturbed, says she can't. The Scarecrow cites her prior help. Glinda explains that after that, she was looking at the Emerald City to see how things fared and learned about Ozma. While she could reconcile herself with the notion leaving him in power because she could not find Ozma, she could not bring herself to intervene in a fight between two illegitimate rulers.

(It would have undermined Glinda's position as the wise soul who knows everything, but that would only help in that many future Oz stories only work as stories because they work around her ability.)

Sometimes it's even frustrating. For instance, the Patrician who appears in the first two Discworld works is nothing like Vetinari, when Pratchett first named him. Fans have reasoned that, therefore, that Patrician in those books was Snapcase, Vetinari's predecessor. Pratchett shot that notion down on the grounds it was meant to be Vetinari, by a younger and less competent writer.

That makes no sense. Vetinari, in that sense, did not exist when Pratchett wrote the first two books. Indeed, the first two books did not even talk as if the Patrician was a post with history and different people serving in it. Therefore the later clarity can as easily change which man held it at that time.

The problem lies in that not all changes can be thus easily smoothed away. Very few can. Famously, throwing Sherlock Holmes over Reichenbach Falls had to be explained away and did not work out entirely neatly, because his motives for keeping Watson in the dark (necessary to keep *The Final Problem* coherent) were weak.

The creator of Zorro brazened it out. Johnston McCulley had Zorro reveal his secret identity at the end of *The Curse of Capistrano*. For sequels, he just ignored that he had done so.

That, of course, is better than some explanations. Jean Gray didn't really die as the Phoenix! It wasn't really Jean! She was asleep in the harbor in stasis all along! Entire stories, for years, were dedicated to neither drama nor humor but merely trying to explain the whole mess—and undermining the heroic tale of Jean Gray as Phoenix, at that.

Infamously, we have Obi-Wan telling Luke why he lied, and since it had not been intended when first he told Luke how his father died, it was awkward. (Personally I would have decreed that Anakin/ Darth Vader had fooled Obi-Wan, which also would have made him still more dangerous.)

Deaths that didn't happen, a la Sherlock Holmes, tend to be the worst. Especially in comics—"comic-book death" is notorious for a reason. Long farragoes of nonsense in which someone woke up in a morgue and mixed up the tags to prevent his disappearance being noticed, and then crawled off and lived in an out-of-character secrecy for years to keep the story line going.

This is not to say that retroactively smoothing out the world of your story is impossible in a series. It may even improve the series. But be wary. Be careful.

Prefer short explanations such "he was mistaken when he said that" or "she lied" to ones that require an entire story to lay out.

Ensure that the story is interesting in itself to someone who doesn't care about the element of history being straightened out in it. You may need to seek an opinion from someone unfamiliar with your series for that one.

Above all else, avoid pure wish-fulfillment. There should be costs as well as benefits from the retcon.

One of the most famous retcons is, of course, that Bucky didn't die in World War II. The writer of the comic book version admits he came up with the core idea as a teen, being unhappy with the way the death was dismissed in a panel, but he tightened up the idea enormously, partly under editorial pressure, and wrote an amazing and dramatic tale in which the question of whether it was better that he lived was a serious matter.

On the other hand, part of its fame is that it does so well something that so many writers have produced aesthetic disasters out of. Remember that when trying to decide whether to rewrite your series' past.

Settings

Those fictional creations that your characters move through, in your stories.

The Ancient Forest

What does your character think of the forest?

In most eras, probably he's not too fond of it. As late as the Romantic era, forests could not be beautiful—no natural landscape could be. They could be sublime, they could be picturesque, but they could not be beautiful. Only agricultural fields and pasture, showing the human touch, could make a land beautiful.

Early tourists coming to the United States, for instance, would go from city to city and see the sights at each one, but treat the intervening miles as just a nuisance. If they took a lingering trip down a river, it would be the Connecticut or the Hudson, both with their banks covered with farms.

Before that, the view of forest was heavily practical, and often deeply hostile. The "druid" of modern fantasy is indeed a modern fantasy.

This can be overstated. The worst forest was the forest at a distance. Trackless. Where such tracks as there were might lead you astray, or fail. Where there is no shelter, and food is hard to find, and once you were caught in the open by nightfall, the branches and boughs blocked out the moonlight and starlight, so the clear night was as dark as the stormy one. Where wolves, or bears, or ogres might live. Or outlaws.

Bear in mind that outlaws have been romanticized as well as the forest. The oldest tales of Robin Hood feature such incidents as everyone fleeing Nottingham on the news of his approach, down to elderly women hobbling away on their canes—and the Merry Men killing a page boy for no more reason than he could bear news of their plans.

Nearby woods were more familiar. The one thing absolutely limiting the dread of the forest was that the forest was essential. There you found your firewood. There you gathered herbs and berries and mushrooms. There you drove your pigs to fatten them on fallen acorns and beechnuts. There you poached, unless you were of high enough birth to hunt game.

This produced noticeable changes to the woodland. Paths, obviously. Not allowing brush to prevent passage. Planting the seeds of the most valued plants, and rooting up the noxious ones. Certainly they would not allow dead, fallen trees to clutter up the forest floor and rot away, to the complete waste of all that wood. As firewood, if nothing else.

Coppicing—cutting down a tree and letting the sprouts grow into saplings, and then cutting them down—and pollarding—the same thing, only higher up so it was harder for the sprouts to be grazed—produced many trees of highly unusual appearance.

I, personally, was greatly surprised the first time I read a work about a forest in England where the writer calmly talked about the grass. Here in America, there may be clearings in a forest, but a place where the trees do not grow so thickly that their boughs overshadow the ground too much for grass to grow is not a forest. (And the clearings are often outcroppings of rock, with lichens and maybe a few plants in the cracks.)

Regional differences like that may be crucial to the world-building.

Some patterns are inherent. The influence of nearby settlements will not reach too far into the forest. This will turn on how far the goods they find can be carried. Carts can only go by the (rare) roads, and even pack animals may find the forest floor impassible. Waterways may vastly improve range, but the perishability of each good comes into play.

Firewood can be stacked up by the woodcutter, brought bit by bit to his cottage, and then be brought to the market by cart or by boat. A huntsman searching for fur-bearing animals can fare much farther than one looking for meat. Herbs had best be brought back fresh, whether for use or drying. Perhaps the herb wife lives in the forest to enable herself to ready them for drying. (Certainly once dried they would be easier to carry, even factoring out that she would trim them down to the useful part.)

The relationship to the forest can grow quite complex, and that's even before we factor in any magic.

The Enchanted Forest

Is the forest magical?

Almost certainly. All you have to do is get lost in the woods, and you will stumble on a witch, an ogre, dwarves, a talking wolf, an enchanted deer, a feather from a firebird—

Well, first of all, you might find herbs. This is the easiest one to slither into a story. Genuine pharmaceuticals might be found there, and the magical plants don't have to wear their powers on their sleeve. Though, of course, a glowing golden flower is possible. Or a garnet-red violet that springs up where blood falls.

Trees are more common in modern fantasy than tales of old, whether fairy tales, or legends. Trees you can walk into more than trees than can talk, though you have both.

The great way that trees are magical lies in how you can get lost in their midst. Paths vanish. Trees shift, or seem to shift. (Part of this is, of course, the extent to which forests are strange to modern audiences.)

It is the beasts, however, that truly bring the magical possibilities.

Starting with some that are even ambiguous. An uncommonly large and fierce wolf might start rumors of werewolfry while being merely a wolf. A deer, particularly a leucistic white deer (all the more before genetics were understood), could lead a huntsman all over the forest without being—clearly—magical.

Though it could be, of course. The deer in (some variants of) *The Famous Flower of Serving Men* led the king to a grave and its ghost. Or the deer that provided for Genevieve of Bradant and her child in the forest.

Talking animals raise this still higher. The ghost at the grave did, after all, take the form of a talking bird. Most talking animals are found in the forest, though oddly enough they never seem to surprise any of the characters.

Then, of course, there are those people you may meet in the forest. Villages and castles are less important, though they may not be welcoming to strangers. The others—the people whose cottages are in the middle of the forest far from everyone—there's where things start to get interesting.

Some are beneficent. Best to mind your manners, of course. Whether they are three dwarfs you meet while looking for strawberries in snow, or an old witch whom you just want to ask for fire, or an old beggar who asks you what you are doing, they may be a test. Many a girl came from the forest with toads and snakes dropping from her mouth with every word, and many a boy lame for life, having tried to build a ship that would fly over sea and land, and having only struck his leg with the ax.

If you start to get into legends, or tales of chivalry, the forest holds beneficent hermits who will tell you where you are going wrong (particularly in your search for the Holy Grail) and damsels errant who know where the evils in the land are, and even how a knight might fight them. (Though the damsel errant is more likely to show up at court and demand that the king send a knight with her. Wise. She knows the way through the forest.)

Even in the fairy tales, they can also be wicked witches, or ogres, or giants. And if you get into legends, they may be dragons. Or men armed with magic, and with enchanted castles. Or possibly merely outlaws and bandits, who are dangerous enough.

Just as it might happen, if you and your wife had to travel in the forest with your twin newborn children because you are the Man Tested By Fate, that one child be carried off by a gryphon—or an eagle. A forest filled with magic generally does not distinguish between the magical and the mundane ones.

Then, from the viewpoint of the characters in tales of chivalry, there is no real difference between the gryphon and the eagle.

Magic works by unknown causality. There is no fundamental difference between a willow-bark tea that dispels a headache and the touch of the unicorn's horn to dispel poisons.

And if your world has modeled magic, so it is known causality that differs, it will still integrate with other things, so your characters don't see the division the way your readers do. Such is the balancing act of writing.

Mountains Cross History

Questions about a setting

What does your character think about mountains?

Not, of course, that they are fun things to climb, not until the Romantic era. And possibly not even then.

No, mountains you try to bypass by whatever way is most convenient, which involve not climbing one inch higher than you have to. Passes were crucial. Sometimes enormous engineering projects hollowed out ways through the mountains, taking immense effort for pre-industrial societies.

And still they were an obstacle. As late as World War II, American advertisements routinely had a disclaimer that prices would be higher west of the Rockies, because they were still an obstacle to transportation.

Then, the Rockies reflect the most difficult situation: two regions blocked entirely by the mountains. Unless you took to the sea, there was no way around them. The Alps pose this problem, though the Mediterranean made them easier to evade than in other cases. The Rockies present it in particularly stiff form since you have to go down to the southernmost tip of South America to get around by sea, and the passage there was so difficult that, in the days of sailing ships, it was considered suicide to try to go from the west to the east.

The Himalayas fall between. They cover the area from India to China, and the sea voyage, while more feasible, was not so easy as to prevent the Silk Road and other travelers.

At that, there are stories told of guides through the Himalayas who would name each mountain as they came it, and were startled when white travelers would say that a new mountain was the other side of one they had already named. Their guides just thought of them as guideposts to the ways through the passes.

On the bright side, mountains were protection from foes on the other sides. Particularly if you fortified the passes. Then, of course, you had to man and supply the fortress. Sending people far away, to what will feel like exile, trudging up all the food (because waterways are, of course, impossible as a means to bring it all the way).

There would be the advantages that all the difficulties of supplying them would militate against the attackers too. Any siege also had to lug all the supplies up the slopes.

But there were people in the mountains, weren't there? Of course there were. Marginal though it was, people lived in the mountains. Fewer than would live in an equivalent area in flatter but reasonably damp regions. In places all over the world, they were noted for their poverty, their lack of education, their mistrust of strangers. The problems of travel they generally solved by remaining put in those regions where they could make their living, poor though it was. They heard little news, they had little contact with those outside, they seldom if ever saw books.

They could not be trusted to man your fortress, because they regard you as a stranger, and they probably did not raise enough food to supply the fortress even if you trusted them to supply it.

Being necessarily rough, little of the mountain land could be farmed. Many mountain folks made their living with herbs, furs, possibly timber if it could be moved. (Not so much mining. The association of mining with mountains is more fantasy than fact, though some mountainous regions can be profitably mined.)

Or preying on travelers. The limited ways through the mountains, the rough terrain, and the limited population made life easier for bandits, both to hide from the law and to attack the law-abiding.

The more elegant solution of tariffs requires some organization among the mountain folks, but has been done. Most of the expense of the silk and spices coming along the Silk Road was the cost of tariffs. This would require fortresses and securing the road to avoid merchants bypassing you.

Fortresses would help against the bandits, too, whether you were a mountain lord ensuring that the merchants didn't regard the route as too dangerous, or a king securing his border. Also with other problems, such as man-eating panthers, or bears, or worse problems such as woodwoses and other magical beings. The extent of the wilderness between settlements gives them more room to be a danger. You might even have fortified villages to give you a safe place to sleep.

At that, even in flatter lands, with fewer refuges for dangers, the highest peak was the logical location for a fortress. In such lands, this was not so much that the attackers would be forced to go past it, as that the fortress took advantage of the height to make it more difficult to break in. And still the fortress's forces could sally forth as soon as your main force had gone by and attack your supply lines. It might prove essential to reduce it, mountain or no mountain.

Consequently, mountains did acquire some connotations of protection.

They had some other beneficial attributes. Not everyone law-abiding regarded mountainous isolation as terrible. Monasteries exploited it to find isolated locations, and hermits, too. (Hence the prefix "mona-".) A band of adventurers may have to fare to one to gain knowledge found only in their books.

And mountain air was good air. A late medieval manuscript talks about doctors ordering patients to move to the mountains. On the other hand, it talks about that in the context of "extraordinary care" specifying that the patient does not have to obey because of the extraordinary cost of doing so. Thus the distance and the difficulties of the mountains came to bear, even for that.

Such were the problems of mountains.

The Desert Land

A setting

What does your character think of the desert?

For that matter, what does your character think is desert? Any deserted land—or, for that matter, any unpopulated land, even if it never had any population?

William Shakespeare referred to the "deserts of Bohemia" in *Winter's Tale*. This is not a demonstration of poor geography, but the "sparse population" meaning. I have read a work from nineteenth century America describing being lost at night in the deserts near Niagara Falls. The dense forests of the region made it easy to be lost.

But, for the moment, let us talk of the arid regions.

Officially, a desert is a region that receives ten inches of rain or less a year. Some regions have never registered rainfall. Others get up to the ten inches. The Sonoran desert, the sole native habitat of the iconic saguaro cactus, is one of them.

The odds are good that your character is in one of the soggier ones. Deciding how much water the desert gets is a crucial decision. (And you should then verify how much vegetation the desert can bear at that rainfall. See the above crack about the saguaro cactus, not really found everywhere where deserts are.)

The problem with food while traveling is that everything that carries food also eats it. (Pre-Industrial Revolution.) This is aggravated with water. Basically, armies never went anywhere where they could not get enough water to supply themselves.

As a lone traveler, your character would have an easier time in that respect. Assuming he could find the springs, the oases, and the other water sources. Assuming that he wasn't killed over them. Waterholes are an excellent place for lions, or cougars—or dragons and gryphons, if you are thus minded—to find prey, and desert dwellers hide their knowledge and may kill over the water rights. That problem with armies? That means that deserts tend to be populated with people who are their own law, and jealously guard their water for their own people. If, indeed, they are not populated with people who fled the law, often for good reason, and continue their lawless ways in the desert.

Wise travelers never camp near the water hole. Drink up, fill up your water bottles, and move quite some distance before camping.

Which, at least, should get you farther on your journey. Unless you are one of the few people living in the desert, you probably go there only to get to the other side. Deciding whether the desert is sandy or rocky influences many things. Rocks make better and more steadfast landmarks, but create more difficulties in getting anywhere.

If the travel goes by a reasonably popular route, you may have a road. You may even have way stations. It's one thing to march an army, but it's often quite feasible to build a fort and thus take over a source of water.

Especially if it's not too far from less arid regions. A narrow band of desert is much more likely to have such a guarded road than a vast region of sand.

This has the additional advantage of taking in account years of knowledge, about the danger of floods. Any region that has rainfall at all is in danger of flash floods, because the ground does not absorb the water quickly. Wise travelers will always camp over the highest flood mark they can see. (And floods have a tendency to turn the desert rocky.)

The wall of water plowing down some gorge and carrying everything before it is the great peril of the rainy season. Still, the lakes, rivers, and streams can also add interest. Their water is, perhaps, the important thing to a traveler, but they do enliven the routes. Even Death Valley, with rainfall annually measured in millimeters, has been known to have a seasonal lake.

On the other hand, the very inhospitability and difficulty of the land gives it a certain interest, even beyond the outlaws noted above. The very oldest monks were known as the Desert Fathers, and they were not the only people who retreated to the desert for religious purposes. The lack of other people and of wealth makes it very suitable for those with austerity in mind, and the difficulties traveling there make it less likely you are pestered by the merely curious, and form an initial test of sincerity for those who wish to join you.

Thus, like the mountains, a character can easily be sent into the desert to find the library that these monks have. (With the added bonus that the desert preserves manuscripts.) Thus your character's attitude is more likely than usual to come up.

The Exotic And The Extraordinary

Meditations on settings.

When John Donne wrote

She baits not at the moon.

he did not mean something far off and exotic. Well, when using "baits." He depicted a soul soaring through the celestial spheres, and commented the equivalent of observing that she didn't hit a fast-food joint on the moon. Or a vending machine. The term "bait" was not an exotic, archaic word to him, it just meant grabbing food and drink on a trip.

This was a deliberate clash, of the strange and heavenly, and the familiar and everyday.

Time has blunted it for us.

The fantasy writer has the advantage of knowing that to the reader, the wizard weaving his spells and the webster weaving her cloth are both strange, if not equally so, to the reader, where the characters regard the first as extraordinary and the second literally every day.

One great advantage of the portal story is that the main character finds it all strange, and so it can be introduced to the readers. The same thing occurs when a newbie learns of the masquerade. A toned-down version occurs when a character leaves an isolated location and travels the world.

Which has its downsides.

The first problem, which is the less common, is that mundane world can actually be more fascinating than the magical one.

I have read a judge in a competition recounting how one submission was about interactions with characters in rural Georgia with a fantasy land filled with powerful magic beings, and the writer's rural parts were vivid and filled with interesting details, strange to him, where her fantasy land was pretty generic.

I myself have read a marvelous opening with magical wonders appearing in the vividly drawn mundane city (in pursuit of a man there) have never been outdone in my experience, in part because of the vivid reactions, down to annoyance when a marvel got in the way of ordinary life, but in which the world of magic was thin, unreal, mechanical with dull and life-less rules that were not, in fact, needed to explain the magic used in the tale, and not actually situated anywhere.

The second and greater problem is that the story must therefore work in a situation where someone is looking at the setting from an outside viewpoint. And you can not actually try to convey the strange world and how it feels to someone to whom it is not strange. One who regards sailing by enchanted wind to be normal, or the reign of the king, or the problems with sea serpents. (This is perhaps part of the realism problem with portals.)

When a writer boldly strides forth to try to depict it from within, various plot devices can be used to introduce knowledge of the world, what is ordinary, and what is extraordinary. I used a school and its history lessons in *Queen Shulamith's Ball*. I used a character's reflecting on his situation in *Spells In Secret*. I've not personally used bridging conflict to get things going, but I've seen it used highly effectively.

But in *A Diabolical Bargain* and in many other tales, I had to feed in the knowledge bit by bit, past the characters' lack of need to tell each other it. There were some plot devices, such as a master wizard drilling a would-be student to find out how much he knew. Most of it had to ground up and spread out. At that, most of the knowledge of *Queen Shulamith's Ball* and *Spells in Secret* had to be fed in that way; the plot devices only enough to orient the reader in the opening.

That is on top of the way *Queen Shulamith's Ball* has a major character arrive for the first time at the city where it takes place; *A Diabolical Bargain* has the main character change what he does in a place so as to be talking mostly with a different social circle; and *Spells in Secret* has the main characters moving about (to keep them in secret). All of these were for other plot reasons, but they did aid as plot devices to have knowledge transmitted.

And, of course, for what is ordinary and what is extraordinary, nothing helps more than the dialog. Characters talk about what is extraordinary to them. That they discuss that *Queen Shulamith* is having a ball shows that is extraordinary; that they do not discuss the other balls except incidentally shows those are ordinary.

Sometimes the narrator can slid in knowledge, but that does depend on how chatty your narrator is. What is more important is that your narrator should not know too much about the reading audience—unless that's plausible in story. An omniscient narrator is all-knowing *about the setting.*

Even a narrator consciously helping audiences whom he knows are not familiar with the setting should make plausibly wrong guesses about what people are ignorant of—which is another form of knowledge. In Poul Anderson's *Operation Chaos*, the narrator warns us that he may ramble, and we should hold on for the important information even if we know who won World War II because too much knowledge is better than too little. Then he plops us into a war scene from World War II—and it turns out that we don't know who *fought* World War II.

The stranger, the more filled with wonders and marvels and horrors, the less like either the mundane world or the generic fantasy that we all know, the more difficult it is to throw the reader into the deep end and give him enough help to swim. But it can create works of art like no other technique.

Libraries in Books

And their purpose

Every now and again, there's an online discussion about which is your favorite library in a work of fiction.

Every time it comes up, I answer the same: my favorite library is the one in Robin McKinley's *Beauty*.

This is because every library in a book is a plot device, and in *Beauty*, it has the rare use of having pleasure reading that facilitates the two main characters getting to know each other.

The vast majority of fictional libraries are there for research purposes.

I have a fair number of libraries myself. And they all serve to forward the story.

The Lion and the Library has the library itself front and center, because Lina is desperately looking for the knowledge to deal with the king and save her beloved.

The Book of Bone has Avice visiting a library as an episode in the story, but she's looking for knowledge, not amusement. Plus, there's a curse on the library to complicate her life, which might also interfere with pleasure reading.

Spells in Secret has a complication in that Kenneth and his companions are, indeed, trying to study spellcraft while in hiding. The problem is that while the locations they go to have libraries, none of them are designed to teach spellcraft at the level they need. The assumption being that all wizards who go to these places have already completed all the basic studies and, anyway, can go and fetch books if any are needed.

They do derive both knowledge and amusement from the libraries—especially knowledge of things that are not routinely taught— but more frustration because they need that basic knowledge first.

A Diabolical Bargain has two significant libraries, and in either one, Nick is looking for something to study. In the university library, others are also looking for it. Though, as the title may warn you, they may also find books that were planted for them.

On the other hand, it also joins hands with *Beauty* in one respect. The pleasure reading helps Beauty and the Beast because they share which books are good reads, discuss the art of reading the enchanted library (not all the books in it have been written yet), and read to each other.

Nick talks about his studies with the other scholars, sometimes brushing on what he read. More important, he tells stories.

Characters telling each other stories do not have do so from memory, if that would fit your story better. A scene in which your characters read to each other makes your pleasure library a plot device, and fits into the world and the story.

Genre

Not all aesthetic principles apply in the same way to all works. Some observations on this variation.

The Adult Problem

A young adult genre issue

Sometimes I quip that the difference between the juveniles of my youth and the young adults of today is that in the juveniles, the main character could be an adult, albeit young, but in the young adults, they have to be juveniles.

That's not entirely true. Some YA books I have read have legal adults as main characters. The thing is, they tend to be in the military.

Now, an adult in the military can reasonably tackle more problems than a minor. But a newly enlisted soldier, or a very junior officer, has to have reason to be the person making the decisions that the plot requires, most of which are often far above their grade. Consequently, it hits—

The Adult Problem

The adult problem is the burning question of why, in the situation, the adults (or the character's seniors in the military) do not intervene, so that the driving problem of the plot is resolved, or at least taken out of the main character's hands.

Thus stopping the story dead. Nevertheless, even making all due allowance for its status as a vital plot device, it is unreasonable for the characters to not do so.

The Adult Problem does not exist when the problems the main character faces are age-appropriate. A teen can have to learn to deal with flirting, to earn spending money, not to abandon interests in the name of popularity or trust flattery, or what have you. Indeed, adult intervention may *be* the problem in those cases.

Likewise, the soldier or junior officer can cope with issues in his sphere. Surviving his first battle, bringing back intelligence, adjusting a plan when they find the enemy in an unexpected location—but not the grand questions of strategy that will win the war.

In a story, other problems can arise. Those that are legitimately within the adult (or superior) sphere. If the protagonist's problem is set as "Adults do not know of this, and I must get word back," that can work.

There is some leeway in the face of crisis. Youngsters may have to rise to the occasion because the adults are busy, but even there, some proportion must be maintained. The adults will drop their work to deal with the graver problem, possibly leaving the original problem to the youngsters.

If the problem is not within the youngster's scope, by necessity or by nature, and the problem is not how to bring the issue to the attention of the right adult (or superior), you must keep the adults from solving the problem—somehow. They can be absent—whether for good or bad reasons—or ~~incompetent~~ *incapable* or evil.

Absent gives the parents the best chance of being good parents. The children were abducted, or at least carried off by magic or the like; the parents were abducted, and the children have to rescue them; the parents have to deal with a serious problem and leave the children alone in what (to their best of knowledge) was a safe place.

The downside of this is that it requires careful handling. "Your father and mother were abducted by the Evil Overlord. You must rescue them!" is a much darker and more dangerous tale than your parents having to rescue *you*. Trying to juggle the difficulty and danger has given many a YA work an air of unreality. Pushing the situation into a problem of reasonable scope for a child the age of the protagonist without making the setup obvious is a real trick, but necessary.

When the adult is absent because the youngster keeps secrets, there's the delicate balancing act between the secrecy and the youngster's judgment. There's only so much folly in a sympathetic character.

Also the parents have to evaluate evidence reasonably for their character. You can make them bad parents, or give them reason to overlook, say, mud and bruises, or ensure that the youngster manages to avoid much evidence, but all of that will interact with other elements of the tale.

Military stories tend to run with this, plausibly enough. There are far more reasons for juniors and newly enlisted soldiers to be out of touch with their superiors than for youngsters. Even when the superiors are evil or incompetent, the juniors tend to skedaddle on the pretext of one of those reasons, often well enough to have plausible deniability about the matter. At that, when the superiors are good, there is often the need for plausible deniability if only as distraction. The superiors may be deploying the forces that would be plausible merely to let the juniors have a chance, since they will not be threats as plausible to the enemy forces.

Children are more likely to have incapable or evil parents—who shade into each other in the middle, though the ends are distinct.

At one end, you have the parent or parents who are the villains of the piece, intent on hunting down the youngster, or conquering the world, or both.

At the other, you have a parent enchanted to be unable to notice the problem or lacking the superpowers that are the only way to fight.

In between we have adults whose response to the youngster's suffering assault and battery is telling the youngster to try harder to get along with the attackers—which is why my first impulse was to think of these parents as incompetent.

The merely incapable ones can, in fact, act as a support system for the mission if they are adequately convinced that the youngsters really have to do it, but the incompetent ones have to be carefully handled because they are obstacles that may complicate the plot, and should do so in a way that contributes to it.

The evil ones, of course, just form the main plot, and have a degree of simplicity from that. Still, it has to be juggled properly, because sending under-aged protagonists against their own parents could easily get very dark, and avoiding that can give the work an air of unreality, as in the absent parents.

Any of these three in some combination at least give the genre a solid footing.

Keep On Wandering

Movement and its motives

When keeping a series from ever ending by using a main character who is endlessly moving, so as to logically meet new situations, new problems, and new stories, there is the question of why he is so endlessly on the road.

There are motives that are productive of stories—I am searching for information about the man who killed my father—and those that are not—as a minstrel, I need new audiences because people are too poor to support me for long.

Obviously this produces a range.

John the Minstrel wanders the hills, playing and singing, and stumbles on haunts or werewolves or their ilk, and puts them down with his superior knowledge because he is generous like that, or

James the Minstrel wanders the hills, playing and singing (for his livelihood) and asking about haunts and werewolves and their ilk so he can hunt them down and prevent other families from being slaughtered, or

Richard the Minstrel wanders the hills, playing and singing (for his livelihood), and asks after haunts and werewolves and hunts them down in search of the ones that killed his father.

Likewise, a wizard can be on a quest for a specific spell, or just hoping to find new magic, or merely for the gold to buy a tower. A paladin can be learning new monsters, or seeking a specific one to slay. A thief can be amassing wealth, or seeking the magical jewel, the Star of Fire, that was stolen from his family.

The unproductive one is the better of the two for an interminable series.

The problem with one that produces motives for particular stories is that it points to an end. Find the spell, the monster, or the jewel, and the story ends.

So, what happens if they just do not find what they are looking for?

That frustrates the reader.

Dangling a bait such as this spell will fix this problem; or this monster is causing too much destruction, and its death will end much harm; or recovering this jewel will reconcile this thief to his family—this raises expectations too much. The readers expect the question to be answered, and answered in a way that isn't anticlimax, and thus end the series.

Even if you end the matter by revealing that the spell that the wizard wants is physically impossible, because the concentration of power it requires can not be held for the duration required; that the monster was slain by someone else, and so the paladin can not fulfill his oath; or that the jewel was destroyed by the family patriarch rather than let it be lost—then the story shifts to the hero having to resolve his new issue, namely, what to do with his loss.

Frustrating though it is to the reader to dangle the Star of Fire before them, the spectacle of the thief in morose despair at having thrown away his family's good opinion to recover it only to find it can't be recovered is even more frustrating. And not productive of good stories. No, the thief must soldier on, perhaps in support of the valiant companions who brought him thus far, and find a new motive to live.

This motive will, of course, need to keep him moving in a way that brings about new stories, or else end the series.

The wizard decides that what she needs is to work out a way to carry out the process gradually, spell by spell, and for that she needs a few more spells, which are known to exist.

The thief, alienated from his family forever, realizes that he should not have been trying to win them over because it would have failed. They would have taken the jewel and shown him the door, they were that self-centered. Instead, he should support this lovely wizard in her quest.

Meanwhile, while his specific oath is void, the paladin still has the duty to protect the innocent. He resolves to shelter the thief and the wizard on their way, and guide them into the path of righteousness, pointing out to the thief that he hasn't been stealing from the innocent, and he should keep it that way.

Thus, of course, setting them up to end when the wizard lines up the spells, the thief settles down with her, and the paladin concludes that the importance of the spell is such that he can justly keep guard on it for life.

Oddly enough, the motive that does not produce stories can generally be resolved whenever you are tired of the series. The character can meet the love of his life, and drop the journey. The character can conclude that he has money enough, or has grown powerful enough. The character can find a crossroads where the travelers will constitute a never-ending audience so that he can stay put.

That can be dangerously anticlimactic; the last story needs to be seriously built up to avoid frustrating the reader by having what appears to be an ordinary story of a new adventure end not only itself, but all the adventures.

The one good thing about a motive that produces stories is that it can, indeed, resolve the series in the end.

Faction, Fiction, Forces

Loose in the world

Reading some old pulp stories, I noticed that how many *factions* they have.

Louis L'Amour wrote Westerns that are too slim to be traditionally published today.

Robert E. Howard's stories seldom rose to the length of a novel.

Both of them had four or five factions in many stories.

After their wagon train was massacred, a boy tries to keep going, to safety, along with a small girl and one horse. One raider realizes what he is doing and that that is a really good horse, and pursues them. Two white ruffians are in the wilderness and out to see what they can get. The boy's father and two friends are out to track him down, thus leading to another viewpoint to follow at least. And there's the weather and a grizzly bear.

OR

A barbarian and a woman who begged for his help escape the lands where the barbarian killed their common foe—common for different reasons—but they are shipwrecked on an island. There is a shrine where enchanted statues stand, an ape-man who lives there, and a pirate ship arrives there. (Also parrots that scream a strange word, which fortunately serves no purpose except infodumping.)

OR

A group of people slowly gather at a defensible spring, for protection against attackers, and stage a last stand there, hoping for rescue. The group includes a lone traveler, a couple trying to elope and escape her rich and powerful father, two men who had fled a town where they were strangers and had to kill in self-defense, the posse that went after them, plus an army patrol and the girl they had found after she escaped from a raiding party—a different party than the one besieging them. (It took more than a third of the book to set this group up.)

OR

A barbarian who seized the throne has a conspiracy act against him, and all of the conspirators act from different motives. The spirit of a dead priest speaks with him in a dream, and a powerful sorcerer regains his power and attacks one of the conspirators at a very inconvenient time for the barbarian.

These did, indeed, stretch the arm of coincidence beyond its usual length.

On the bright side, this keeps the action moving. It does require some care to juggle all the balls at once, but things can collide and rebound and produce complications.

(As with conflict between two forces, what matters is not so much how powerful the characters what they want, as that what they want is in direct opposition. What one character, or set of characters, wants must be incompatible with what another character wants.)

Still, all these complications ensued without pushing the story beyond the bounds of a short novel, or even a novella.

This is because the complications are all between the factions, and hence, exterior to the characters. In the last stand, the woman trying to elope realizes that her beloved is not what she thought he was, and falls for the lone traveler instead. And this is the subject of a few conversations, and the depth of internal conflict involved.

The conflicts are therefore sharp and dramatic. Those who want the young, junior military officer to lead the last stand against those who want the experienced Western traveler—no one changes sides, no one has doubts, and the entire conflict is dramatized in arguments and voting.

Likewise, the pirates have fights among their number about whether they should avenge the pirate that the barbarian killed, or whether the barbarian obeyed the pirate code in doing so and thus is free from guilt, but every pirate knows his view on the matter.

Factions can be used in stories with internal conflict, of course, but that's a way of making the story more complicated.

Try to make it more complex as well. The elements should echo each other, reflect aspects of the theme, and have causal interactions. Otherwise it's just a muddle. But if you do it right, you can add a lot to the story.

The License And The Limits

Historical fiction and other problems

Sometimes I philosophically contemplate historical fiction. Not just the problems it elides, but the liberties it takes.

Some people do not mind the number of dukes in Regencies. There is, after all, only one more duke in any given Regency romance than there was in reality. That there are scads and scads of Regencies, many, perhaps most of them, with an additional duke, doesn't change that this one has only one.

After all, science fiction stories have all those different forms of faster-than-light travel in different stories.

Some of us, however, are bugged by it. The SF stories are not pretending to be in the same universe. The Regencies are pretending to be in the same era.

It's not a problem in them alone. The tendency of historical fiction to congregate on small periods of time aggravates it. England's Anarchy, when Empress Matilda and Stephan of Blois contended for the throne, is popular in historical romances, and the writers often have to invent characterization details for them, and for Stephan's wife, also a Matilda, to fill out the story. When you face half a dozen different characters for each of them, I am uneasily remembering that allegedly this is all the same person.

Not that the writer can evade it. For instance, the Emperor Constantine did execute his son Crispus by his first wife, and then a few months later, his second wife Fausta.

Later historical accounts say that Fausta tried to seduce Crispus and, when he repulsed her, accused him of trying to rape her to Constantine, thus prompting his execution—followed by hers when the truth came out.

This is, of course, the same story as Theseus, Phaedra, and Hippolytus, minus the fantastical elements. Yet historians have been known to say that it does, after all, include nothing that hasn't been known to happen, because there is so little else to go on.

But you can't just let it hang. When Dorothy L. Sayers wrote her play, *Emperor Constantine*, she depicted Fausta as an obsessively jealous woman. Finally, she read the story of Phaedra and devised the plan to rid herself of Crispus, as another woman's son, by the false accusation. It's a crucial part of the play and works quite dramatically, but—it is, after all, something that Sayers had to devise to fill in the reasons.

At that, she had only to invent motives.

The story of Suppiluliuma, an ancient Hittite king, despite its drama, has problems for many stories. He received a letter from an Egyptian woman identified only as Dahamunzu—king's wife—asking him to send a son, whom she would marry and make Pharaoh because her late husband had no son. He finally decided to send his fourth son, Zannanza, who was murdered on the way. Suppiluliuma invaded, defeated armies, and brought back many captives—who carried a plague with them. Many Hittites, including Suppiluliuma himself, died in the epidemic.

Ending with an epidemic is only dramatic if you can write it up as a tragedy with Suppiluliuma taking it as revenge from the gods for his folly in agreeing in the first place or some such.

Even if using him as the villain of the piece, the writer will have to make the viewpoint character regard the death as divine vindication or the like.

(I have seen this done. A writer sent her hero after King John to kill him, and King John's actual, historical death shocked him out of his quest for revenge. So I know it is possible. But I have only seen it once.)

Still, in order to weave Suppiluliuma's tale into any other kind of story while maintaining the pretext that it's historical, you would need to invent new history to go after it, or alongside it, in a way that actual history precludes. (Possibly even throw in some functional magic, which would really change the genre.)

Not that history precluding it is much hindrance to many writers of historical fiction. Works on Francesco Foscari and his son Jacopo have been more based on Lord Byron's fictionalized version of their lives—and gone on to change the crime, and insist on his innocence for dramatic effect. Innocence is, as best I can tell, a colorable argument, but Jacopo was definitely sent to the exile in which he died for treason, not for murder.

Whereupon his father Francesco, who had had to sign the order, was forced to abdicate as doge, and died within days. It's a very dramatic situation, and I can see the temptation to touch it up a little and pretend it's the same one.

Some readers will still feel the niggling awareness that this is claiming to be historical when it's not.

Peopling Alternate History

The working out of paths

Those who describe the genre of alternate history as describing what would happen if one change were made, and then working out the consequences—

I notice that very quickly, it would be impossible to simply work it out.

Consider some changes:

- Prince Arthur lives long enough that Catherine of Aragon becomes pregnant with a son

- Catherine of Aragon's son lives, and lives to outlive his father.

- Henry VIII dies shortly after naming Mary Princess of Wales, and Catherine of Aragon marries her off to an English nobleman for stability. Their children carry on the royal line.

Now, what sort of alternate history would ensue from these changes?

Despite all of these occurring at the exact time, place, and position where their mere existence (or prolonged life) would change history—and, in fact, change it enormously—it would be impossible to tell what happens next for long without giving these children all characters.

Since the only one who existed historically died so very young, it's going to be a matter of pure invention, and any of them would have enormous effects, somehow, on the Reformation.

And then there's the ripple effect of the possibility of other people existing, or not existing, to have a role in history and changing things impossible to extrapolate. Catherine of Aragon having a son, Prince Henry is married off to someone else—probably not one of his historical other brides, as it would likely be much earlier than when he married Anne Boleyn. Even a second son is too valuable, especially since he has only a young nephew between him and the throne.

The existence of people who never existed is only an aspect of the alternate history issue, to be certain.

Bring the Jubilee by Ward Moore features a world in which the South won the American Civil War, by winning the Battle of Gettysburg. The issue is not so much the dubiousness of the point of divergence, but that it depicts the North as, basically, having done nothing since the war. The North lapsed into economic depression and stagnated there. (The international consequences, given that the novel starts in 1956, would also be large.)

Likewise, in the *Lord Darcy* series, one bit of potted history comes up again and again, how Richard the Lion-Hearted survived his death wound of our world, and his heir was his nephew Arthur, and how magic was codified in this world.

There is one mention, once, of how a Plantagenet king became the Holy Roman Emperor, and now the heir is always chosen from that line.

The rest is blank. Presumably there's some history about the Americas, which are part of their kingdom now, and how Poland rose to power, to be their great rival, but it's not even hinted at.

It gives the impression of a blank world, where nothing happened. The kings after Arthur are new characters, and they have not been delineated. Neither have those about them, who would rapidly become someone new because all sorts of marriages would be different, people would die or not die at different times—

Actually, the almost utopian set-up of the *Lord Darcy* world adds to this: how did they get there? The lack of history makes it rather bland.

Worse than that, however, is the "in spite of a nail" stories. These tend to be alternate histories spawned by a time traveler. Such as *The Sound of Thunder*, where stepping on a butterfly in the time of the dinosaurs changed who won the latest election.

Instead of, oh, the country being conquered in the last war, and still occupied.

Elections being called instead of scheduled, so that there hadn't been an election.

The time traveling place they visited landing in a new place so they return to a shopping mall, or a swamp.

The Industrial Revolution never have started so there are no machines, let alone time travel ones.

Or a civilization evolved from intelligent packrats, or maiasaurae, or ants.

It's as if everything else was held in abeyance until that election.

Arguing that *most* effects wash out works just fine—there are a lot of butterflies—and both Poul Anderson and Connie Willis do an excellent job of reasoning it out.

But a change in history will either fade out quickly or produce great effects. An alternate history that is actually trying to extrapolate the effects rapidly becomes guesswork.

The Villainess, Live

The console vs the story

There's a popular manga trope.

Heroine plays a romance/fantasy dating game. Heroine wakes up in a fantasy world. Heroine is—horrors!—the doomed villainess of the story! She must pick her way with care because every path the game had led to death, or *perhaps* exile or imprisonment. She has no way to safety except bucking the game.

Many discussions of this trope point out that it's actually very rare in dating games for there to be a villainess. At that, most games that do have a villainess have a path for the heroine to befriend and so neutralize her—safely, for the villainess.

True, one of the oldest games of this type is atypical, and has a villainess, but that's probably not the reason.

The reason is that this set-up works so marvelously well in a story such as a manga or a novel, as a multi-purpose plot device.

It gives an excuse for info-dumping as the heroine reviews her knowledge from the game and compares it to the reality of the world, and hunts for more knowledge for her own safety.

It gives the heroine a problem with vastly high stakes and a tight time-frame.

It makes the heroine the underdog, with the world against her. Often the villainess already has a well-deserved bad reputation by the time the character enters the scene and can do anything about it.

True, it also raises metaphysical questions: how she got there; whether anyone is responsible, and how trustworthy that character is; what happened to the person there before her; whether this is real. Still, you can elide those to just use it as a plot device. (Not always. *Kill The Villainess* does consider how she got there and what that means.)

One thing they also pick up from the game is the love tangle. This is a trope that is actually better suited to the game than to the story.

The game allows the player to choose the love target to taste. Or even re-run the game and choose a new one. After all, the game heroine has the personality that the player gives her. Some games choose one pairing as the true route, and some players are quite annoyed by it. The love interests who do not become the chosen target do not interfere with the play.

This, obviously, does not fit a book. It starts with the additional targets being clutter, which never adds to the story, but on top of that, a character so bland that she could fit any of the various love interests is—well, not unknown in stories, but never a virtue. A situation where the love interests are not varied enough to make the choice between them one of real thematic significance might work in a game—I haven't played them to know—but it does not work in a story.

Then there's the situation where they all represent real choices. The problem with that is that four, five, six love interests all offering a real difference, such that it will determine her future and the story's theme, is that the clutter makes the theme indistinct.

This could be evaded by making them solely obstacles to her life and happiness. This route is seldom taken. (I have heard of a series where the villainess realizes that all the love targets are horrible and sets out to rescue the heroine from ending up with any of them. I do not know how the execution went, but the idea itself is excellent.)

Ideally, she would tackle each obstacle one by one, so that each one would be a different arc.

It would be truly amusing if she were to get help from another character, who was not a target, not even a hidden target, only to find that she's fallen in love with him by the end.

But the plot where she actually wins one of them is not aesthetically flawed, as long as the tangle is managed.

It does hit on the problem that the very reason why so many are offered in the game works against you: tastes differ. Even when a reader admits that the character as drawn would choose the love interest, the other love interest may be more to the reader's taste.

This can be a problem with romance novels, where the other man is often not even really a rival, except in the thoughts of the love interest. A common resort is to make the next novel be about the other man.

Having even four love interests and matching up all three of the others before the end would make for a long series. You would need eight characters in all, and all would have to be developed. Perhaps more if you yourself don't marry one of the game ones—and perhaps you match up the heroine with another character at that.

And all this for following the game so strictly. There are even games with fewer interests, if you want that escape.

Who Are You, And What Have You Done With The Villainess?

A plot hole

I've found them. Not one, but two, isekai where the question of how the heroine takes over the villainess's role in the story is answered, resoundingly.

Whodunit? The villainess!

Past that, the tales are very different.

One has a wizard villainess working a spell for evil purposes despite warnings that the one summoned is a danger to the summoner. The heroine, it is revealed in due course, has magical power; that's probably why she was chosen.

One has a despairing woman trapped in a situation that would push her to the villainy—and the book the summoned heroine had read was, in fact, unjust to her—and who expresses an ill-advised wish in a situation where it would be fulfilled, and she didn't even realize that.

This one doesn't explain why the heroine was chosen, or brush on what happened to the original character.

On the other hand, it does have the heroine want to go back. To what is, after all, her home.

And in both of them, other characters realize that she's not the original.

It is very common for these series to just have the other characters not bother to notice. Maybe with a hand-wave about her suffering a head injury or the like. Maybe not. All the characters, including all the members of her immediate family, ignore vast changes in her habits, personality, ambitions, likes, dislikes, and everything else.

Even if the old villainess completely lacked acting skills and wore her villainy on her sleeve. (And would not have wished herself away and thus drawn the innocent heroine in. She tends to have been so arrogantly full of herself that she would not think to run away. The despairing woman I mentioned is an oddball.)

Yet what we have is people who even only sometimes wonder why she changed. It is an unusual step for them even to think that the character is growing up. (Or he. This requires neither the sex, nor, for that matter, the role of villain. Any drastic switch would do it.)

If they do not think that she was taken over by someone by another universe—which is very plausible for them to not think (though it does make the isekai replacement of the character unusual in that world)—why are they not considering the possibilities of magic? Charming or other bewitchment? Head injury requiring magical healing? Diabolical possession? Doubles? In any given world, abrupt personality changes will have some extremely drastic explanations.

Now, obviously, as plot devices go, ignoring an abrupt change of character is implausible—but vital. Whatever happens when someone notices will determine the story. The character is apt to be slapped into a hospital, or sent off to a shrine, or locked up in a tower or possibly a dungeon if they are certainly enough that the impostor is an evil being. They will send for a priest, or a doctor, or a wizard as the era calls for.

Some effects can be mitigated by having her plopped into the story before the serious villainy begins. If she was something of a spoiled brat but only started to show her truly dark side when her parents brought her orphaned cousin into the house, the change isn't so drastic; she must prevent herself from developing into the villainess.

Another technique is to send her somewhere else, so that those who meet her know her only by reputation. It may surprise them that the rumors are so wildly off, but not so much as witnessing a radical personality change. Also, this would buy her some time away from those who knew her. They might still be surprised, but the change would not be so abrupt.

The problem with both of those, of course, is that they radically restrict the number of plots. As do telling the other characters, and having them react to the personality change as if it were an in-universe effect.

It is rather like the "a tiny mask hides your secret identity" plot device of superheroes: central to the genre, absurd on the surface, and sliding by its convention status because of the centrality.

Experience In The Dungeons

Can this trope be justified?

Off the characters go, into the depths of the dungeon, clearing it level by level. And going up in level each time.

As a consequence, they rise from easily killed weaklings to beings of extraordinary, if not god-like, powers. (All right, god-like chiefly if the Game Master wimps out on the gods. But many GMs do.)

Can this work in a story?

Besides, of course, a GameLit story where the hero is thrown into the world and told it works like a game, or where he grows up in it, and the mechanics of it have always been the way the world worked. Where a thief can cheerfully explain to a wizard that the real trick to improving is adventuring—she went on an adventure, and her lockpicking improved even though she hadn't picked a single lock on the trip.

But can it work in a fantasy world?

One notes it is very unlike myths and legends, or fairy tales either, for that matter. Hercules does not grow in strength in his labors, only in fame. Indeed, even in his cradle, he was strong enough to strangle venomous snakes sent to kill him.

When legendary characters grow in power, it's usually because they have been handed a sword, an invisibility helmet, a winged horse—a *means* of being more powerful.

Then, fantasy can differ from legend.

So, this might work in a fantasy world, but one thing that's impossible is to conceal it entirely. Perhaps well enough that a reader unfamiliar with RPGs can read it and think it a quirk of the world, perhaps even a charming or dramatic quirk, but you can not conceal it so well that a person familiar with RPGs will not notice that it's leveling up.

One hopes it serves some plot purposes in your story, to justify the kludge.

The Powers That Be have decreed it? That those who fight monsters shall be rewarded with the power to fight monsters? That fighting magical beings causes the "mana" to flow free and empower you? While the explanation does have the advantage of brevity, it doesn't do much to disguise the plot device. Even if you invoke the gods, the readers know that the gods do what you decree.

For a more detailed reason, there's always the old "Dungeon as Mythic Underworld." This goes back to the early days of D&D, when all adventures were deemed to occur in underground dungeons. And not just because the underground was where the DM put the monsters.

It was another world.

All the monsters could see in the dark, and your characters needed light sources. Indeed, monsters that started to work for the characters needed light sources.

All the doors had to be unlocked and sometimes forced open for the characters. They would spontaneously shut after them unless spiked open, and even then the spikes might "slip."

On the other hand, doors, unless spiked shut, would open spontaneously for the monsters.

Wandering monsters could find you despite that type of monster having no lairs in the dungeon, or your party having cleaned out their lair. Indeed, they could lair—or wander—without doors large enough for them to pass though. The dungeon contains no visible ecology.

Gold and curses and magical objects abound. Perhaps that explains why the rules to make magical objects are so ill-defined: the dungeon spontaneously makes them as a lure. It fits such a region, and its odd nature.

Uncanny nature, in fact. Eerie. Unearthly. Liminal. Possibly without limits in either space or time, having no known origin or purpose, changing in form over time, non-linear, even non-Euclidean.

Not all underground adventures have to happen in such an underworld, and not all such "underworlds" have to be underground, though the need for paths and barriers limit the possibilities. Still, you can put them in a forest, an enormous edifice—a rocky desert provided the formations can't easily be surmounted.

Then you have it. The sort of place where odd things happen. Having passed through so liminal a place, it would not be out of the ordinary for the characters to pick up some numinous aspects of it for themselves. To grow in power, toward that of legends, would be one element of it.

In a game this can be a bit of flavor, or even utterly ignored as the justification the GM and players don't care about. It can even be an excuse for jovial, free-wheeling, random dungeons of the true old school.

In a story, however, getting readers to care means taking the dungeon seriously, and building up the mythic and uncanny aspects as something felt as well as a plot device allowing for free-wheeling adventures. If the risk of death is real, the characters have to treat it as serious if the story is not to be absurd.

But it does give a fictional reason for experience and leveling. One does note that all the adventures have to be in such mythic zones, or that the other ones can't grant experience. That, in itself, would require a lot of juggling in a story. But it would be epic if you could pull it off.

A Problem With Portals

Convincing the reader

The thing I've found about portal stories, as opposed to high fantasies, is that they make the fantasy world seem less real. More artificial. Less dangerous, as a consequence, with lower stakes because both what is imperiled and the peril are less genuine.

Sometimes you want that for a light-hearted fantasy. Particularly a children's book, which may help explain why so many portal fantasies are children's books. Still, you may want a portal fantasy where the world on the other side is realistic and carries weight, and portal fantasies are less good at that.

On the whole, on average. The use of the same sort of tropes in a high fantasy does tend to import the same sort of problems. In particular, the Chosen One.

Obviously if you send out a magic spell to grab a person and drop him into a land to deliver it from an evil, the land and the character have to fit together neatly. Very neatly indeed.

This creates the impression that the land has been made for the character, as in as tidy a manner as any of the Victorian fantasy lands created solely for the edification of the child who is dropped in it. Even if the character arc is to stop being so self-centered.

There are isekai where the character seems comically misfit for the situation, but then, the character turns out to fit after all. What, after all, are you going to do? Drop the character in, and have the disaster happen anyway? That's no fun.

Still, the feeling of being contrived undermines the reality of the other world. Among other things contributing to the unreality.

In one respect, the isekai where many people are thrown into a Gamelit world handles it more graciously, except that the story, naturally, follows the one with the most effect on the world.

But if an isekai is to feel as real as the best high fantasy works, work must be done.

Something could be done with lowering the stakes, perhaps. A certain school of evil sorcerers has devised a magic that no one in the world can counter. A wise wizard devised a magic to summon a person who can fight it—and whose situation in his own world is such that he will not be missed, except perhaps by the evil characters. These sorcerers do not have to be powerful. Perhaps one cursed seven children for laughing at him, and the newly summoned hero needs only to master the magics to heal them. And find a new place in his new world.

Who knows? Perhaps the wizard casts the spell, and if it works, the summoned person has to figure out what the problem is. One thing that contributes to the "fit together" situation is that the character usually lands where the problem is known, and he is known to be the solution, but perhaps more important, the quest to figure out the problem gives the tale a chance to show the world, and make it look real and convincing—and worth fighting for.

Trickling out history also helps. A world that can deliver its history in one chunk is a problem, even if one character is clearly motivated to tell it, and another to listen. Tracking over the world helps there.

One thing to be very wary of is the Gamelit situation. If the characters gain classes, and see their stats, and other things, it's very hard to be convincing. I won't say it's impossible, because Kit Sun Cheah pulled it off in *Dungeon Samurai*. On the other hand, he both limited the number of stats—if you can't pack the stats in the size of a paragraph you have too many; pages and pages are right out—and, more importantly, gave a reason for it that fit into the world-building. (It does get revealed rather deep in the story, to be sure. On the other hand, it was clearly built in, and illuminates events before.)

A way to increase the effect would be to make the change less intentional. Gates, stairways, and portals lead from one world to another. Pass through, even if you just followed some strangers out of curiosity, and you are in a new world. There would probably be something to make them one way—perhaps a labyrinth to bewilder the path, perhaps something so simple as a door that locks behind you, perhaps something to escape on the other side—though some characters might just want to stay.

A fixed portal might even have an order with its monastery standing by. Among their other duties is taking in those who stumble through, orienting them, and sending them out into the world to forge a new life.

There is nothing like making the character one of many to stumble through to curb the effect of the world's seeming as if made for them.

The Chosen One

Can this trope work?

I mentioned, a while back, that the Chosen One trope can make a high fantasy have problems like a portal fantasy.

But that's not the big problem with the Chosen One.

The big problem with the Chosen One trope is whether you introduced anyone to Choose him.

Who is this person? What is his character? What are his motives in choosing someone? Did he set up the situation to require a Chosen One, and if so, why? How wisely would he go about it? Is he even human? Or a rational being equivalent to human?

The missing parts are a sign of a plot device plopped in the middle of the story, where they are hard to miss. And this one is generally used as a way of evading the hard work of writing.

Why is this character the main character? He's the Chosen One?

Why is he pursuing the Evil Overlord? He's the Chosen One?

What drives him to risk his life without reward? He's the Chosen One?

Why does everyone support him? He's the Chosen One?

I read a fantasy once in which a wizard had, long ago, described who was needed to do something, the main character had been deliberately set up to fit the conditions (shoved into a body of water, for instance), and a wizard in his day asked him (after he survived doing it) to consider his fate as the chosen instrument. He cheerfully explained that the long-ago wizard would have considered such things, foreseeing them in his crystal ball, and set up the conditions such that they would set up the right person anyway.

This is better than most, but it doesn't lean into the issue the way it should. Why did the wizard chose this one? What made him suited more than anyone else? Why does he blandly accept this fate?

Even having him be affected by the thing that he did would have worked better. Perhaps he passed through a liminal region with all that implies. Though it would not answer all the questions, it would clear up some.

Harry Potter being called "The Chosen One" is not so bad because it's clear that someone just dreamed it up. Still, it would be better if someone actually pointed out that calling him that without the idea of who chose him is silly.

This is one of the chief uses of that hoary cliche, the prophecy. The problem is that many people use the prophecy without remembering that it is inspired speech. Who inspired it? With what motives? For what purpose? That's the Chooser of the One.

The more the Chooser of the One stays off stage, the more important it is to depict the Choice as wise. If Odin shows up at a wedding, drives a sword into a tree, and tells everyone that the man who pulls it out gets it—well, it's Odin. He's probably out to cause trouble and war. He's not known as the Necromancer for nothing.

If the age-old sword was destined for the hand of the farm boy, and he defeats the dragon, the old warriors who guarded him on the way can give him a side eye and ask about his fighting style, only to learn that the sword guided him in it, and his lack of knowledge was the only thing that let him not fight against its ancient teachings—perhaps not so good as modern for battles, but much wiser for dragons—and thus was the wisdom of the sword's forger revealed.

If at the last moment, the young farmer's lad realizes that all his companions had axes to grind in the civil war, and that he must act without consulting them because he alone just wants the war to end, so that he uses the mysterious Celestial Pearl—the celestial wisdom behind choosing him is revealed.

Such are the complications.

Historically Ever After

Happy endings in historical fiction

One downside of plotting historical fiction is that, despite all voids that you have to invent plausible and plot-worthy incidents, characters, settings, and motivations to fill, there are also hard historical facts that have to be left in place, because no amount of poetical license will enable you to work around them.

An agent of George Washington, sent to capture Benedict Arnold during the American Revolution, failed. There is no way to rewrite his story to make him successful and keep it historical. (And his cover story for this task had him, and his family, fleeing to the frontier afterwards, with some assistance from Washington to make a new life.)

Or a romance in the Middle East, a Bronze Age king being the love interest. There is no real way to avoid that he would have a harem, and the Song of Solomon presents an improbable conclusion.

> There are sixty queens, and eighty concubines, and virgins without number. My dove, my pure one, is unique; she is the only one of her mother, she is the favorite one of her that bare her. The daughters saw her, and blessed her; yea, the queens and the concubines, and they praised her.

The queens and concubines are entirely dependent on the king's favor for their future, and their children's.

Likewise, marriages, children, and deaths—including remarriages after deaths—are fixed for many figures of royalty and nobility.

True, one can do lesser figures, even adding imaginary ones. But royalty and nobility—besides all the appeal of wealth and position—have far more ability to affect their own lives. And their position did help to cut down on the unpleasant effects of history.

One common solution for this is to *stop early.*

If you write a tale of Robin Hood and put the tale, as it has been put from the sixteenth century, in the reign of King Richard the Lion-Hearted (from being in the reign of an unspecified "King Edward"), you can end your tale with Robin being reconciled with the king and entering his service. You can even make your tale about his clashing with Prince John and helping ensure that Richard's ransom is raised and delivered, as has been done from the twentieth century.

What you can't help is that many readers know enough history to realize that Richard will die without an heir, leaving Robin exposed to Prince John's ire, or at least without a royal protector.

Likewise, if you are retelling the tale of the Man in the Iron Mask, and sticking to the notion that he was Louis XIV's identical twin, you can give whichever twin is the hero a love interest. Perhaps Maria Theresa of Spain, his wife. But if you do that, your readers may remember that later, she was deeply humiliated by his mistresses.

One retelling had the Man be the older twin, the rightful heir, so a conspiracy took him from the mask and had him replace his crowned and incompetent younger twin, who was pursuing Louise de La Vallière. She repulsed him and fell in love with the older twin after meeting him before the replacement. The queen indicates that she is aware of the replacement but will say nothing as long as the twin does not share her bed or disinherit her children, and looks tolerantly on the affair with Louise.

Leaving aside the poetic license of the romance—Louise in fact did not resist Louis's attentions, for instance, among many other things on top of the whole Man in the Iron Mask—your readers may remember how deeply Louise was humiliated when Louis cast her aside for another mistress but, since the new mistress was a married woman, kept Louise about to provide cover for this new affair.

History is full of problems like that, though seldom that convoluted, but it's like having a sequel that undermines the happy ending of your story, and one that the readers read first.

A royal couple rejoices over their beautiful and healthy firstborn son, and the reader knows they will have seven sons, only the youngest of which will reach the age of five.

A king triumphantly unites a kingdom, and the reader knows that his sons will tear it apart.

A lowly knight and his bride take a position within the War of the Roses that win them quiet on his estate, but the reader realizes that the shifts of the war will mean future trouble for them.

Writers who manage to artfully select things so that they work out can be astonishing, though I do note they tend to have plausible but not actually historical characters in historical settings.

Other times, well, a helping of suspension of disbelief helps.

The GM Versus The Writer, Magically Mechanical

The mechanics of magic

The goblins fill the pass behind your party, roaring for blood. The wizard steps on the path behind everyone else, and blasts them with fire.

If you are in a game, the damage is totted up, the goblins fall or don't according to the math, and the wizard's player gets to decide whether to try a stone wall, another fire ball, or an ice storm. Whether they are fire or ice goblins may be a factor in his decisions (including to cast the fireball originally) but nothing more.

If you are in a story—

The first effect should be that if this occurs at night, or if there are shadows from the mountains or from trees about, the magical fire illuminates the scene, perhaps giving the party the first glimpse of the horde's size.

The fire sets combustible things in its path on fire. Even if that peters out, there will be smoke. Enough to smell, perhaps enough to obscure vision (are there more goblins behind?), maybe enough to make them cough. If it doesn't peter out, the party may be running from a raging forest fire faster than they ever did from the goblins.

And if the goblins are carrying any incendiaries, the party, and any surviving goblins, should scramble for their lives. (All right, some role-playing games have such things roll against damage and then explode if they fall, but not all.)

In that classic work of fantasy, *The Hobbit*, Gandalf nearly gets himself, the dwarves, and Bilbo all killed because his fire, used against the wolves, lights things on fire, and the wolves are crafty enough to use it against the trees that are their refuge.

On the other hand, in *The Lord of the Rings*, Gandalf can light a fire for the party, even if it betrays his presence.

Because there is another way—

Well, the light would be hard to explain away. At least, not without foreshadowing. Perhaps the wizard showed his "dark fire" earlier? Or perhaps you run with the light.

The others—well, the wizard casts his fire.

A glob of pure yellow flame hurls toward the goblin horde and splinters.

Goblins scream in agony as the yellow leaps up on them, and fall silent as they shrivel up.

Minutes later, the party stands in darkness again. The clear mountain air about them remains clear. Their torchlight reaches as far, and they can't even smell smoke.

Their guide grunts and tells the wizard that he should have lit the campfire.

The wizard carefully explains that the spell fire would have consumed the log it was cast upon in moments, and then not lit the rest. It is true there are magical fires that set things ablaze, but they tend to ensure that nobody wins the battle.

Also, he can't tone the spell down, so it would have consumed many massive logs too quickly. Not only a waste of firewood, but of heat, because you could not get close to the fire.

Not only can you go with compartmentalized spells like this in fantasy, but you can then go either way: either the wizards have worked very hard to prevent their spells from having untoward side effects, or else the very nature of magic compels spells to work like that.

The wizard explains that kings and emperors tend to be annoyed with wizards who burn down the royal forest, so they learned to contain them. And in fact, normally learn only the compartmentalized spells unless they study history.

Or the wizard explains that conjuring fire out of thin air is of course working against the mundane rules of fire, and the wizard can only designate so much to happen. Hmmm. If you don't want him to light the fire at night, you might have to add that it's not a matter of scaling. Large amounts of fire versus small amounts of fire have to be different spells entirely.

But whichever way you go, what you can not forgo is the description and the reactions. Firelight? Smoke? Setting things on fire? Wondering why this is limited to this use?

The players can dismiss the magical fire as a game effect. The readers need to be shown that the characters react to the situation. If you have dropped them into a situation where the characters are inured to the spell, you will have to show that. The captain cynically thinks that the wizard didn't get half of the horde that old Tabitha used to get, perhaps.

The mechanics of magic are, in fiction, the plot devices. The writer needs to artfully disguise their status with rhetoric in a way that the game master doesn't.

Style

And what are all these ideas without their being conveyed to the reader? Some points on how to do so.

It Figures

Genre and language

One thing to be wary of, in any genre, is the use of language that is meant to be figurative in a context where it could be taken literally.

By the readers, that is. If your hero tells a companion automaton that his heart is broken, that the automaton offers to fetch him a new one from the storeroom—of finest ruby, too!—is a moment of comic culture clash.

Saying of the automaton that his heart was broken—except in situations where it is very clear whether he needs someone to run to the storeroom and back with all speed, or he has fully realized why humans refer with such language to emotional trauma—does not work.

Neither does having a character have "his hand on his chin and his eyes on the gun before them." That is the wrong place for metonymy; put his actual *gaze* on it.

But that this can be an issue for mundane writers does not mean that it is the same across all genres.

I have heard of a writers' group, half mundane, half fantastic, where the second group, including the professional writer presiding, found the phrase "snake train" baffling. The first group thought it obviously that it mean the train moved sinuously, like a snake. What else could it mean?

It could mean that this was the train that the snakes took—intelligent snakes, or there was a reason for shipping snakes about. It could mean a train run by intelligent snakes. It could mean that the train went to the area noted for snakes, which could even be mundane. It could mean that the train itself was a genetically or magically engineered snake.

The grave problem is, of course, that when you open up a story that isn't hemmed in, because it's in a fantastic genre, all metaphors could be literal. A baby found under a lilac tree might be a foundling, but might just have come from the lilac tree.

There's always the quick signaling that this is a generic sort of fantasy, with mankind and elves and dwarves and dragons, and all the rest of the baggage, but while those writers have made it easier for themselves, they have made it harder for the rest of us.

I particularly noticed it when I was reading one of Patricia McKillip's works. She writes with a lovely, lyrical style. And similes. Many, many, many similes.

In a work where a major character is confused about whether she was really a human child, or had been fashioned out of wax by another character, and this is a reasonable confusion, this is an important way to distinguish between what really was possible, and what was only a comparison in this world.

You may wonder how long this has to last. After all, the tone of the setting has to be set. Once it's established that this is a world where children can be formed out of wax rather than (really) found under lilac bushes, or (really) brought in the doctor's bag, the readers won't be confused by a metaphor.

The thing is that you have also set the tone of the style. It's easier to shift it than to shift the rules of the world, because it does not dictate things, but it's not unbounded.

If, after all the queen's efforts to form a child out of wax, it turns out that the doctor just brought a heir to the throne in his black bag, and now the king won't repudiate his wife, that throws the whole story out of whack. Without going to back and revising in that this way of finding a child also works, it will fail.

But if the story opens with chunks of wax, as lifeless as snow, spreading over the table, and ends a rosy and golden dawn (literally the newborn princess) taken from the doctor's black bag, it takes real art to pull off the change in voice.

What's In A Name?

Monsters and language

In the deep woods, a creature enters the scene. A rabbit, it seems, but it has antlers like a deer, fangs, and wings.

Ah, a wolpertinger, you say.

But no, the author comes along to inform you that this beast is a jackalope.

blink, blink, blink

Jackalopes are creatures of the plains, like the jack rabbit (actually a hare) and the pronghorn antelope that it is a chimera of. Furthermore, it has the horns, and only the horns, on the jack rabbit body.

Unfortunately you get this quite a bit in fantasy fiction, what with the people who call winged horses "unicorns" or "hippogriffs" or worse.

Indeed, I once surprised a woman who saw a book where the title referred to a manticore, and the cover showed a chimera, by explaining that the manticore was a proper manticore in the story, AND the story actually had a proper chimera, appearing in a scene very like the one depicted.

This sort of confusion is not even very recent. I have read people blaming RPGs for the belief that a lamia is part snake rather than the mythological part lion, but there are artworks as far back as the Pre-Raphaelites showing a lamia as a snake woman. (Indeed, there are jumbles, if not that particular one, as far back as we can determine.)

You don't want to call a rabbit a smeerp, as the saying goes. Likewise, you don't want to call a wolpertinger a smeerp, or a jackalope. Or a jackalope a wolpertinger.

This is complicated by the way the legendary creatures slip, slid, will not stay in place. Is a cockatrice a serpent, or a wyvern with a rooster's head?

Nevertheless, you want to call the monsters by their rightful names. Failure will annoy readers—some at the time, some when they discover that the name they picked up from your work is wrong.

(If the monster is strange to the characters, you may get away with it. Have them pick a descriptive name based on its most obvious traits. A fire lion. A golden bird. A horned rabbit. But it would have to be strange.)

This is another reason to limit the number of monsters, on top of unity of monsters. If you introduce a term every other page, the reader will have trouble keeping track of them.

The real problem arises when you hit on situations like that of the lamia—snake or lion—where the monster has grown confused. I have run across a person who said that everyone knows what fairies look like.

The truthful and accurate description is that fairies look like humans of every size from tiny to gigantic, that they frequently have such deformities as feet that are on backward, tails, and pointy ears, but they never ever have wings. Even the smallest of fairies would fly on dried yarrow stalks rather than by wings. (Plus, of course, the tendency to use glamour, which would result in their appearing however they liked.)

What this person meant, however, was that the fairies were small and had butterfly wings, per Victorian pictures. That is very far from the folklore.

You do the best you can. Sometimes you can use a more obscure name—fae, perhaps—or a different spelling, such as faery. Or one of the euphemisms. I went the euphemism route myself; in *The Princess Seeks Her Fortune*, no one talks of the fairies. They talk of the lords and ladies, and so thoroughly that men and women are noblemen and noblewomen, instead.

Likewise, a dragon can be a drake or a wyrm even within European tradition.

Sometimes that does not work. There are no other terms, or the other terms have also have inaccurate baggage. (Historically, gnomes are actually more associated with earth and rock than dwarves are, but that is little help to the writer. As for kobolds, RPGs have stepped in, and nickels will just baffle readers.)

Sometimes, you just have to put your part-lion lamia on the page, and realize that those who think that you are wrong because of it are just something you have to live with.

Perhaps you can help spread the knowledge of the old, deep lore about monsters.

Dialect Do's and Don'ts

Mostly don'ts

Ah, dialects. The subtle variants in phrasing, pronunciation, and vocabulary, which can range from mild shades to "only a linguist would not say that this is a different language."

The reason why, having forged into the mountains to find out what this mysterious trow is, you get to fight a plain old ordinary troll. A tough fight, I grant you, but the big mystery that they sent you after was that the dialectal term for "troll" is "trow." (True in the Shetland Islands, by the way)

Avoid in your writing. Not quite at all costs, but unless it adds to the story, avoid it. Even when it adds to the story, it detracts from it as well, by making it more difficult for the reader to understand what is being said. Unless this is put into the story as the characters' difficulty, it pushes against the effect of the story, and even when the characters echo the reader's thoughts, it's frustrating.

This goes double for high fantasy and SF, because in other genres, you can rip off a dialect from real life. It takes a careful ear and a lot of work to pull it off well, but it can be done.

In those genres, however, you have to be careful indeed to avoid calling back to a real-life dialect. Unless you want to raise questions about why your extraterrestrial colony speaks Cockney.

If you want to convey that a character speaks differently, it is wiser to resort to unusual grammatical patterns. (This can also be useful to convey an accent.) Ursula Vernon used it well in *Castle Hangnail,* where Cook is speaking always in the present tense and is using the progressive voice in contexts where typical English speakers are not using it. Arranging your sentence order can also have a vivid effect.

If it is essential to show that the pronunciation is different, and makes it hard to understand, it may be wise to use a sound shift. Perhaps the dialect pronounces all S's as Z's. I have seen very effective uses of such shift, and also watched while the writer subtly toned down what was first unintelligible until finally only one sound shift was used, because the characters grew better and better at fathoming it.

(It helped that at one point, they sang to a child to calm her, and when she sang the next verse, already knowing the words let them decipher them. But that turned on a common historical culture.)

I note that you should never ever use phonetic spelling in a first-person account unless it is clearly an oral retelling. *You* think that the character says "Zally," but that's just a reflection of *your* dialect. From his point of view, he's just saying "Sally"—it's no odder than his saying "iland" instead of "isssland." This does indeed give a problem when strangers come through and refer to her as—well, how do you indicate "Sally" is pronounced with an S? Any more than that "island" is pronounced without one?

Dialectical words are the hardest things to use. If your characters talk to those who speak of haunts, or even haints, rather than ghosts, it adds to the dialect, but violates the wise old rule about not calling a rabbit a smerp. Multiplication of terms for the same thing adds confusion, and it's hard to pull off in a way that adds depth to recompense for it.

Lesser used synonyms may help—do your characters speak of *schools* of fish or *shoals* of fish?—but a lot of terms have no real synonyms in standard English. It's dialectal (real or invented) or nothing.

It's especially hard if you want to use it to create communication problems. (The alternative being local color. Local color definitively helps with stories by making their settings real, but it helps best when it's not confusing.)

The thing is that using *one* term for the problem betrays at once that the term is significant.

On the other hand, using enough terms to lose the problem one in the clutter makes the story confusing for readers.

It's a problem. I'm not sure it's a soluble problem in the general case.

There is nothing for it except to wrestle with it in your particular story and see what can be done.

Lumping And Splitting The Lore

What was that thing?

I have seen people wondering why every culture has a dragon.

Wonder no more.

It's because every vaguely reptilian creature gets labeled a dragon.

Partly this is an element of translation: turning oni, rakshasa, and trolls into ogres may be defended as translating the term like the rest of the words in the original. Too many foreign terms, and the ability to memorize them all is swamped.

Still, it does lead to problems. Rakshasa may feature in fairy tales as ogre-like creatures, but they do tend to be the most powerful of all four. (Especially in tales outside of the fairy tale set.) Trolls are far more likely to be beneficent, or at least kindly, than ogres. Oni have weather powers and can be driven off by throwing beans.

(As a side note, because this is folklore, there can then be drift. The *fenghuang* was immortal. Simply immortal. Then it became the "Chinese phoenix." Stories about how a phoenix grew old, made itself a nest of spices, and burned itself alive to regenerate its youth were apparently too cool to avoid picking it up. But this applies to your world-building only if your creatures are folklore, not for real. If they are for real, you can just pick the one you want.)

But even within a region with common folklore, there is the question of whether a pixie is the same being as a pisky, a pixy, a pixi, a pizkie, a piskie, or a pigsie. Is it just dialectal terms for the same being? Are there regional difference for some or all of them? If there are regional differences, are they large enough to draw a distinction?

The last question is where the distinction between lumpers and splitters arises. The terms are much more widespread, indicating all sorts of scientists who prefer to put more things in bigger and fewer groups, or fewer things in smaller and more groups.

Role-playing games go for splitting. Every difference in stats is, if not a different monster, a different subtype of the monster.

This is less likely in folklore, which can go either way from it.

Frequently, the being is not a type at all, but a unique and named being: the Cauld Lad of Hilton, Jennie Greentooth, or some other specific being.

But once you get past that, there can be specific names for specific types of beings, but they tend to be vague, and general, and very different. You could not draw up a stat block and manage to encompass it all.

I recommend going for lumping.

For one thing, it helps with the problem of making them all different. Perhaps *this* fae lives in households, and *that* one in the forest, and *this other one* lives in the marshes and tries to mislead travelers with its lights.

All right, that's a little loose. Most cultures would distinguish between a pixie who confuses your path; a brownie who does household work and must given milk but no clothes, to avoid insult; and a redcap who haunts old castles and will murder you to keep his cap red with blood.

But within such broad strokes you can lump. It may even be wise to have the terms be unrealistically uniform—after all, having your characters have to wade through dialects is a pain whatever they talk about—even as your characters ponder how the redcaps of the plains differ from those of the hills, and those from the ones of the seashore—or, for that matter, among themselves—because those differences are crucial.

Whether you do opt to use the terms broadly or narrowly, ensure that the characters know about that, sometimes even before they reach the region.

Remember how sheltered Bilbo Baggins knew how a dragon's undersides are somewhat tender. In many RPGs, characters are blindsided by the traits of monsters they meet.

Realistically, they could know through tales what the monsters are like, and how they are vulnerable. That a redcap, regardless of region, needs to keep its cap red with fresh blood or die. That being pixy-led can be undone by turning an article of clothing inside out.

They could also know that you have to stop by the tavern and fish for stories to find the details of the local monsters. Possibly even if their knowledge was sufficient normally. This would apply regardless of the terms. They would know that either the Cauld Lad the peasants talk of is a unique being, and they should fish for knowledge, or that this region had redcaps, but that's not to say that they have to be like redcaps in the lands they came from.

Finally, if neither of those worked, they would know that, and they would have at hand a lot of magic, or whatever other technique, devised to exactly test *this* monster, given the known variability. (RPGs have unrealistically few ways to glean the vulnerabilities of monsters, given how many oddball vulnerabilities the monsters have.)

Perhaps they even document these things, noting that the Cauld Lad was a ghost; that the redcaps of the shore can live off shore-birds as well as humans; and what are called pixies in the marsh are, in reality, not true pixies but will-o-wisps filled with malice. Depending on whether it is helpful to the story. Tracking down old lore is an old story technique.

Then the characters have to consider whether the writer was a lumper or a splitter.

Style And Semantic Drift

Old words and old meanings

I've recommended old books for your style. Picking up the vocabulary and sentence structure of old helps write in a "timeless" style that at least does not smack of your exact year while you are writing in a historical era, or a far-distant future, or a high-fantasy world where you are no longer in the fields we know.

Some vocabulary changes are easy if you have the words. Obviously, some are important because they tie into world-building. You should speak of a kingdom's subjects, not its citizens, since it is not a republic. Your hero should court his sweetheart, not date his girlfriend.

But even when you are not world-building and suggesting the changes by your words, it is wise to use older words. Your characters should not say, "Okay," but "All right" or some such. They should not speak of data but of knowledge.

Should they speak of information?

Ah, that's where the fun really starts. Would your characters think of information as you do? Or would it still be colored by the usage that correlates to "informer"—which still means a sneak who passes information secretly to people, especially to the police?

Obscure, archaic, or obsolete words do not have this problem. If you write of a farrier, you may baffle readers, particularly if you provide no clues to hint that he's a fitter of horseshoes, but you will not mislead them. Misleading is the grave danger.

For instance, suppose you run across a reference to "ancient." Let us suppose it is in Edmund Burke's speech on conciliation with America:

> we wholly abrogated the ancient government of Massachusetts

Now, nowadays I do not think anyone would describe Massachusetts as "ancient" even with the addition of a century and a half, but it was ancient at that time. Indeed, I have run across references to "ancient" practices that were instituted within the lifetime of people still alive.

Loaded terms are particularly fraught with danger. Take Ivan the Terrible. At the time when that became the standard translation of his byname *grozny*, "terrible" still meant "inspiring terror." "Formidable" would be a more reasonable term nowadays.

Many terms meaning high praise have now come to mean insults. I suspect envy, but the effect is nevertheless there. You can not use "condescending" to mean "gracious to those in inferior positions" or "specious" to mean actually attractive, instead of only apparently so.

When talking of the Fair Folk, many people talk of the Seelie Court and the Unseelie Court. This remains in a regional spelling because the alternative of Silly Court and Unsilly Court conveys the wrong idea entirely. At the time it was originally used, it mean the Holy Court and the Unholy Court.

This is, on the whole, a bad thing because it makes language less useful. It blunts fine distinctions so that the writer must express in many words what could have been said in one without it. I recommend C.S. Lewis's *Studies in Words* to look at the prolonged decay of words. (Not all of them. Some have useful meanings to this day.)

As writers, sometimes we can put up a struggle for a distinction before it's lost.

> If the changes we fear be thus irresistible, what remains but to acquiesce with silence, as in the other insurmountable distresses of humanity? it remains that we retard what we cannot repel, that we palliate what we cannot cure. Life may be lengthened by care, though death can-

> not be ultimately defeated: tongues, like governments, have a natural tendency to degeneration; we have long preserved our constitution, let us make some struggles for our language. Samuel Johnson

Alas, some distinctions are lost to us. We must sigh and go on, paraphrasing to try to get the timeless effect without confusing our readers.

Or So He Said

How to indicate speakers

I still see memes with long lists of said-bookisms. Even though the memes don't accumulate enough to write a book, I think I shall discuss the gentle art of attributing speech to characters.

A "said book" is a book simply consisting of a long list of synonyms you can use for "said." In the sense that using the term does not actually make the sentence grammatically incorrect, not that it's a good idea, nor even that the term actually makes sense in context.

On the whole, the word "said" is all but invisible. You have to really belabor it to make it noticeable to the reader, generally in dialog-heavy passages. But for those passages—

The first rule, if you choose to alter the term, is that you must not use any word that is not actually a synonym for "said." This rules out

"That's unexpected," he frowned.

You can not "frown" anything audibly.

If it's important that the readers know he's frowning while he says it, you need

Frowning, he said, "That's unexpected."

If it's not so important, you can hang it in a sentence before or after. (More on action tags later.)

On the actual synonyms, it's wise to be chary, because a passage of dialog with only the "said" changed out in every single line draws attention even more blatantly than using "said" in every one. Still, the synonyms have their uses.

On the whole, it's better to favor those that describe something a viewpoint character could experience directly. Which is to say,

"That's unexpected," he whispered.

works better than

"That's unexpected," he answered.

A viewpoint character can hear the whisper, but "answer" is a logical deduction of intent from its position in the conversation.

Still, play it by ear. There's times when even the synonym that describes intent fits the passage better.

Hanging an adverb on the "said" can also shake things up a bit to avoid monotony, but do not do this except when the adverb is useful in itself. In

"That's unexpected," he said slowly.

the adverb also conveys his tone, and adds some conviction to his words.

Sometimes, especially in passages where there are two speakers, you can just omit it. It's important not to confuse the reader about who's speaking, though.

"I checked the third engine," said Joan.

"How's it doing?" said Horatio.

"Running a bit rough."

"That's a possible problem. I checked the supplies, and we're a bit low on the lubricant."

Having one character address another can also work:

"Horatio, what's the reading?" said Joan.
"That's unexpected. It's exactly what it was an hour ago."

Now, characters in fiction address each other by name much more than would be realistic in real life. That such references can also clue readers in what the names are, and who is where is another influence. Still, don't overdo it; it's invisible only for small amounts of unrealistic use.

The real workhorse of the said-substitutes is the action tag. The character does something before, after, or while speaking. This not only clues the reader into the speaker, it grounds the speech, making it seem like it takes place somewhere real.

The convention is that paragraphs hold not only the speech of a character, but his actions.

> "That's unexpected." John scowled.

links the tag and the speech, where

"That's unexpected."

John scowled.

"Well, it is."

in a two-person situation tags the other character as the speaker as clearly as if John had said something.

If it's important that the readers know that the speech and the action occur simultaneously, the action tag by itself does not work because it's a separate sentence. You must hang it off "said" or one of its synonyms.

> "That's unexpected," John said while turning some gauges.

Emphasis may call for

> While turning some gauges, John said, "That's unexpected."

Or even

> John turned some gauges, saying, "That's unexpected."

One place where greater care than usual is needed is when you mix up the page by adding actions from characters, or things, that aren't speaking. This is not to say it's unwise. It adds greater conviction and realism to the setting. If there's a moment of silence, what the character actually experiences will be the bird song outside, the ticking of the clock, or the breeze and the way the sunlight on the carpet vanishes and returns as the breeze blows a cloud by. A writer can even chose those for symbolic elements—but he does have to return to the issue of telling who said what, using one, or all, of these techniques.

Using any one of these for too long in a passage heavy with dialog will draw attention to it. Mix 'em up and let them make the page less monotonous.

Whom Do I Have The Honor of Speaking To?

The style of names.

Once you named your characters, you aren't out of the woods.

How do people refer to each other?

If they each have one name, or one nickname, and everyone calls everyone else by it, and refers to everyone else to other people by it, you have simplified your task, and defined a lot of your world. Perhaps you did not realize it, but addressing one another has a whole slew of systems that relate to a lot of social issues.

You probably want to choose a somewhat simple one to avoid confusing your readers. But a system with a few complications can be worth it. Having your viewpoint character refer to the other characters as he thinks of them—and thus changing, if necessary, when the viewpoint changed—can add a great deal to a story.

The way Alfred addresses Bruce Wayne as "Master Bruce" is not just old-fashioned. It is the appropriate form of address from a servant to a child of the family, and it is permissible for an old retainer to continue address the now-grown child as such. Witness in *Jane Eyre*, where Jane speaks to the servants:

> "I telled Mary how it would be," he said: "I knew what Mr. Edward" (John was an old servant, and had known his master when he was the cadet of the house, therefore, he often gave him his Christian name)—"I knew what Mr. Edward would do;"

Thus, it indicates both that he's a servant, and that he has the advantage of age.

Readers will not always pick up on such things, but you want to get them right, or at least consistent. With the real world as well with each other. I have read manwha where the main character, a woman of noble birth, is addressed as "lady" and it makes me flinch a little; proper address would be "my lady" or "Lady Name" unless you have a taxi driver going "Hey lady," or the like.

(I once heard a writer talking of her frustration of trying to track down how peasants would have addressed each other in medieval Italy. The modern day "signore"—*lord*—struck her as improbable. She ended up evading the issue.)

Above all else, you want to avoid the *Pirates of the Caribbean* situation. In scenes, the trilogy handled address as a matter of delicacy and with historical accuracy, to great effect. That Elizabeth and Will knew each other as children is the sort of thing that would lead to addressing each other by first name—except for their social differences, hence "Miss Swann." The way Gibbs knew her when she was young and he was subordinate shows in the way he addresses her as "Miss Elizabeth"—like "Master Bruce." "Captain Swann" when Captain Jack Sparrow voted for her. And then "Mrs. Turner" at the end.

However—between those scenes, *everyone* just called her Elizabeth.

Don't do that. You need to carry through.

In whatever rule you are using. Even if it's an imaginary one. Especially if it's an imaginary one. You should devise it to show off social status and personal relationships in the most effective way that does not betray its plot device nature.

For instance, a less formal address can indicate contempt—you are beneath politeness—or closeness—we are too close to use formality. But even less formal address may go by rules. Note that no one calls Sherlock Holmes Sherlock except his brother Mycroft. Holmes and Watson show how close they are by not referring to each other by title, only by last name. Deft handling is needed to indicate it properly.

Genevieve Cogman uses this in her Invisible Library series. The generally-Victorian-era detective Vale calls Irene "Winters" when he's on good terms with her—out of respect for her intrepid conduct in adventures—and "Miss Winters" when he's annoyed.

That, of course, shows off some quirks of his nature, because he is addressing her like a man. G.K. Chesterton observed that the Bright Young Things of his day casually called anyone by first name, and missed out the delight of being asked by a lady to call her by her first name, instead of "Miss Lastname", indicating that you had entered her circle of close friends.

This is all the more fun in that etiquette like this is something you have to carefully slither into the story, because it's a rare character who needs instruction in a way that makes info-dumping easy. But it has its many uses, down to doing its own info-dumping, when you introduce characters and tell volumes by how the others address them.

I Just Made The Door Red

Details and what they say

I once was in an online discussion where one writer said, rather sulkily, that he had just made the door red because it was his favorite color, and that it didn't mean anything.

Well, he may not have meant to mean anything, but that does not prevent its meaning anything.

If your hero calls another character a dingbat, it will characterize him whether you mean it or not.

Likewise, just making the door red still will raise questions.

Why did you make the door red?

Why did you give its color rather than refer to it just as a door?

Why did you mention the door at all? Doors are commonplace enough to pass notice.

Sometimes, of course, the answer is simple. "Take the third door on the left. It's red."

Even then, if the character walks into a blandly white corridor, with blandly white doors marking the way, that red door will stick out. One admits that if it's likely that many people will be directed there, painting it a different color makes directions easier. On the other hand, there may be just a twinge of question. Of —why not blue or green, or other vivid color?

Then there's the house where the roof is purple, the trim is blue, the walls are green, the windows are yellow, the porch is orange, and the door is—red.

Much depends on whether the houses about are likewise vivid (whether this is the only one with an actual red door, or the paint used is uniform in this town) or this house is the eccentric loner in a more subdued town.

It is also important whether this is surrounded by houses smaller than it, or the same size. A larger house may indicate the classic financial difference between a lunatic and an eccentric.

Then, if you come to a village, and all the houses are neatly white with brown doors and gray slate roofs, and one door is red though the rest of the house appears the same as the rest, you know something is odd. You would know it if the door were black, or green, or blue, as well, but then red has a certain punch that the other colors lack.

What, of course, is left open. Though, of course, it does matter whether it's a rose-red or a blood-red door, that's only another way to clue in the reader.

It could be that there was a shortage of brown paint at one point, to be sure, though even there one would expect something to pan out from that. Either it's important when that door was put up, or else it's foreshadowing the dangers of shortages and other such problems.

Or perhaps someone will tell how the door got stove in one day, and putting up the door in a hurry did not allow for waiting for brown paint, and the characters will realize that the villain they were chasing did the deed.

Or the making of brown paint was rendered impossible by a feud, and the embittered refusal to allow the ingredients for this person's door. And so the door was painted red.

Or the door remains a puzzling anomaly, symbolic of the way that the townsfolk regard the party, despite being explicitly authorized by the king, as intruders and vagabonds entitled to no knowledge. (Enough to make you suspicious of them. Until all is revealed, and they are just that insular, and idiotic.)

Or perhaps you just leave the red door hanging until the end of the novel, and the reader finally concludes that you were just that sloppy.

If you are lucky.

If you are unlucky and popular, you may find thousands of words expended in fan theories on why the door is red, which no explanation that it means nothing will derail.

That's why the door should have a reason to be red.

Writing Process

A few techniques for when it comes to apply all this to the document.

A Brief Account Of Rubber Duck Debugging For Writers

Quack

You have a problem, you do not know how to fix it, it is time to ask for advice. . . .

The classic piece of advice for a computer programmer is to explain it to a rubber duck. Or any other inanimate object—or plant or animal—that is to hand.

The only problem with an actual duck is that it might fly off.

The point is that to frame the problem clearly enough that you can verbalize it is often to see where it actually lies.

In real life, what generally happens is that one programmer calls over another for advice, and then halfway through the explanation, says, "Never mind." (To which the correct response is "Glad I could be of assistance" or "Quack," depending on your office.)

I have also gotten this effect from writing most of an email to ask another programmer for help.

At that, I have also gotten this effect by writing a blog post about the difficulties of plotting, or character, or setting. Sometimes by reasoning out the process while writing it, sometimes by having my thoughts set in new order after I was done grousing and posted my grouse.

Not always, mind you.

This has its affinities to dropping everything and going for a walk, which technique I have also used in both fields, but, of course, different. You are still attacking the problem, from a complete different angle.

The only advice I can give is that the duck needs you to be able to explain what the problem is, but even the vaguest of notions can suffice to open the matter up.

How Did That Get In There?

The art of revision

Ah, revision. You finish your first draft. Sagely, you put it aside and let it stew on the back burner. Perhaps you give it a week, or longer. Perhaps when you pull it off for the second draft, you change the font, or the color of the font, in order to give yourself a chance to read what you wrote instead of what you imagined you wrote.

Or perhaps what the gremlins introduced instead of what you actually wrote. Drafts can be unrecognizable.

So you are looking through your work and carefully excising all the misspelled words, and unnecessary progressive voice—are you?

That's not where you should start. Fixing grammar and style is possible but extremely peripheral in your concerns if you're doing it right.

It doesn't do you any good to turn a scene into a marvel of description and voice when it's entirely too long for the work it does for the story and should be reduced to a sentence of dialog in another scene.

Or, worse, is entirely superfluous because it supports neither plot nor character development nor world-building nor theme.

Or, worst of all, undermines the plot by turning the hero into a misguided fool, or falsifies the world-building for magic, or reveals to the hero something that should have solved the entire issue in one page because the hero would have known what it meant at once.

The issue that should be foremost in your mind is whether the story hangs together. Does the conflict triggered by the inciting incident come to a head in the climax? Are the characters adequately motivated for all their actions? Is it plausible that your hero, having shrunk back twice, from entering the Golden Tower, will dare on the third attempt? Is the love interest's characterization in the opening compatible with her position at the end? Is the middle just a plodding thread of episodes, or does it hold some important changes in the direction of the story?

I have heard of people who pull out the plot skeleton at this point to ensure they have a full story, and there's no reason why you can't if that helps you.

I plow into the story myself. And yes, I do tweak the sentences as I go. And untangle sentences once I figured out what I meant them to mean. And elaborate settings so the characters aren't talking in a void, and the reader can figure out where it happens.

I also look at any notes I made along the way—either in the first draft or while revising—about things that needed revision in other parts of the story. (And I cross them off when I'm done. Otherwise, on another pass, I may find myself having foreshadowed something seventeen times and needing to chop out sixteen of them.)

The paradox of revising is that you need to look at the big picture but you can only work page by page. I'm good at keeping it in memory, but I have to ensure I do at least one pass at *speed*, so I can notice that the king whom I said was widowed in an early chapter does not show up with a queen without having remarried.

Still, if the main conflict of the story does not get resolved, however obfuscated the matter is, the details of the prose do not matter.

If the hero wants to attend the wizards' school, it must end with his either attaining it or ceasing to strive toward it (for whatever reason from resignation to contempt).

It can not be resolved by his killing the Evil Overlord, and therefore you must ensure that the death results in his being offered a place and his either accepting or refusing; a master wizard taking him on an apprentice, far more prestigious; the wizards awarding him the status of master wizard in honor of his demonstrated skill; or the hero deciding the wizard school is filled with contemptible wizards whom he does not want to learn from.

This must be foreshadowed, the characterization must be deployed, and the setting must be set to make this work.

Likewise, it does not matter how you phrase the description of the school if the scene makes it look wonderful and marvelous, and your hero has to be stunned that he aspired to go there—or, conversely, lowly and contemptible, and the hero has to long to go.

The details of the prose come last in importance, because revising to fix larger problems is likely to eliminate many of the problem details—and introduce new ones.

Order is important.

Juggling Time, Or Maybe Weaving

Handling plot threads and time

How I envy the juggler, working with discrete, compact objects.

Or the weaver, with the whole apparatus of the loom and all its moving parts to hold the threads in order.

When you are weaving together plot threads—if you are weaving together plot threads, which is the first thing to be considered.

There is, of course, a main plot thread, the great conflict that moves the story forward.

And for anything longer than a short-short, or maybe a story, there's some clutter in the background to be a convincing world. Sometimes it interacts and makes the main plot line more complicated.

No matter how much something interacts and complicates matters, it's not a separate plot thread until it has its own timeline.

Then—well, sometimes you need a calendar to plot it all out. Sometimes even that won't help because you need to remember to avoid a narrow focus. Concentrate too hard on the prince's dealing with the monster, or his romance, or his political problems with becoming the crown prince, or those with nobles resisting royal authority, and the other elements fall by the wayside.

Which is a balancing act in itself. All these separate elements do help build up a convincingly full world, but they also have to contribute to the story in a way that gives it unity of theme.

If the other elements turn out to be distractions from the main plot, and indeed the theme is that he should focus on the important thing, that's one thing, but that only serves some stories.

This grows all the worse when they do not interact causally early in the story. (If they do not grow increasingly in contact and affecting each other by the end of the story, you may want to fall back and regroup. It is a rare story that can have a thread that only resonates thematically.)

Worse yet, when the subplots have different viewpoint characters, you have to interweave them. Chronologically is nice but may not work aesthetically. And you have to keep the readers' interest in all of them, because if they skip the characters they don't like, they miss essential knowledge. (If they do not miss essential knowledge, of course, you have an easy solution. Simplify the tale.)

Or, of course, they have different characters whose viewpoint we never see.

You still have to figure out the timelines.

Then you have to figure out how they affect the viewpoint character, or characters, and whether those characters figure it why this effect is happening, and when they realize it, or if they do, and if so, whether you can hint to the readers that it happened, and if not, whether the readers will find the plot line plausible.

With foreshadowing and set-up on top of that. Particularly set-up.

Which can be awkward. I remember a series in which characters wondered about some evidence and came to a conclusion that they leapt to. It was only in the later books that it was vindicated.

That was an extreme case of a common problem.

To explicate: foreshadowing is alerting the reader to something coming up, and set-up is justifying latter occurrences.

If Miss Victorine Smith is sent to the seashore for her health, and as she disembarks from the train and heads to the cottage where she will stay, old sea captains grumble out what a bad season it is for storms, the reader will expect storms. If they talk about rescuing sailors from wrecks after storms, the readers will expect wrecks and rescues. All foreshadowing as well as set-up.

Now, if they mention that Lord Jonathan, the duke's grandson, is actively involved with the rescue service, we know he will be involved in at least one rescue, despite the danger, despite having met and fallen in love with Miss Smith. Foreshadowing and set-up.

On the other hand, if there are only mentions that the family is involved with the rescue service, and such like touches, the reader may not expect it, any more than Miss Smith, when Lord Jonathan says that he will of course have to take the boat out with the other seamen to rescue sailors.

The thing is that all this set-up has to be artfully woven in at the right time, to seem plausible in place, so that the reader does not think that the only reason you would write that is to set up something. Even foreshadowing can be difficult because it shows the writer's hand, when done unartfully.

Indeed, it may turn out that you need a subplot, with all the problems of weaving it in, in which, say, Lady Graycliffe, Lord Jonathan's mother and the duke's daughter-in-law, visits the widows of sailors for good works and brings along Miss Smith. Then you have excuses for the knowledge, and the problem of weaving in the thread.

Such are the complexities of stories.

Knowing Thyself, and Outlining

Ways to outline

If you are a plotter, if you know that you can not sit down and story without the story petering out, if you must force the story to take form before you begin it—know what you need.

There's no way to get around it but experiment, as writers need all sorts of different levels of detail.

Or sometimes several different levels of detail. C.J. Cherryh writes a series of outlines with increasing detail, and when she puts in dialog, she calls it a first draft.

Me, I couldn't do that. I often put bits of dialog in my very first outline. I don't need to, but why lose the perfect line just because I think of it then?

What I do need to do is to have every single scene that will occur in the story. That is how I nail down the plot and ensure that it is actually a plot.

At least the main plot. Stories have been known to sprout subplots. And sometimes I realize that I elided important points, and what I wrote has to be elaborated and turned into scenes. This annoys me because it takes more time, but as long as the scenes can actually be written and do not steer me off the main plot, it works.

You may have noticed that this doesn't fit the formats that various writing advice offers.

(It also doesn't fit the format that your English teacher had you write in. That's because no one writes an outline for a novel like those requirements. Roman numerals and indents—well, if you like them, you can use them. But particularly remember that you can have as many or as few on any level as fits, and that it doesn't have to be even. See above about dialog. You can put in one line of dialog if you like.)

But—writers offer higher-level outlines than my simple list of scenes. Things like the snowflake method, which starts with one sentence, turns to a paragraph of four, adds the major characters' profiles—

I do keep a list of characters with notes such as names, appearance, traits, jobs, if these come up. But I don't classify them as major. Indeed, keeping a character list is more important for the bit characters. Who was that gossip who said something snide about the hero in the third chapter? And what was her hair color?

And the snowflake method does get down to the same list I start with. The thing is that I couldn't start with the one-sentence, because I start with lower-level things generally. A fraction of the ending. A moment in the middle. A hint at the beginning.

Always, always, always be wary of outlines that tell you to start with one thing. They can work if you know that thing. If not—they don't.

Plot skeletons can be useful for me. Not as a substitute for scene-by-scene outlines, but as a way to add some structure to a tale that turns out to be one thing after another. I have to stop and consider how I can give it a sharp swerve in the middle, and a couple of lesser but still more significant than usual events.

Which is a point to consider. A scene-by-scene outline is very, very loose. Arguably, I'm just pantsing a very sketchy first draft. If that doesn't give you enough structure to form your story on, you can look for something with more.

One thing is that you do not have to fill them out in the order they give. You can work backwards and forwards to put your ideas in places where they might fit, shuffle them around, and try to figure out the earlier parts from the later ones.

Or perhaps you must. Perhaps your foundation needs to be secure before you build on it.

This is why you must know your own writing process rather than anyone else's.

Reflecting On Fanfic First

Whether that's wise

I have heard people recommending writing fanfic as a way to begin writing with the intention to switch to original fiction.

To which I say—I don't.

Some habits and skills that writing fanfic cultivates may be useful for original fiction.

Others are positively detrimental.

Devising new plots may help.

Writing the story without taking care to clue in the reader with the world it is taking place in, and the characters who are living it out—because the fans already know—weakens an important skill.

Not devising the world and the characters but keeping (more or less) within canon also weakens important skills.

The thing is that while we have certainly seen works where writers could devise plots, but the characters were cardboard, or in which a cliche plot moves through a vivid setting, the skills still all work together.

If you don't like how the hero and heroine quarreled, or think that it should have led to a permanent rupture, or resent that a character was killed off—or not—you go ahead and steal that. This is a perfectly commonplace way to start writing original fiction, and it is better than just being inspired by the work because it gives you a motive to change.

But consider what to change.

For instance, what plot purpose did the death serve?

It's one thing to fix it by making another character, whom you never liked anyway, make a mistake that prevents the character get to the place where he died. (Or, of course, to get himself killed if his survival was what you objected to.)

It's another thing to reorganize the setting to prevent (or enable) the death. This is much more likely to break canon, but it enables you to do much.

It's still another to consider whether you should change the magic system to facilitate it. Particularly if you are considering a profound uprooting of the system from the bottom. It was generic, it didn't serve your theme, it killed off the character you liked and not the character you didn't.

It's wonderful thing to do. For the final work, it's best if it is actually an improvement on the work you are deriving inspiration from, being less generic, more colorful and vivid, less obviously a plot device, plus fitting your themes more elegantly—but if you are doing it for practice, it doesn't matter if you end up with a worse magical system. You tried. You exercised your ability to pull the ideas loose.

Some elements really do have to be pulled loose for an aesthetically complete work. The reason why the hero and heroine never commit is that it would change the series, and their unending battle with the evil shadow creatures has no real resolution. Both of them are so driven that they would not give up even so much attention as a marriage would take.

You could just hook them and override their characters, but you could also tear them out of that situation and give them a finite problem to deal with, such that they can conclusively end it, and marry securely in the knowledge that the future will be better for their heroism.

This is because you are developing the art of making your own canon, and making it aesthetically sound. The great art of it is realizing that all the parts have to hang together, and any of the parts can be changed in order to make it hang better. You are juggling characters and plots and settings because in the end, all of these act and react on each other.

Would this work better in a high fantasy world, without characters who did not know anything of magic before it started?

Can you put the school in a labyrinth?

Is dark magic just destructive magic, such as you would use to knock down a building after it had been rendered unsafe in an earthquake?

If these children hadn't been trapped in the painting, would it be better if the results were told from the viewpoint of one of them? Or even the entire story?

Everything is an option.

The more you practice, the better you get.

You can start with being annoyed at how shallow and selfish an assassin being presented as a love interest is, and consider how he could defend his trade if he weren't in solely for the money and shameless enough to admit it.

First you set up a land with endemic warfare.

Then you set up a quarrel with paladins where he argues that they go into the field to kill knights and men-at-arms who had no say in the battle, where he cuts straight to the heart and kills the man who decided.

One paladin counter-argues that he kills people in their own homes, leaving all people in dread where they should feel most secure; another that he pays no heed to the right and wrong of the war when assassinating important people, just for who pays.

After that, the paladins are attacked, and the assassin saves the day by killing the nobleman in command, whose idea it was, without pay.

Then, of course, you have to elaborate the plot to set up that conversation and that attack.

During which, perhaps, you realize that you dropped the romance. The assassin is no longer a love interest.

You have forged so far into original fiction that the original inspiration has stolen away.

And if you can't imagine getting that far—well, there are story ideas to this day where it's a surprise how little, if any, of the original ripped-off idea makes it in.

Timely Revision

And its questions

What is the best time for a writer to revise a story?

At least a week after the latest draft. A month is generally better.

But on the whole, it helps to not wait too long. Sometimes, if you are stymied on it—and working on something else—but not often.

In part this is, of course, because if you take too long to loop around, you get very few works done and out the door, and that irregularly, which doesn't help.

But an important part of it is to have the work sufficiently fresh in mind that, when you come across a sentence that makes no sense as written and say "What on earth did I mean by that?" you have a chance to rummage around your memory and dredge the originally intended meaning up.

Then you can rewrite to actually express what you meant.

Rewriting on the spur of the moment, as soon as you finish the draft before, is fine if you know you have things to fix, but it precedes rather than substitutes for revising in cold blood.

It is only in revising in cold blood that you can notice that your sentences do not actually make sense as written.

It is only in revising in cold blood that you can notice that the lengthy discussion in the garden doesn't actually mention that it's happening in the garden, let alone give the vivid details that illuminate the discussion (which is the reason for setting it there).

It is only in revising in cold blood that you realize that at no point do you actually depict, or even describe, the friendship between two men that makes their current quarrel so bitter and painful to them both.

I particularly note that if you notice the later, it is wise to make note of it. It is even wiser to, after adding the information, to scratch the note off the list of things to do. I have, on more than one occasion, discovered that I realized some knowledge had to be given, and had put it in six times. Since they were written weeks apart, it did not occur to me at the time, but reading in cold blood, and at a good clip, cured that.

(If you do not revise your work in progress but go back and rewrite as soon as the draft is done, that noting that work is needed and then scratching it off is vital.)

A month or so is enough to let you keep the story in mind, also. At least, enough so that when you open the work and start to re-read it, you realize what a shift in mood the story undertook. How a character changed in purpose and characterization. All sorts of swerves, down to realizing that you had assumed that you had put in all the foreshadowing, but you hadn't, because you hadn't even seen what was emerging.

On the other hand, if you dig up a trunked novel and remember that plot bunny, and it starts to bound about again, all is not lost.

Sit down and re-read the novel. Get it in mind that way.

If you start revising while re-reading, you may find yourself in a tangle as you discover things you did not remember. Or that you have to knock out what are structural supports and so have to totally overhaul the work. Which may explain why you were so stymied on it. (Major issues tend to take longer to resolve than small ones.)

Possibly even the wisest thing to do is toss the manuscript back into the trunk and then start with an outline or whatever you start with. This works best when you are throwing away the characters, their names, their world, and their situation to entirely rehome the plot bunny. If you conclude that it was stymied because you had hared off after the wrong tale entirely. Then the gap may have been the best way to, since it let you see clearly that you did it badly the first time that you need to start over entirely.

Timing is not quite everything, but it can be important.

A Brief Note On Back And Forth

Writing vs revision

Do you go back to revise while working on the first draft?

This, above all else, is a thing where you, as a writer, must obey the famous injunction of Delphi:

Know Yourself

Me, I frequently go back to revise before I finish the first draft. Even when I went to write a novel in a month. Which worked for me because I generally added enough to plump up the novel.

This works particularly well when I realize that the scene I'm working on really should build up to the actual scene, so I shift back and write what happened just before it—sometimes a scene, sometimes two.

Other times I go way back. To add a new scene. To embellish an old scene. To rewrite a scene. Always to add the support to the foundation for the story.

At least, that would be the intent of the revision.

There are those who tell you to never ever revise when you are working on the first draft.

They have a point.

There are the times when I am vacuuming the cat, as they say. I need to go on, and I'm avoiding doing it with tweaking this and that.

Sometimes this is a wise thing. Gathering up the strength, or working out the details, and then tackling it. Like circling around to other works, it gives the forward motion a chance to refresh itself.

But, like circling around, it can mean that you never make progress. Indeed, unlike circling around, there's no criterion to judge how you've been running away—circling around lets you count the works you've jumped to.

So—Know Yourself. If going back is always vacuuming the cat, or too frequently vacuuming the cat, you have to learn to avoid it.

Writing Times

When do you write?

The first great rule of writing is: Write.

I have run across writing advice that derides it as insufficient, but really, that's the rule that most would-be writers fail at. You have to write. That is more important even than finishing what you write, because it is foundational to all the rest.

You have to write, and writing takes time.

Much writing advice advises aspiring writers to write every single day.

This is one of the great writing questions that turns on the great principle:

Know Yourself

If you must write every single day or fail to write for weeks or months on end because you have lost the habit, write every single day. (Or decide that you are not a writer. Which also works.)

It can help to have a quota. Choose it with care. One that is too large will discourage you because you know you will not reach it, and some writing is better than none. But it should be longer than it normally takes you to warm up.

Furthermore, since its purpose is to keep you coming back to writing, you can and must make the quota up after missing it for a day—or a week—but you can not do it in advance.

You can write many multiples of the quota, of course. Ideally you would, because that's progress. You just can't count it against future quotas. Advance writing creates a temptation to avoid the quota the next day. Even if you know you will be unable to write for a week, the accumulated debt can help motivate you to get started again.

You also have to edit. This is trickier because I've never been able to devise a good quota for rewriting. Ten pages a day? Or an amount of rewriting to reach quota? What do you do if you are mostly deleting the extraneous? But to re-write is also to write, as long as it's every day. (The question of how to stop rewriting, like how to finish the story, is built on this foundation.)

Other writers require a schedule. This is particularly useful for people who can't write every day for whatever other conflicting activities are involved. Given the number of activities, a calendar and writing down the designated time are generally useful.

Flannery O'Connor worked like this. Three hours every morning. The big difference between this and the writing-every-day rule was that she didn't actually require herself to write in that period of time. She could write not a word while she sat at her desk. She just didn't allow herself to do anything else in that time.

If that works for you, it works for you. Perhaps boredom alone will drive you to write. But you may have to insist that you write in that time. Perhaps to a quota?

Still other writers can keep returning to writing after a time away. This is liable to decrease your output—unless you will suddenly, after months of silence, start pouring out thousands upon thousands of words in a day.

Possibly even then. If you can always return, the thing is that you have to keep returning to become an actual writer. The more you write, the more practice you get in writing. Furthermore, the more works you can actually write, and rewrite, and eventually kick out the door to face the cruel, hard world.

Writing only when inspired is a good way to not get anything done. Unless you're William Faulkner, who observed that it was fortunate that he felt inspired every morning at eight o'clock. That is how you build a sound foundation.

Considering A Cold

writing, and not

It has the sore throat and the stuffed nose, and it has exhausted me, but worst of all, it has the tendency to muzzy my thoughts. Even beyond the need for judicious naps, very little is getting written.

Life happens. Crunch time at work. Family visits. Preparations for a holiday, and then the holiday. (Many a soul has observed online that choosing November for NaNoWriMo because of the holiday said a lot about the founders of NaNoWriMo.)

The big question is getting back on the horse.

A cold is a hard case. So is something like helping a family member though a transition where the help tapers off rather than ceases.

Once you are improving, once more of your time is free, if you don't start to get back to writing, you may never return.

Habits, once broken, are hard to reform.

To Increase, To Decrease

Revision and word count

Once I got a comment in a writer's group by a somewhat baffled writer. He had read Stephan King's comment about the second draft being 90% of the first draft, and did not feel comfortable telling me I had to fill my story out more.

In nothing is it more important to know yourself than in the revision process. You will have to add things, and remove things, but which are specific to you.

To this instance of your work.

And to the particular passage you are working on.

Fortunately, you learn to recognize patterns. King apparently added more than was needed. You may too, but you need to know what.

Elaborate descriptions?

Scenes that don't actually move the story forward?

Too much foreshadowing, which not only pads the story but means the dramatic climax is thundering anticlimax?

Foreshadowing the wrong things because your notions changed half way?

Sentences that could be half the length if you removed the dead weight and verbiage?

Meanwhile—did you omit foreshadowing?

Or description because it was clear to you where characters were talking, so they appear as nothing but disembodied dialog?

Or characters' motives? (There was a time, when I was young, when I could only figure out what the characters did on the first pass. Once I had the story in hand, only then their motives for it were clear. Not until.)

And, of course, any given thing can be both lacking and superfluous in the same story.

This witty banter scene does not move the story forward, and makes the wits look more important than they are.

Meanwhile the heroes are supposed to be friends, so you need to—hmm, have them walk down the street together to reach the HQ and talk on the way. Maybe buy a snack from the vendor and laugh at how a small dog, barking at a goose, discovers that the goose can chase it. Or whatever other byplay fits the story and convinces the reader that they are friends. (Double points if it sets up their skill set, but first and foremost, it convinces the readers they are friends.)

One complication arises if you want to have it a certain length for an anthology. Or even to fill out a collection of your own.

As every writer who settles into a 12,000 word story to pare it down to 10,000 words only to end up with a 16,000 one—whether to add or remove can be surprising.

Sometimes you can simplify a story to contract it. Sometimes you can throw in complications to expand it. And sometimes you just have to live with it.

Writing can be like that.

Also by Mary Catelli

Writing And Reflections
Writing And Reflections
Writing And Reflections Volume 2

Standalone
Curses And Wonders
Dragon Slayer
Eyes of the Sorceress
Fever and Snow
Mermaids' Song
Sword and Shadow
The Book of Bone
Witch-Prince Ways
Dragonfire and Time
Enchantments And Dragons
Jewel of the Tiger
Over the Sea, To Me
The Dragon's Cottage
The Maze, the Manor, and the Unicorn
The White Menagerie
A Diabolical Bargain
Madeleine and the Mists

About the Author

Mary Catelli is an avid reader of fantasy, science fiction, history, fairy tales, philosophy, folklore and a lot of other things. (Including the backs of cereal boxes.) Which, in due course, overflowed into writing fantasy (and some science fiction).

www.ingramcontent.com/pod-product-compliance
Lightning Source LLC
LaVergne TN
LVHW010050110826
845155LV00028B/275

* 9 7 8 1 9 4 2 5 6 4 8 3 6 *